THREE STRIKES

*Labor's Heartland Losses and What
They Mean for Working Americans*

STEPHEN FRANKLIN

Foreword by William Serrin

gp

THE GUILFORD PRESS
New York   London

©2001 Stephen Franklin
Published by The Guilford Press
A Division of Guilford Publications, Inc.
72 Spring Street, New York, NY 10012
www.guilford.com

Printed in the United States of America

This book is printed on acid-free paper.

Last digit is print number: 9   8   7   6   5   4   3   2   1

Library of Congress Cataloging-in-Publication Data

Franklin, Stephen.
    Three strikes: labor's heartland losses and what they mean for working
  Americans / Stephen Franklin.
       p. cm.
    Includes bibliographical references and index.
    ISBN 1-57230-477-4 (hardcover : alk. paper)
    1. Strikes and lockouts—Illinois—Decatur—History—20th century.
  2. Working class—Illinois—Decatur—History—20th century.
  3. Decatur (Ill.)—Social conditions. 4. Decatur (Ill.)—
  Economic conditions. I. Title.
  HD5326.I3 F73 2001
  331.892′9773582—dc21
                                                          2001023194

Contents

Foreword

I told reporters they should go to Decatur. This was in the early and mid-1990s, at the time of the Decatur labor wars. I was receiving calls from people involved in three great fights there: one between Caterpillar and the United Automobile Workers; the second between Staley and an old, small union, the Allied Industrial Workers; the third between Bridgestone/Firestone and the old, once radical United Rubber Workers, now subsumed into the United Steel Workers. The callers said someone should go there and tell the story of an American heartland town riven by three bitter strikes. In Decatur, economic lessons had come alive and rubbed the town raw.

The scenarios were familiar but important: picket lines being crossed, families and friends split between strikers and line crossers, strikers putting themselves and their unions on the line, the economy of the town in peril. On top of that, though, the broad issues of the American economy—globalization, free trade, consolidation of local companies into national firms, competition with foreign markets—were being brought home.

Nobody took my advice. Steve Franklin did not need it. He went on his own.

What he found in Decatur is one of the fascinating labor stories of that decade, far more important, I believe, than the street protests on free trade in Seattle, Washington, D.C., and Quebec. While not unimportant, events like these often receive undue attention because of the telegenic nature of protests that feature picket signs and tear gas and protesters with their faces masked and riot police, and because of the tendency of reporters to fit all protests into a master narrative left over from the 1960s. And do not forget: It is easier to cover organized protests, which occur in front of the reporter in a major city, than to drive unfamiliar Midwestern streets looking for strange addresses and knocking on strange doors to convince strangers to invite a reporter in to tell their stories.

But behind those doors in Decatur—and in many other towns like Decatur—are true stories of work, the labor movement, and what is happening today in the American economy. In Decatur in the 1990s, workers who had lost their jobs were slipping out of the working class and the middle class, a status they had fought so hard for so long to gain. Old industrial unions were challenging, without much of a plan, corporations that operated under new rules. Two of the most innovative of American labor voices—Ray Rogers and Jerry Tucker, iconoclasts both, who were trying, as they had before, now with some dissension between them, to breathe excitement into the American labor movement—were on the scene.

Franklin tells this ignored story with detail and compassion. But he does more, for he interlaces his narrative with the stories of globalization; new management techniques (essentially old management techniques, seemingly more representative of the 1930s than of the 1990s and the new century); international ownership of long-standing American companies; an often weak, bureaucratized American labor movement; and the proposal of new, aggressive labor techniques often opposed by old-fashioned, hidebound union leadership. He also tells, in a moving manner, of the transformation of Decatur, on the edge of the Illinois prairie, from an agricultural to a manufacturing center, and in so doing tells the story of what has happened, unhappily so often, to many communities in America.

Much of the labor movement and much of the United States—including the nation's newsrooms—believed in the 1980s and 1990s that nothing was going on in labor. The truth was, everything was going on in labor—in Decatur and elsewhere. In truth, industrial America, the labor movement, and the lives of America's working people were being turned upside down. It was just that almost no one could see this, including the last few labor correspondents and a handful of reporters often reduced to covering work, not labor, and quickly ready to say so.

Steve Franklin did not buy this. He knew there was a sad and important story in Decatur to cover and write, and he went there and did what a good reporter and writer does. The result is this fine book. He unearths much. He writes of the return of the strikebreaker, once thought extinct in America; of the new foreign ownership of U.S. companies; of the new uniformed rent-a-guards (the new Pinkertons, as Franklin calls them); labor leaders who keen and are cautious and do not know what to do, and would not receive Decatur workers at the labor barons' winter retreat in Florida; of the work, unsuccessful in the end although perhaps it did not have to be, of mavericks Tucker and Rogers. He writes, also movingly, of the death of United Rubber Workers' union activist Suzie Watts, the abandonment of downtown Decatur, the kind of abandonment that is occurring so often in America, and, in a sad epilogue, what happened to other ordinary men and women who fought the Decatur wars. Labor largely lost in Decatur. (Franklin says there has been a "superficial healing.") But there are some things worse than losing, and one of them is not fighting.

I am glad that one reporter went to Decatur to tell this important story of three strikes and their losses for labor, which otherwise, I believe, would not have been told.

WILLIAM SERRIN
Associate Professor of Journalism
New York University

Acknowledgments

Without the inspiration of everyday believers in workers' rights like Tom Geoghegan, without the open-hearted acceptance of the people of Decatur, without the foresight and determination of Editor-in-Chief Seymour Weingarten at The Guilford Press, without the brilliance of my editor, Christine M. Benton, and without my wife, Suzanne's, ever insightful patience, I could not have told this story. I owe them and so many more so much.

Introduction

On Work, Writing about Work, and the Workers in Decatur

This is the story of a mostly blue-collar Midwestern town consumed by labor unrest in the 1990s. It is the story of a typical American community on the edge of the prairie caught up in a struggle more typical of the 1930s than of the last decade in the second millennium.

It begins with three monolithic companies, global giants all, that decided it was time for an abrupt change in the rules between themselves and their workers in Decatur, Illinois, a heartland community nurtured on such rules.

It grinds on through the inability of labor's breathless old guard to catch up with corporate America's new tactics and defend the workers' rights that had been so hard won 60 years earlier.

It gets lost in the chasm between workers and the world of work that now surrounds them, shoved aside in the conspiracy of amnesia that overcomes most of our labor–management conflicts today.

Families are divided. Neighbors turn their backs on each other. Marriages collapse. The financial dreams of workers caught up in the struggles flitter away.

When all is said and done, some of the people I have come to know over the years in Decatur will never be the same again.

Of course, the story doesn't really end there. In Decatur I was struck by how the confluence of events in one town had created a small paradigm

1

for what has been happening all over the United States and elsewhere around the globe: a darkening fate for America's blue-collar workers, their families, and communities, American unions' long stumbling struggle to regain stability, a return to a more brutal style of labor–management relations, and the unprincipled drive for success carried out by global companies that operate without national flags or morality.

Like many, I had listened to the corporate song about the new global reality and applied it across the board. We had to get tough and swallow the bitter medicine of job losses and pay cuts and harder, more tiring jobs so we could get strong and run the world's economy. That made sense. Or so I thought.

But in Decatur the three global giants that were taking on the unions—Caterpillar, Bridgestone/Firestone, and A. E. Staley—were the reigning powers in their industries. They were not fighting to stay alive. They were not racing to keep ahead of ruthless competitors about to overtake them. They were monoliths, and they had prevailed because they had had the power to do so.

This was not the new global economics. It was the old rule of the strong making the rules. When the unions had the upper hand, they did the same. But those days were gone. The unions had squandered their talent and insight. The tables had turned in favor of the companies, which lost no time in dealing a new hand to their workers.

No longer garbed in the words of a simple contract dispute, Decatur's labor battles took on universal themes: the battle for and against global capitalism, for American companies, for workers, and, ultimately, for competing visions of the American dream and the phantom reality known as the new economy.

They became almost religious battles for some and socially redeeming missions for others. They reopened wounds left by Vietnam. And they exposed workers to feelings of helplessness and economic freefall in an era of incredible prosperity.

This is an American drama that has continued across generations, one that I have been watching for three decades of reporting. For over eight years I traveled back and forth to the medium-sized community in south central Illinois where the lives and dramas that unfolded before me were riveting, compelling, baffling. But not many others seemed to care, and that struck me. It seemed more than the chronic forgetfulness that afflicts our recollection of our history. And more than the impulse to heal wounds by buffing over the rough edges of things that went wrong.

I think it is like an unplugged telephone or a wire cut inside a computer. It's a disconnect between workers and the world of work around them: a separation between the larger problems faced by many and the reality some of us deal with on our jobs today. It is a way of thinking that looks the other way, that says, "It is their problem, not mine," that urges us to move on.

Because of this disconnect, which seems almost impossible to get repaired, few hear about workers snarled in endless legal battles with companies or about those coping silently with exhausting on-the-job demands. Our politicians and leaders don't seem to care much about telling this story. Not the center-focused Democrats. Nor the Republicans, for sure. And organized labor has few champions who can transcend and magnify the world of low-paid warehouse workers complaining about the overtime they can no longer bear.

But there is a need for someone to speak out, because the problems workers face today are surely as important to them, as their predecessors' problems were to them. The sweatshops haven't been eradicated; they have merely been hidden away at the back of small buildings. The workers—immigrants, others who fear speaking up, and, yes, you and I—haven't disappeared; they are simply scattered and, in many cases, have changed the tint of their collars from blue to pink, to gray and to white.

More than ever corporate America is keen on dispensing new rules, and it has become more Orwellian with every passing financial quarter. In return for helping their companies prosper and, in some cases, facing the companies' ever daunting global imperatives, corporate America's workers outside the executive ranks have mostly been asked to tighten their belts. Fewer pensions, less job security, and a heavier work load are their rewards for surviving the downsizing and reengineering fevers. For those who were not in hot jobs, corporate America's rank and file learned to accept measly pay increases through most of the 1990s, while ogling their CEOs' stock-option-enriched lifestyles. Where factory workers once fought for an 8-hour day, their descendants today fight to hold the line against 12-hour days.

No surprise that workplace grumbling is pervasive. But it's disparate and incoherent. It is a Babel of whines. And in Decatur, this Babel erupted into a cacophony of howls.

Progress is wonderful. But progress without a safety net or a vow to put humanity before the bottom line is cruel.

Nevertheless, American workers, including you and me, abide, as always, by the belief that they are in control of their fate and must seek their own fixes. So we each fend for ourselves. We browse the bookstores, sorting through a flood of titles promising workplace redemption. Or we head for the drugstore and fill our carts with medicine chest supplies. Individually we reduce our own howls to whines again. Collectively we see, speak, and hear no evil.

That's just fine with many of those who were involved in Decatur's disputes. Exhausted by the years of conflict, some survivors set aside their memories and went on with their lives. Some looked the other way, confused by all that had happened to them. Some welcomed the opportunity to bury the painful evidence of organized labor's shortcomings, of the disintegration of the myth of union solidarity. Many people I encountered over the last decade—from both the companies and the unions—were reluctant, suspicious, guarded in talking to me. But of all those whose cooperation I sought in reporting on the struggles in Decatur, only officials with Caterpillar Inc. absolutely refused to tell their side of the story or to offer any guidance. I repeatedly asked and repeatedly was told that the company would not cooperate. The last thing the company wanted, said a top-ranking spokesman, was another "sad story about workers."

And so, one frigid winter afternoon in Peoria outside Caterpillar headquarters, I decided to give over the story to the workers, not their unions or their employers. They were the ones whose voices were least heard and least acknowledged. That is why this story is told largely through the eyes of a handful whose lives defined this drama that was played out on a very large stage.

"It was like a tragedy, a human tragedy, an American tragedy. It was as if they were locked into roles and they could not get out of them," said John Calhoun Wells, former head of the Federal Mediation and Conciliation Service, who had spent hundreds of hours trying to work out deals for two of Decatur's disputes.

That is the way I saw it too, as an American tragedy. But I think it is a story that reaches far beyond the factories' steam clouds billowing high over Decatur. I offer it as a witness's account of what happens when workplace rules are broken, when unions no longer make workers strong, and when the fruits of progress are no longer meant to be shared, but rather worshiped by most of us from afar.

Chicago, 2001

PART I

They Lead the Way

Destined to Do Right

Larry Solomon, Union Man, versus Caterpillar

December 1991

Fog hopscotching streets. Fog everywhere. Fog layered across Eldorado, a four-lane main street that slices straight east to west through town. Fog mingling with clouds of steam emerging from hundreds of smokestacks at the rambling, nearly 400-acre A. E. Staley Manufacturing Company facility. It crawls over a steep bridge just north of Eldorado, crosses the railroad tracks that feed the mill, and marches by a low-slung bar, a grungy-looking discount gas station, a bunch of auto repair shops, a used car lot, a time-worn bowling alley, a grain mill and silos, a closed factory, an old meat processing factory.

The fog pushes beyond an old two-story, red-brown brick tire plant and an outdoor athletic field and bleachers on its grounds that look as through they belong next to a high school. The street goes past a state prison halfway house set up in an old motel's group of bungalows at a bend in the road. Around the bend is another gas station, selling really cheap gas and flying the largest American flag you've ever seen. In the other direction is the large Caterpillar Inc. factory. It sits at the end of a long driveway.

There the fog surrounds clumps of United Automobile Workers pickets, who gather by red-hot barrels stuffed with piles of freshly cut

7

wood delivered regularly by the union. Night and day the barrels flicker and burn to warm the mostly middle-aged strikers and to keep their fledgling strike alive.

On a cold winter's day in 1991 the UAW strikers seemed like ghosts. In a sense they were.

They were survivors of another time, leftovers from a much-remembered era of prospering American manufacturers and their workers. They were stragglers cut off from the widespread retreat of unions no longer in charge of their fates. They were well-paid blue-collar workers, who mostly came to work decades ago with strong backs, a grudging willingness to take orders, and a hunger for a decent, regular wage.

They earned a decent salary and more. They received a raise every year, several weeks of vacation, generous benefits, and completely company-paid health care—almost all the fruits of union bargaining. In good years, which were many, ample overtime pay helped them buy bigger houses, newer cars, newer pickup trucks, vacations, and other blue-collar dreams.

Years later older workers would recall how much it meant to get a job in the factory and how their lives were uplifted. Caterpillar's arrival in town in the 1950s had been a godsend, a financial blessing for them and for Decatur, many believed.

In the fall of 1991, however, Caterpillar hardly seemed beneficent. Into one contract proposal, the company had stuffed a number of changes. It wanted a six-year contract. Never before had the union agreed to one so long. The company would not give annual pay increases to workers on lower-skilled jobs, who numbered about one in five of the hourly workforce. These workers would receive only cost-of-living adjustments.

The company wanted to set up a second tier of wages at half the $17 an hour paid to the others. This category would take in all newly hired employees and others called back to work at its parts facilities. The contract offer wiped out job security for a fixed number of workers, replacing it with a job guarantee for those on the job currently. That was critical for the company, which wanted to undo an arrangement the union had established with the auto industry that set a base number of employees, thereby blocking the companies from reducing their work-forces unless they could pose a strong argument to the union about technological changes. The contract offer created a new schedule that meant weekend work might not be considered overtime. It shifted the workers into a health maintenance plan.

Refusing to make such sweeping concessions and anxious to resist Caterpillar's perceived efforts to break the union's power, the UAW called out its 1,800 Caterpillar workers in Decatur and 1,000 in neighboring Peoria.

The striking workers' leader was Larry Solomon, president of UAW Local 75, a short, paunchy, grandfatherly man with wavy silver hair, small, dark eyes, puffy cheeks, and broad, thick arms. He spoke in a soft, almost squeaky voice, and his accent immediately placed him somewhere between southern Illinois and the mid-South. He showed up at the union's modest one-level meeting hall almost always in the same uniform: a short-sleeved shirt, blue jeans, and a thick leather belt with a metal buckle. Solomon was a symbol of the old ways of doing things, ways that had largely disappeared since American unions first took power in the 1930s. He distrusted his company leaders and saw no danger in pressing the union's demands. Driven by loyalty to his fellow workers, he was an anachronism of sorts, a maverick among the union officials of the 1990s, who operated more like insurance agents than blue-collar shepherds. He recalled the kind of union leader who had filled the ranks of the United Automobile Workers at its birth, an image he favored highly.

FIRE AND BRIMSTONE AND LABOR'S PIETY

Larry Solomon prided himself on his moxie and the wisdom he had gleaned from studying the labor history books that filled two metal bookshelves in a tiny, crowded office he had set up at his small house. He lived at the end of a road in a flat, windswept town just east of Decatur, Cerro Gordo, population 1,600. Two separate railroad tracks, remnants of Decatur's days as a major railroad hub, still ran through his time-battered town, and the frequent roar of the railroad horn rattled through his house. One of his favorite books was a perfectly preserved edition of the minutes of the first convention of the Industrial Workers of the World, "the Wobblies," held in 1905 in Chicago. Radical unionists, the Wobblies tore through organized labor's ranks with great ambitions, built a membership of over 100,000 by 1917, but then collapsed and virtually vanished as a presence in organized labor within three decades of their founding. Another of Solomon's prizes was a vintage collection of speeches and writings from the 1920s by fiery miners' union leader John L. Lewis.

Solomon would hold up his more valued books delicately and carefully, as if they were prized paintings, opening to their front pages and then proudly showing them off, though he had bought some at used-book stores for less than $1. History repeats itself, he would point out, book in hand. These volumes had taught him that there was a repeating pattern of victories and losses, that union movements bravely fought and lost in one generation, only to resurface in another. His deterministic view of labor history was as clear as a wall calendar: Only new dates had to be filled in to update the old events. "I learned from my books that the poorer class of people have always been second-class people," he said.

His readings also gave Solomon a deep admiration for the high-sounding words that describe average workers' rights and freedoms. He had a number of basic books about the U.S. government and its history, and he would read to his children from the Bill of Rights and the Constitution on the Fourth of July.

Solomon's admiration for groups like the Wobblies was fueled by a powerful sense of justice. "It made me feel good that people would give their lives for what was right," he said. A fierce and passionate believer himself, he came from a family who had little but their fierce religious beliefs about the Christian way to lead one's life and the determination to abide by a proper moral code.

"I ALWAYS THOUGHT I HAD TO DO WHAT WAS RIGHT"

The Solomons lived on a ramshackle farm on the banks of the Skillet Fork River in southeastern Illinois. Larry was one of nine children raised in a home without running water, electricity, or a bathroom. The kids were constantly reminded to help people who sought their assistance or who got lost on the muddy country roads, but they were never to take any money offered to them. That was not the Christian way. When the river did not flood, the family prospered. When the river flooded, as it often did, and the water rose up the steps of the house, the family lost everything. Most neighbors for miles around were dirt-poor farmers, though Larry's father was one of the lucky ones who had a job on one of the few oil rigs that had sprung up.

Larry's mother, Opal, was the task master for the house, directing and guiding her children, who spent their days hustling to take care of the gardens that surrounded the house. Every day Opal took at least an hour out in the afternoon to sit in the family's living room and pray. She prayed aloud for herself, for her children, for the community, for the country, for everyone. She prayed hard, raising her voice and working herself into a sweat. The sound of Opal praying became as much a part of the family's daily environment as the drone of cars going by or the normal neighborhood noises. The children listened.

Opal taught Larry that "anyone who went away from God's laws would be deteriorated and destroyed." He knew early on, he said, what he would do with his life: "I always thought I had to do what was right."

But things around us, he soon learned, do not always go right. The unpredictable river could wash away a family's crop. A farm season could be destroyed by drought. All of the best-intentioned efforts could collapse without a trace.

There was only one way to respond: to put the grief behind you and go ahead. Life had to be lived and endured. In the Bible, Opal had taught her son, "all of the things that happened . . . happened for a purpose." But in life, Larry explained, as if revealing an everyday truth, "people can just have bad luck. And just by being poor, we learned that we had to move on."

During Larry's childhood Opal would jokingly say she didn't know how her children were going to survive in life with the legacy of their father's temper and her stubbornness. Larry didn't seem to inherit the fierce temper, but he brought his stubbornness, his firm conviction, to the unions that dominated his adult life. As a youngster, however, he was quiet and unassuming and was stunned when his eighth-grade classmates voted to give him the American Legion award for leadership.

AN APPRENTICESHIP IN BLUE-COLLAR EXPECTATIONS

When he turned 18, Larry married, left his family's endlessly struggling corn and soybean farm, and put in for a job at Caterpillar in Decatur. Caterpillar was not hiring, so he searched and found work at a gas station in South Bend, Indiana. It was 1960.

Larry quickly became fascinated by the men who stopped for gas on their way to and from the Studebaker plant in South Bend. He found himself intrigued by the ebb and flow of factory life, how the workers were recalled and laid off as the small auto company struggled. With each layoff, he told himself that Studebaker was certainly dying.

It was. After 113 years, the manufacturer that had long defied setbacks, that had been founded in the back of a small blacksmith shop and later turned itself into the world's largest builder of wagons, closed its doors.

In 1963, Caterpillar sent a letter telling Larry he had a job if he could get to Decatur by a certain date. So he quit his new job delivering fresh chickens in South Bend and hurried back to Illinois to start earning $2.34 an hour, enough to move his wife and his first son, born six days after he started with Caterpillar, into a small house near the plant. He started on the burr bench, then worked at a small gearing machine, then a milling machine, then a lathe. From there he went to assembly, then shipping, then inspection. Finally he stepped full-time into union affairs, which filled him with a day-to-day mission.

Larry had been on the job only a short while when he got into a feud with a foreman and demanded to see his union's chief steward. Cliff Weaver came upon an angry, curly-haired worker who looked too young to be working in a factory and who could not believe that the union did not speak up more for its members. Sensing Solomon's innate drive, Weaver made a quick decision. The local steward in the area where Solomon was working was a farmer who cared little about fighting the union's battles. "Do you believe in unions?" Weaver asked—he remembered the moment clearly years later when I interviewed him. When Solomon nodded, Weaver made him the new local union steward.

Larry's perspective was clear from the start. For him, there were three kinds of workers: those who sucked up to the company; those who wanted to fit in and not draw any attention, who were the majority; and those who stood up to the company. He fell in line with the last group, the minority.

His outward daring struck many in the union. Some were respectful of it, and some thought it strange. The first time Ron Kramer, a veteran worker, came upon Solomon, the union had just called a wildcat strike against the company, as it often did. There was Solomon, standing with two hammers in hand in the middle of the factory, asking what he should do to help the strike. Kramer was amazed, but as time passed, he thought he understood Solomon. "I never saw anyone give to the union the way Larry did," said Kramer, who retired soon after the union struck in 1991.

From their first encounter onward, Weaver and Solomon remained close, although they did not always see eye to eye. Weaver was continually astounded by his friend's devotion to the union. Solomon would spend weekends at the union hall, poring over files for a grievance hearing. He would come to the factory in the middle of the night if he thought he could make a difference. "He didn't hunt. He didn't fish. He had no hobbies," said Weaver, who had his own interests, among which was raising dogs.

The company once fired Solomon, and Weaver was dumbfounded when Solomon fought the issue for nearly a year without pay. Anyone else, Weaver said, would have quit the union and moved on. But not Solomon. "He wouldn't back down." Weaver retired in 1988. He had asked Solomon over the years to bend more, to give in, to show more compromise at the union hall. But, Weaver said, "Larry is the kind of guy who can't change, who can't give a little." He had also asked Larry to heed his history books less. "Larry was too much on history," he said with a frown and shake of his head.

NOT TOO RADICAL TO RULE

By the time Solomon was elected the local's president in 1987, winning by a slim margin of 100 votes, he had been fired twice and suspended six times for infractions, which he flatly considered injustices inasmuch as he had been speaking up for his rights. One of his suspensions was for refusing to stand up when filling out a grievance complaint. The company didn't want visitors to think that its employees sat down on the job and so ordered workers to complete the forms while standing. Solomon thought that was a violation of his rights as a union member and decided to sit down and complete the form.

Solomon was unbending, especially when he thought the company was trying somehow to take advantage of union members. When all was added up, he became respected mainly for his loyalty to the job and his grit. He was not a powerful or inspiring speaker nor a skillful negotiator. He tended to state his case and stand by it, some in the local said, not planning ahead for compromises.

He also knew his reputation among the membership. "For a long time," he recalled, "a lot of the people said I was too radical." He won his second election by only 16 votes. Still, he thought he got along well with the plant's supervisors and was able to deal with them as the head of the union. Most supervisors were Decatur people. Most had come off the factory floor to become managers. They talked the way he did. His real battle, he was convinced, was not with them but with the company, with "the suits," the ambitious corporate climbers, the bosses who were eager to make a name and move up the ladder to Caterpillar headquarters in Peoria.

If he stood up to the company, he did the same to the Detroit-based union, telling its officials what he was convinced the other local leaders really felt but hesitated to reveal. "I would be the guy that had to crack their tails, 'cause it had to be done," he said. It was his job, he was sure, to take the heat for challenging the union, and he did it repeatedly in the late 1980s as the local signed company-wide agreements calling for more cooperation between the union and the company. He was convinced that this was not the way to go and that such deals would only backfire for the union. His reaction: "I saw the union moving with the company, and it was souring my stomach."

UNION DEMOCRACY—NOT A WELL-KNOWN SONG

Many of the members of Larry Solomon's union local didn't share his drive. Rarely would more than 50 show up for regular meetings. Rarely did they come out in overwhelming support for him at election time. They weren't very different from most American union members—they knew they had a union and little else.

Most of today's unions take care of their members' problems on the job and send them forms to fill out about their pensions, their health insurance, and other benefits that the unions negotiate for them. When and how they gained their benefits, most do not know. Many do not even know the exact name of the union they belong to. It's simply "the union" or "the local." Typically, rank-and-file union members do not elect the leaders of their unions. Only a handful of U.S. unions throw open the balloting for their highest positions to all of their members. Usually, union leaders are elected by delegates sent to national conventions.

In some cases, the gap between the union and its members is a divide that even the most well-intentioned, socially conscious unions cannot bridge. In others, the union leadership long ago gave up on relating to its membership. And in a small handful of unions, the members do not count. From the ground up, they are terrified to raise their voices or have little experience with democracy. For years unions such as the Teamsters, the Laborers, and the Hotel Employees and Restaurant Employees operated this way. A clique of union bosses decided who would run the union. Or, as government prosecutors learned, the mob made that decision for the Teamsters and Laborers unions.

Under pressure from the government and union dissidents, one-party, one-boss rule began to crumble. In the 1990s, democracy began to flourish, albeit slowly, for these unions as a result of government investigations and agreements reached with federal prosecutors.

The problem for most unions was not corruption or autocratic rulers. It was more insidious. It was an apathy that came with the business unionism espoused by union leaders from the 1950s onward. As unions surrendered their militancy for a guaranteed seat at the bargaining table, as they rewarded their members with higher wages but failed to instill in them a sense that they had a broader agenda than filling their wallets, the unions' importance to the average worker ebbed.

Among U.S. unions, the UAW, however, had a reputation for honesty and a history of rank-and-file activism. But over the years its hold on union members' lives had weakened. This was a fact Solomon knew very well. Not long after the 1991 strike against Caterpillar began, he philosophized about it: "We should've been doing more as a union between 1982 and 1992 to make our members aware of union issues. We more or less operated as a union from the top up. We didn't put the emphasis on the members."

Searching for a Strategy

Staley, a Small-Town Family Business, Goes Global

August 1992

The plant had almost always been there, looming in the back of his mind as that large place where people found good-paying factory jobs, always a rock of stability in town. He had grown up in a small wooden bungalow, one of a long row of modest buildings on the 2500 block of Eldorado, across from the giant wheezing complex of buildings that filled the air with great white sheets of clouds, that hissed and clanked and covered the town with the sweet–sour stink of its ovens baking the soy. He remembered how its smoke left a yellow dust on the fresh snow in winter before they cleaned up its smokestacks. And how the plant was where he went almost immediately when he wanted a job, a newly married youngster, cocky and sure he would be as good a blue-collar worker as any of his friends in town. It was a natural choice. Its reputation around town was that it was top-notch in caring for its workers.

He had grown up inside the plant. Had raised a family. Had learned what he didn't like to do with his hands—carry hefty bags all day long—and that he liked to use his head more. What he hadn't learned from all of his years as a union worker inside the A. E. Staley mills was a strategy he could use to stand up to a giant company and negotiate a contract when the company wanted massive changes, as it did in 1992.

And so Dave Watts felt a great uncertainty about the future. With few resources, he feared his union local was slipping into a bargaining quagmire. If he could have relied on expert advice from someone higher up in his union, life would have been much easier for him. But Watts, a tall, well-built man with a salt-and-pepper moustache and an unblinking stare, the president of the union local at the A. E. Staley facility, had no such backup. He was a worker, not a lawyer, not a trained negotiator. He needed all the help he could get.

He was the head of a small local with limited resources, someone way down at the bottom of organized labor's ladder. He shared with many other locals a precarious fate. They bargained on their own, and they normally got close to what they considered acceptable—if not because their union was strong enough to push the company around, then because of tradition. They counted on expectations, built up over years, about what the company wanted from its workers and what the union could get. Historically, they did not count on the company's changing the rules. Now they do.

A new reality had emerged over the past few decades, as long-time family businesses handed over their firms to larger corporations, as small firms merged with larger ones, as investors scooped up failing businesses going for bargain rates, and as competition and new technology pushed old-line businesses to the edge of financial ruin. U.S. companies like the one Watts worked for no longer play by the old rules.

TRAPPED ON THE SHELVES OF U.S. LABOR HISTORY

True believer. Idealist. Die-hard activist. Watts fit all the clichés about leaders of small union locals who saw themselves fighting not legal battles but moral ones, battles that measure what kind of people they are and display their ability to stand up for what they believe in.

Staley, now owned by a London-based conglomerate, viewed the changes it wanted in 1992 as ways of lowering its labor costs and erasing out-of-date job restrictions written into contracts over the years. It wanted a more flexible workforce in terms of hours and assignments. Workers should be able to float between jobs. They would not be not tied down to strict job categories. The company did not want to be limited by the burden of job seniority when assigning shifts. It wanted to go to 12-hour shifts that would rotate every month. That meant workers would live in a half-world of light and darkness, floating between night- and daytime jobs. It would wipe out the ability of senior workers to control the more preferred daytime jobs, and, much to the company's liking, let the bosses, who worked in the daytime, get to know the younger workers. By the company's calculations, 20 of its 23 similar plants in the United States operated on some form of rotating shifts. This plant was already running around the clock, so establishing 12-hour shifts was just another way to make the labor force more efficient.

It was not a matter of pay, as the company saw it, since it was not putting up a squabble over pay increases. The workers' pay ranged from $11.55 an hour to $14.37 per hour, and the company was offering to raise wages by about 10 percent over three years. Plus it was offering a $2,000 signing bonus and a pension plan and a 401(k) savings plan and 10 paid holidays and up to five weeks of vacation yearly. Company officials felt that they were being very generous.

It was simply a matter, as the company saw it, of rules and control. Who ran the place? The company felt that the union had been in control for too long and that weak managers over the years had pampered the union. But money was involved, because the new shifts proposed by the company eliminated nighttime differential, weekend, and overtime pay. That may have seemed like pocket money to corporate higher-ups, but it mattered in Decatur.

To Watts, all of the changes were vehicles for wiping out a chunk of workers' lives and jobs. Take away these benefits, and what did the workers need the union for? What good was it to have a union if it couldn't stand up for what workers had won year after year? It was not just the workers who stood to lose, but the union and the local too. All the danger signs were clear to him.

Watts's problem was that he had been president only since 1990, and when he sat down to bargain with the company he realized that he had little experience in a complex bargaining situation. His union, the Allied Industrial Workers, was a skeleton of its former self, a relic of the labor feuds of the 1930s. It could not offer any help.

The Allied Industrial Workers was the alternative to the United Automobile Workers union backed by the American Federation of Labor (AFL). In the early 1990s there were more than 80 unions in the United States, and a number were running on the fumes of their past. They should have merged with larger, more powerful unions, but old rivalries and pride blocked them. There were a handful of postal unions that should have merged, but they could not see eye to eye. The same was true for railroad transportation unions. The once mighty United Mine Workers union operated out of a building in downtown Washington that should have been a museum, not a union headquarters. Decorated with timeworn pictures of pictures of John L. Lewis, its flamboyant leader, it still burned coal. Its membership had fallen to a fraction of its former size, but it could not relinquish its identity or independence.

These unions clung to images nurtured 50 years ago, when there had been trade unions under the wings of the AFL and mass industrial unions under the auspices of the Congress of Industrial Organizations (CIO). They had pigeonholed themselves by their narrow job titles. They were arthritic pensioners, clinging to a more glorious past and struggling to keep their old jobs with insufficient resources.

In a newsletter sent to employees as a form of psychological warfare, Staley, citing the union's most recent newsletter, pointed out the dire situation facing the Milwaukee-based union: The union's membership was hovering at just below 50,000. It was operating at a serious deficit. Its own personnel had not had a wage hike in three years, and the headquarters operations were being run by two staffers, an international representative, and four clerical workers. The message: Just as the company had to change to keep up—meaning change its contract with the workers—the troubled union had to evolve. The underlying message: The union was barely capable of supporting its members. The workers shouldn't take the risk.

When the company spoke about new technology and looking to the future, Watts knew the union would have to accept a cut in the workforce down the road. What worried him was how the changes were going to be carried out.

From 2,300 workers in 1967, when he first came to work at the plant, the workforce had dropped to 700. He feared that jobs would be sliced left and right, that the idea of seniority would be obliterated, that the company would hand the work out to lower-paying contractors, that the local would have little say over work conditions, and that it would eventually have little say over anything at the plant.

Among all the terms the company wanted in its contract, the death of the eight-hour shift and the scheduled switching back and forth between days and nights without regard for weekends provoked the most upset. What would happen, workers complained, to their family life, to the time they spent at PTA meetings, their time bowling, their time off on weekends? What about single moms and their need to be home at sundown?

WORK WITHOUT END, AMEN

Companies pushing 12-hour shifts talk of the freedom workers gain with a shorter workweek. But like a life-threatening force, the spread of 12-hour shifts has stirred deep anxieties among workers in wealthy nations like the United States. And some of their fears have been justified. When workers cannot adjust to the longer hours as well as reversed schedules, and when companies flip-flop the shifts too frequently, greater fatigue, sleepiness, depression, and increased heart problems have typically resulted. Workers complain about "highway hypnosis," the problem of staying alert on the way home from the job. Social burnout and isolation creep in.

The *Exxon Valdez* oil spill, the Three Mile Island nuclear malfunction, the Bophal, India, chemical plant explosion, and the Chernobyl nuclear mishap all took place on the night shift.

At A. E. Staley the longer shifts were to be only for the blue-collar workers, not the white-collar professionals who ran the company out of the large office building nearby. But Staley was not an exception. Elsewhere factories had been putting their workers on 12-hour schedules. All-night drug stores and copy printing businesses suddenly discovered new markets with 24-hour operations and 12-hour shifts. In a service-obsessed world, banks, credit card companies, and computer fixit hotlines erased the differences between day and night work for their employees. Hospitals were among the first to do away with 8-hour shifts, saying that working 12 hours was a more efficient use of nurses' and doctors' time, especially in emergencies. It also meant that the hospitals could cut some of their staffing costs. Weary hospital workers and others working these long shifts have run into the same problems driving home from work as experienced by factory workers.

For the factory worker, who does more than watch a dial or answer a telephone, 12 hours of hard work can be grueling. From the late 1880s onward, this fact is what led thousands of American workers to protest and what drove the demonstrators at the bloody Chicago Haymarket riot. At a time when the average workday across the country was

14 to 18 hours, the idea of an 8-hour day seemed outlandish. "Strikes to enforce the demand for eight hours' work a day may do much to paralyze industry, depress business and check the reviving prosperity of the country," wrote the *New York Times* in May 1886, when the Haymarket riot occurred, "but they cannot succeed."

The shorter workday that labor had sought and companies opposed did come to pass during Franklin Delano Roosevelt's New Deal and the nation's first true extension of workers' rights. "A self-supporting and self-respecting democracy can plead no justification for the existence of child labor, no economic reason for chiseling workers' wages or stretching workers' hours," FDR declared in May 1937 amid strong opposition to his workplace proposals from the business community.

In June 1938, he won the battle. The Fair Labor Standards Act passed after months of opposition in Congress. It prohibited child labor by barring employers covered by federal laws from hiring workers under 16 years old. It established a minimum wage for the first time— set then at 25 cents an hour—and it created a 44-hour workweek, which was trimmed to 40 hours within three years.

For more than 100 years workers in the United States and most of the industrialized world had marched steadily forward toward the point at which they were able to cut down their hours on the job. Then the march stalled or reversed for some.

As unions lost their power, as laws protecting them were rolled back, and as their industries faced greater competition, they began to surrender their eight-hour time cards to the time clock of a longer day. As inequality grew and workers were less difficult to find, companies discovered that they could keep wages down and also hire more workers for longer periods. The more some workers fell behind financially, the more they were willing to put in longer hours on the job.

Pressed by these and other forces, American workers steadily lost out on the time clock in the 1990s. By 1997 they were putting in the longest hours on the job of any workers in the world's industrialized nations, according to the International Labour Organization—about 2,000 hours a year, nearly two working weeks more than in Japan, for example, where workplace hours fell steadily throughout the 1990s.

While the silent, largely unpunishable crime of time clock theft has grown in the United States and other industrialized countries where unions and workers have been facing losses, it has meant an even greater defeat for workers in the poorest nations of the globe. For them, a newborn trend has vanished. Instead of less time on the job, they find themselves lashed to longer and longer days. In some underdeveloped countries, as a 1999 study by the International Labour Office pointed out, workers put in more than twice the hours of those in the richest nations. "Indeed, in many parts of the world, the achievement of an eight-hour day and 48-hour week, a guaranteed weekly rest period and maximum working times in order to prevent accidents and protect workers' health remain highly topical issues," wrote Gerhard Bosch, a German labor expert, in the *International Labour Review* in 1999.

A BATTLE IN THE MAKING

As was the case at Caterpillar, there were omens of what was to take place at A. E. Staley. The company's request to open negotiations seven months before the contract expired was a red flag to the local. And there was something else. Staley officials increasingly spoke about the need for change, and the need for the company to take a stand on changing the way things operated at the plant. Fearful of such talk and of the precedent of beginning bargaining so early, the union would not budge. It rejected the company's bid to begin the talks early. It knew it had to take a stand, but it didn't realize how serious that commitment would become. Dave Watts had a clearer picture of what was to come true later, but when he started at Staley in 1967, earning $2.67 an hour, he had no idea he would end up championing the battle for Allied Industrial Workers Local 837.

He had followed the same route as hundreds like him in Decatur. He always figured he would work in a factory. His father had worked on the railroad before suffering a series of heart attacks, and everyone he knew in the East End of town worked in a factory. He was an athlete and a leader at St. Theresa's High School, where he was captain of the high school basketball team. He left high school at 17 without his diploma, eager to go into the military and full of dreams of becoming a Navy diver. It was 1965, a year that saw the buildup of the Vietnam War, and his enlistment seemed a very normal and patriotic thing to do. After two years in the U.S. Navy, serving on a supply ship off the coast of Vietnam, he came home with a wife and a newborn child.

Five days after he returned to Decatur, Watts went directly to Staley before visiting the other factories in town. They hired him on the spot, and he took a two-week vacation before starting to climb the catwalks and ladders that filled the milling plant like vines. Two years later he was promoted to the mechanics section. That gave him a great new sense of pride because this was a more highly skilled job, plus it paid more than other positions in the factory. He felt respected. The possibility of moving up into management didn't interest him, although his younger brother, Mike, became a manager. As the union and company eventually parted ways years later, so did the two brothers, rarely speaking except when their family gathered.

Being a mechanic wasn't enough, however, as time passed. "I wasn't satisfied with work. I wanted something to give me direction," Watts recalled. So he threw himself into the union, climbing the ladder of elected positions. What he liked about the union was that every time he climbed a step higher, there was more learning involved.

He put in six years on the executive board and then six years as the local's vice-president before being elected president. Soft-spoken and a good listener, possessed of a certain serenity that cooled hot heads and checked impulses, he seemed to take well to the job. Not good at public speaking at first, he soon developed a talent for it. Watts took the job very seriously, treating it as a great responsibility. As local president, he didn't sit with the others who drank in the bar the union operated on the first floor of its meeting hall, always regretting the bar's existence in the union hall.

Some of the greatest emotional wounds of the epidemic factory closings of the preceding decade had been suffered by local union presidents, who had tried to deal with the pressures single-handedly. They couldn't, and in a culture where working-class men reveal so little about themselves, they were suffocated by the burdens they tried to carry. It was not uncommon in the 1980s to visit a blue-collar town where a factory had shut down a few years earlier and learn that the president of the union local had died too. Too much heartache, people would say.

PREPARING FOR TROUBLES AHEAD

Once it was clear that the union was going to have problems with the company, Watts sat down with his wife, Pat, to talk about the trouble he saw ahead and what road he would take. At times over the years Pat had become impatient with her husband's belief in letting everyone have a voice and then trying to be the congenial peacemaker. "[But] we had identical views," she recalled. "We said that you stand up for what is right and it will come out okay in the end." As the union work took more of his time and Dave could not put in enough hours at his factory job, Pat, a nurse, took a second job to keep up the family's income.

Meanwhile, fearful of the future, Watts had pushed for his local to educate itself. He opened the local's meetings to wives of the largely male membership, saying they needed to be part of the solution. Not all of the men agreed, but he stuck to the point that the women had a role to play.

Though he couldn't explain it, Watts was intensely suspicious of Staley's intentions as soon as negotiations for a new contract began in August 1992. He did not trust the company's talk about how it would go about cutting jobs.

It didn't take long for his fears to be realized, a little at a time.

When the company hired the former personnel manager from International Paper's plant in Jay, Maine, and Watts heard from others that International Paper had taken an extra-tough stance against the union, including bringing in replacement workers to break a union strike, he visited Maine. The trip unnerved him. Was Staley planning to repeat what had happened in Maine? Was it prepared to bring in replacement workers if the local didn't buckle under to a contract full of concessions? The paper workers had taken a terrible beating in Maine. How would his small local fare in a similar battle?

Before the union and company negotiators sat down, Staley's president, Larry Cunningham, had visited company headquarters in London. Soon after, he resigned, later joining Archer Daniels Midland, the giant agribusiness firm based in Decatur. Just before Cunningham left Staley, Watts remembers the former president telling him that officials in London had their plans for negotiations and, "They are going to come after you." Asked about the remark, Cunningham would not comment.

REWRITING EXPECTATIONS

As it turned out, the contract negotiations were not as much a showdown as a tug-of-war. Staley and its parent of the last four years, Tate & Lyle PLC, had jumped on a bandwagon increasingly filled with large corporations that wanted to do away with long-embedded traditions. Besides shift changes, Staley wanted, for example, bonuses paid to workers based on their skills, not their seniority. Protecting seniority was a bottom-line issue with the union.

"This is an issue over change," J. Patrick Mohan, a soft-spoken attorney and executive vice-president for Staley in his late forties, insisted repeatedly.

As Mohan would calmly explain throughout the dispute, the company no longer needed workers hired because of their brawn or ability to heft large sacks. It needed people who knew how to operate computers and read industrial measurements. For its rambling complex of 100 buildings it would never again need as many workers as it once had.

WHOM DO YOU BELIEVE?

Staley's workers had had no problems with management since 1970, when the union had struck for 82 days. By 1991, however, Staley was not the same company. It was no longer a local icon of Midwestern self-assurance and evangelizing Corn Belt business ethics, no longer a staid patriarch of Decatur's business elite, but a folder in a portfolio of companies owned by Tate & Lyle PLC of London, the world's leading sugar processor. When the company made its offer available to the factory workers despite the union's overwhelming rejection, most of the union members were terrified. But when the contract expired in September 1992, they did not strike. So much had changed that union leaders like Dave Watts simply didn't know what to do.

The local brought in labor lawyers and labor studies professors from colleges across the Midwest to explain at the local's meetings what options it had. These professors told the members that they needed to stay on the job and not strike when the contract expired, that they needed to wage a sophisticated, high-pressure campaign from the outside, and that the company's British owners had a history of playing very tough with workers. And, they added, the British company was likely going to make a heap of money from Staley.

At the time, the local had about $30,000 in the treasury. To pay for its education in modern-day union strategy, the local gradually raised the monthly dues from $23 to $100 a month. For its investment, the local got a firm statement that striking was not a real option. It also got

Ray Rogers, a man who supposedly would run a campaign that would allow the tiny local to stand up to the giant British conglomerate. Watts had heard of Rogers, but only dimly, so he did some checking. He heard that there had been a documentary movie about a union where Rogers had played a major role, but decided not to see it.

Danny Wirges, the union's regional representative, said, "It appears that they are going to do you, and if you want to do them, get Rogers." Wirges did not really know much about Rogers. He was not completely familiar with what had happened in Austin, Minnesota, a few years before.

Others at his union's small headquarters in Milwaukee told Watts that if he went with Rogers, he would get hell from the AFL-CIO. But Watts figured that the AFL-CIO had done so little so far for his group that he could afford to take the chance.

They needed somebody extra special, Watts believed, because they were up against a force they had never faced before. And, as he and Pat always agreed, when you stand up for what's right, it will come out okay in the end.

Labor's Savior?

Ray Rogers, Slayer of Corporate Battle Plans

June 1992
New York City

The call came from out of the blue. Someone talking on a speaker phone from somewhere in Illinois. The man represented a small group of workers with a company Ray Rogers had never heard of. Their contract expired in September, and they needed help. They didn't want to strike, didn't want to risk getting replaced, or lose their jobs. But they didn't want to give in to the company, either. They had serious problems on their hands, really serious. The union couldn't help them, the local had only $30,000 in the bank, and no one else seemed capable of helping—or was interested.

Would he take the job?

"Man, do I need another one of these?" Ray Rogers asked himself, thinking quickly about what he might get himself into.

Then Dave Watts added the clincher: The local was growing desperate.

"Oh boy," Rogers said to himself.

His life had been one heartbreaking setback after another lately—though he insisted that he never suffered heartbreaks, never felt any remorse. He was a workaholic who couldn't find work, a lifetime bachelor who was wedded to work that was no longer there, a believer in self-improvement who could not overcome the adversity he faced. He was an ascetic who could not easily define for others the rewards he wanted for the sacrifices he made. He was a loner who transformed himself in the midst of his campaigns into a different persona. He had gone from serving as a symbol of organized labor's best hopes to being banished by organized labor's Brahmins, branded an untouchable.

He was the brains that unions hired when their strategies went flat or failed. He had a small, struggling company based in New York City, and he promoted himself to unions as one of the masters of corporate campaigns. Indeed, the term "corporate campaign" had been his idea, he bragged. A handful of others did similar work. Some were in upscale established businesses where people wore suits and also did public relations for unions. And some were veteran union activists who had struck off on their own and became crusaders, traveling from job to job. Many unions, however, set up their own corporate campaign offices, as did the AFL-CIO.

Rogers was both similar to and very different from them all.

No matter how organized labor labeled him, Ray Rogers carried the banner of the maverick, innovative labor troublemaker, one of the few of his kind at the end of the 20th century. He brought a fervor to labor unions that had once flowed through them via the self-made labor radicals in the 1930s and the fiery activists at the turn of the century. His exile and his failed struggles to make his visions real were, likewise, no different from theirs.

Rogers appealed to labor's left with his attacks on unions' autocratic leaders and his inclination to go after corporations' wealth and greed. But he was not an unbending ideologue. He was more a pragmatist, mixing good organizing ideas with basic notions about what seemed to pan out as a successful strategy.

THE PROPHET DEFEATED

There had been problems before, but Rogers's ultimate undoing had been a battle between George A. Hormel & Co. and Local P-9, a 1,400-worker local in Austin, Minnesota, that had refused to go along with the decision of the United Food and Commercial Workers (UCFW) union to take a 23 percent pay cut. The union's thinking was to hold the line on wages industry-wide if possible, as it carried out a controlled retreat in the meat packing industry while reserving its strength for fighting an increasingly unorganized beef industry. Wage cuts and shrinking union workforces had clobbered the union in the 1980s. The UCFW's strategy was not unique for unions in the 1980s. Self-preservation became the dominant theme for many.

With Rogers guiding it, Local P-9 struck in August 1985. But the company was able to run the plant with 450 strikebreakers and another 400 workers, who crossed their own picket lines. The national union leadership, furious about the strike, withdrew the local's strike pay, replaced the local leadership, and bargained for peace with the company on contract terms that the workers had previously rejected.

Refusing to concede defeat, Rogers blamed the UCFW for undermining the local and the bosses of organized labor for failing to come to the local's rescue. Rather than admitting surrender, he urged unions to savor the daring of the national campaign, financed by donations from across the country, that the workers had waged. Ever an optimist, at one point when he was jailed for obstructing justice in Austin, Rogers enthusiastically told a reporter for the *New York Times*, "Hey, we got them where we want them now."

After the Hormel campaign failed, Rogers, already an outsider in organized labor's view, was a pariah. Few unions called on him. He had waged war against a major union and had flouted the AFL-CIO's authority. His business dwindled. He was forced to lay off most of the small group of workers at his cluttered second-floor office on the edge of Greenwich Village in lower Manhattan. Financially, he was near ruin. The Hormel campaign had practically destroyed him. The bad publicity was so fierce it didn't look as though anyone in organized labor would ever rely on him again.

At a 1990 screening in New York City of the award-winning documentary about the Hormel dispute, *American Dream* by Barbara Kopple, audience members hissed at Rogers during a postfilm question and answer session. The documentary had captured his image well: short, muscular, fast-talking, energetic. His clipped New England speech stood out amid the flat Midwestern accents.

Still, Rogers seemed to have boundless optimism in the midst of defeat. But, as one reporter stated, in writing about the screening, he also came across as a charismatic charlatan. That was the major indictment of Rogers after Hormel: He had stirred and incited the workers and then led them haplessly to their defeat.

Rogers resented the documentary, deeply hurt that it had portrayed him, as he said, as a "flimflam man."

DOING WHAT HAS TO BE DONE

Rogers's supporters also considered the film a cruel rendering of the history of the Hormel battle. They saw the local's defeat as a plot by the AFL-CIO and food workers union to kill the "virus" of activism that threatened their control over union locals nationally. "A lot of times he doesn't win, but the goal is to mobilize and educate people," said Peter Kellman, a labor activist in Maine who worked for Rogers over the years. Rogers, in the eyes of supporters like Kellman, is a generous person who often pays himself no more than anyone else on his staff. His generosity is boundless even though he may be financially strapped himself. "He [Rogers] once knew I didn't have any work for a long time, and he said, 'Will you go up to this summer camp I have and mow it for me? I'll give you $1,000,'" Kellman recalled.

To his foes in organized labor, however, the documentary confirmed Rogers's fatal weaknesses: his inability to set limits and to protect his clients against absolute wipeouts, absolute losses that would set the union back for years. They faulted him for relying on one major strategy and being unable to shift to find other ways of winning a battle. They saw him as someone who had a great hunger for claiming all the fame from the successful union fights he had taken part in—battles such as the long one with the southern textile manufacturer J. P. Stevens. While he boasted about his ability to bring the company to the bargaining table, others quickly pointed out that it was not he alone who had been the savior of the textile workers.

THE KNIGHT OF LAST RESORTS
FOR THE DOWN AND ALMOST OUT

Familiar with the criticism against him, Rogers had always maintained that he did the best he could in a tough situation and that those who called on him should have realized what the odds of winning were. They usually sought him out, he would say, at the last minute when everything else had gone wrong. He was the cleanup man for those who would have him. He was the one they called in when all else failed. He was the closer, if there was to be one. This made sense to him.

And he had never lost a night's sleep, he insisted, because he had always tried his best. In addition, he too had suffered.

So when the call came from Decatur, Rogers could not shake from his mind a similar call he had gotten one day from the head of Local P-9 of the UCFW in Austin, Minnesota. But he was intrigued. After some research he thought he saw a way he could do something for Watts's local. He was convinced that he had found the corporate weaknesses that he could mine. That was his specialty, finding the soft spots in companies where unions could apply pressure. He would come up with a strategy for the workers in Decatur that would not be much different from what he had done for years.

He would divide and conquer, wage a form of labor–industrial warfare, an amalgam of guerilla publicity, financial detective work, street-level populism, and upfront, brazen confrontation tactics. It was a style of battle he felt very comfortable with. After all, as he often pointed out, he, Ray Rogers, had pioneered corporate campaigns for organized labor.

PLOTTING AND WINNING CORPORATE WARS

It was true: One campaign, one victory, had made him famous, changing his career forever. For years the giant textile firm J. P. Stevens Company had battled with the Amalgamated Clothing and Textile Workers Union. Finally, in 1980, the company grudgingly agreed to a settlement, a victory of mythic proportions for unions and especially for unions struggling in the fierce battleground of the South and the staunchly anti-union textile mills.

What Rogers added to the union's battle with J. P. Stevens was a lunge at the company's financial throat. He targeted the insurance firms and financial backers the company relied on. He put public pressure on J. P. Stevens board members. He engineered efforts to elect dissident directors for the company. The textile firm was so enraged over Rogers's efforts that it made the union agree not to wage another corporate campaign against it, and it spread the word quickly among southern textile manufacturers to be on the alert for such movements because they were very dangerous.

The victory did not turn out the way the unions had expected. After years of lengthy legal skirmishes, the giant textile manufacturer would recognize the union in only a handful of its more than 80 plants.

But at the time, organized labor, stuck in what seemed like a downhill roller coaster, was electrified by the image of this 36-year-old, boyish-looking, weight-lifting workaholic. "What Norma Rae started on the shop floor, [Ray] Rogers helped the union finish in the financial markets," a Canadian labor activist wrote in 1996, urging Canadian unions to learn from Rogers's efforts. The business world was electrified too, but by fear rather than admiration.

"Where will Ray Rogers strike corporate America next?" asked a glowing profile of Rogers in the *Wall Street Journal* in October 1980. With little doubt about his potential, the paper freely quoted him as saying that he would take his corporate strategy a step higher to help poor and working people. "The important thing isn't organizing people into unions. It's disorganizing the power structure."

As much as he relished the article's praise, Rogers penciled in the word "just" before the word "organizing."

In many ways, Rogers reflected a bigger trend: the entrance into organized labor of young, idealistic Americans, guided by the wide-eyed optimism of the 1960s. Years later some of them would rise to top positions in unions. Some would spend years as organizers. Some would give up, surrendering to the awesome deadening weight of union politics.

By the end of the 1990s, those who had stayed on, and who had managed to gain some power, were beginning to exercise their voices in a handful of unions. But there were not enough of them, though they were needed more than ever.

A COME-FROM-BEHIND PUNCH

If Rogers had given anything to labor, it was the idea of going after companies from a different direction. In his own way, Cesar Chavez, the visionary founder of the United Farm Workers union, had already waged corporate campaigns in the 1960s. Rather than attacking the farmers who refused to hire his union members, he had waged a campaign of moral rectitude, hoping to win over or shame consumers into boycotting the nonunion farm products. But organized labor was deaf to the uproar that Chavez had raised. If it heard his outcry at all, it misinterpreted his crusade for workers as strictly a moral crusade for lowly paid, mostly Hispanic farm workers.

By the 1980s a handful of unions had already tried out their own corporate campaigns, and corporate America was up in arms. In most cases the unions lost. Still, they won in a few instances in which they probably would have fallen flat on their faces using more traditional strategies. The publicity given these union victories and the perception of a turnaround brought new business for management attorneys, consultants, and public relations firms. As the union campaigns proliferated, some companies retaliated with law suits against the union campaigns. Business groups called for legislative barriers to stop corporate campaigns but failed to win them.

To mount corporate campaigns at this point, unions needed new skills.

The goal was the same as before: putting pressure on the companies. But they had to exert such pressure in different ways. The picket line no longer worked. They needed to understand companies' financial underpinnings so they could point out to stockholders not only the mistakes being made by the corporate leadership but also the dangers the company faced. They needed to be able to document abuses of federal and state laws and then bring the agencies down on the companies for violating these laws. They needed to translate their battles into confrontations with higher social and moral intentions so that they would gain broader support from religious and community groups.

They needed to be able to mount publicity campaigns, a whole new area for organizations unaccustomed to opening themselves up to outside scrutiny. For the first time, they had to look outside the United States to form alliances with other unions or to put pressure on international corporations. They needed imagination and the kind of spontaneous brilliance that came to the civil rights demonstrators when they faced overwhelming setbacks. They needed activists, not union bureaucrats who had slowly worked their way up the union's political ranks and into jobs in the organizing office. They needed to keep the pot boiling, so that after one campaign ended, they had activists and staff who could move on to the next. And when they were caught up in these disputes, they needed to be able to sustain solidarity within their ranks. That meant constantly letting the workers know where the dispute was going and where they continued to play a role. And, most important of all, they needed to assure the people putting their lives on the line that the union would not desert them if everything failed.

The problem facing many U.S. unions was that they were not open to new ideas or to new faces, especially from outside their own ranks— even as their troubles mounted year after year.

WANTED: ON-THE-GROUND BLUE-COLLAR CREDENTIALS

Once he had passed through organized labor's doors, Rogers pushed his way ahead. His advancement came despite the fact that he did not have the credentials, as some noted, often demanded of those on the way up: specifically, time on the job.

What he did have was identity appeal. In many ways he resembled the people he was leading. He wore jeans and casual shirts, even to meetings with corporate officials. He baffled union officials, who would urge him to dress up for important occasions. His explanation was that he worked and lived and dressed like working people. The workers don't own suits, so I don't own one either, he would say.

If he raised his arms too much, if he spat out his words so hurriedly that they were garbled, that was fine with some of the people he was leading. Others were put off by his loud, forceful way. But for those who believed and trusted in him, he would become their motivator, their guide, not just their intellectual guru. His roots in middle-class Beverly, Massachusetts, were blue-collar. His mother had worked on an electronics plant's assembly line. His father had operated a lathe for General Electric Company in Lynn, Massachusetts.

Rogers was clearly cut from the 1960s and the era's fervent embrace of unorthodox routes to find oneself. In his last year at the University of Massachusetts he changed his major from sociology to astronomy. Appealing to his draft board as a conscientious objector, he joined VISTA, the domestic Peace Corps, in 1967 and was sent to work in the Appalachian mountain communities of Tennessee. Rogers then drifted through several jobs as a political consultant before working on the winning campaign of union reformer Arnold Miller to lead the troubled United Mine Workers Union. The rebellion among the miners became the breeding ground for more than one high-minded recruit to organized labor's ranks.

In 1969 a union reformer, Joseph A. Yablonski, lost out in a campaign to clean up the union. He was killed a few weeks later. A federal judge overturned the union election, and Arnold Miller stepped up to replace the slain reformer. In 1974, W. A. "Tony" Boyle, the union's former president, who had ordered Yablonski to be killed, was convicted of conspiracy to murder. The down-and-out miners, a dwindling workforce faced with miserable working conditions and corruption, were a magnet for idealists like Rogers.

Rogers's first real union campaign was in Birmingham, Alabama, for the Amalgamated Clothing and Textile Workers Union, where he led a crusade to dry up sales of Farah slacks in an area where the manufacturing company had high sales. Because of the union's overall effort, Farah eventually sought a deal.

Not all of Rogers's campaigns were as successful, however, and he grew increasingly hostile toward union leaders, calling them paper tigers and condemning them for cooperating with companies. In turn, some of the unions he had worked with turned away from him, saying that he had inflated his importance and stubbornly stuck to his own variety of corporate pressure tactics while other methods would have served as well. They were right, but only to a degree. He sometimes turned a blind eye to other tactics, repeating his campaign strategies one after another without blending the mix.

Between striking and publicly pressuring corporate officials, unions were exploring other ways of waging their battles. These were nuances, however, not entirely new strategies. They were slowly discovering, for example, how to use the clout provided by their pension funds and other investments in corporate America. The last thing corporations wanted was an emergence of shareholder revolts, union-led campaigns that focused on how much they paid their executives or how they carried on their business.

Likewise, unions were slowly exploring ways of cooperating with each other so that their disputes would not be isolated ones.

Rogers did not ignore such steps. It was just that when he arrived on the scene, a dervish spinning with ideas, he did not always wage a campaign on all fronts.

THE ART OF BEATING THE BULLIES

A common theme runs through most of Rogers's efforts: standing up to the bully, finding one's strength and not backing down. Corporate executives who took on a union were not only tough-minded in Rogers's view. They were bad guys. They were goons. They were thieves. There were no gray areas. They were out to make life miserable for the workers because they were simply bullies.

This theme echoed from Rogers's childhood, and even today he willingly calls it up to explain himself. He was beaten up in the fourth grade by neighborhood toughs, and the experience stayed with him. For the next few years he lifted weights with the idea of making himself less vulnerable. By the end of the seventh grade he had gotten back at every one of those who had bullied him. From then on he kept up his weightlifting and exercise, always holding himself ready.

Ed Allen, who first worked with Rogers during his campaign against J. P. Stevens and later became his partner, thought Rogers's fixation with bodybuilding was his way of standing up to a bully of a different kind. "While Ray likes to talk about deciding to build himself up," Allen said, "the real thing that motivated him was his desire to try to put himself in a good position to deal with what was a life-threatening disease." Rogers's father, a sister, and his two uncles had died of crippling hereditary diseases, and Rogers's father had been sick for most of his son's teenage years. According to Allen, these events deeply touched Rogers.

As time went on, Allen watched Rogers develop his stance against bullies into an astute understanding of the world of labor and management. "I was always astounded by Ray," said Allen. "We would think from the outset that these people [the workers] are getting screwed, and Ray always, always had a clear sense of what it was that the group could do to magnify its resources."

Despite such admiration, Allen struck out on his own, motivated by "middle-aged angst" following the setbacks in Minnesota and another on behalf of the paper workers union in Maine. Frustration with the criticism Rogers was getting from people who had known him for years and who now held powerful jobs at unions or the AFL-CIO, drove Allen to seek a new career altogether. "There were people who were criticizing Ray who were making $75,000 a year and had a car and a pension and were living a good lifestyle," he explained, "whereas we were struggling from day to day to keep the doors open. And it seemed like that criticism was unlikely to change."

As compared with some of his critics, Rogers lived a monklike existence during most of his organizing years. He did not own a car. He took care of others who depended on him, especially his mother. He was always ready to extend a helping hand to friends and colleagues, like Peter Kellman.

Norm Komich was his childhood friend, a member of the same Boy Scout group—his father was the troop leader—and later his college roommate at the University of Massachusetts. During the Vietnam War, Komich, who later became a commercial airline pilot, was headed overseas when he stopped in Washington, D.C., to visit Rogers and say a nostalgic good-bye. Rogers made him a promise he never forgot. "He said to me, 'Norm, if you ditch, I'll come and get you. I'll come to Vietnam and find you.' That took me through the whole tour. I just accepted it. I believed that he would do it. It really gave me great peace of mind."

Rogers's major fault, according to Ed Allen, was his inability to realize that not everyone is that steadfast. "The hardest thing for Ray to believe is that somebody who was his friend could be his enemy," Allen said. "Ray just presumes that everyone is in it to do the right thing. You have to beat him over the head to make him realize that is not always so."

Rogers's greatest strength, for those who know him well, has been his ability to motivate. He didn't offer small visions to factory workers. He showed them the skies, and some discovered that this was a liberating vision. They were not just fighting for a better contract. They were fighting for a better labor movement. He led those who followed him in Austin and elsewhere into campaigns with grand moral goals, a difficult feat considering the conservative nature of most blue-collar workers. They are moral people, but most blue-collar workers do not like to rock the boat. They are not seething with fury over their oppression by their bosses. They may hate their jobs, but they don't hate the system, they don't get up in the morning grumbling about what an inherently rotten deal they have. They still put their faith in an America as idealistically pristine as the kind that Hollywood used for years in its boilerplate plot.

But Rogers knew where to reach them. He would speak to their self-pride and their dignity and their sense that they could make a difference if only they tried. At one point, Rogers told the workers in Austin, "You can create a moment in history where people will turn to Austin and say, 'That is where they turned back the onslaught against the labor movement.'"

It didn't happen in Austin. But in Decatur, Rogers thought, things might be different.

A Leader for the New World Business Order

Don Fites Remakes Caterpillar's Ambitions

January 1992

He hardly seemed a radical or maverick. He had all the classic trappings of an executive with Caterpillar Inc., a company in which you do not stand out if you want to get ahead and where you quickly learn that the mold is conservative Midwestern. He could have been one of the early prototypes.

Born in 1934 on a 90-acre farm in rural Indiana, high school valedictorian, he went to a small Midwestern college, Valparaiso University, studied civil engineering, and then started his career, earning points with the company. He became a corporate suit, another middle-class white man on the corporate ladder.

He was tall, six feet and more, gangly, reserved, slightly stoop-shouldered. A decent athlete, he had kept in shape over the years, playing golf and going to early morning aerobics classes in Peoria. One spring he splurged on a fantasy baseball training camp in Arizona, a haven of reveries for middle-aged jocks. He had a deep passion for baseball. Perennial losers, the Chicago Cubs were a big favorite.

He was not a marvelous speaker. He did not show much patience for waiting for things to get done or with those who did not agree with him. But ambitious corporate climbers often don't. He was not unique, and to Caterpillar's way of thinking that was what made him eligible to carry the corporate mantle.

But as soon as Don Fites took over the company, the world's largest manufacturer of heavy equipment, he became very different, and so did his company.

In the 1990s, Fites was an archetype of a new kind of corporate executive, a pragmatic ideologue. In the 1990s it was easy to pinpoint these seemingly clear-eyed, forward-thinking CEOs. Their thinking almost always seemed grounded in basic economic realties. The daunting global challenge. The threat of bureaucratic sloth. The needless obstacles thrown in the way of global companies by governments, human rights groups, labor organizations, environmentalists. Without these barriers, they could move their companies forward. Their companies would prosper, they swore, and they would ultimately engineer a better economy and better world than those who had preceded them.

They would move factories across continents, slash thousands of jobs, undo years of bargaining traditions, cut loose whole divisions, and remake corporate identities with what seemed to be a clear sense of mission. They were different from their predecessors, they insisted, because they were breaking free of unneeded ties and traditions that had fettered and constrained their companies. They flattened corporate layers, squeezing out thousands of managers and creating parallel universes of consultants and spin-off companies that did the same work but at much less cost for their parent companies. They spoke a new language, a corporate Esperanto, a sort of globalese. They were answering new mandates, they said, since their companies were no longer protected by national trade barriers. So, too, because they had spread their corporate roots far and wide, they behaved like companies no longer tethered to one flag or one single loyalty.

If they succeeded, their salaries exploded, like Las Vegas jackpots. Even if their companies did not succeed, their salaries often soared, because corporate America in the 1990s was seduced by the allure of high-priced CEOs. To hold on to them and to continue to reap the beneficence of the stock market that they seemed to bring to their companies, corporate boards threw stock options and other cash rewards their way. And, in the 1990s, if they just drew a fresh breath daily, Wall Street filled their pockets as it rang up the values of their companies' stocks.

HEARTLAND INSTINCTS, GLOBAL VISIONS

Don Fites's advancement at Caterpillar was predictable, because the company preferred Midwesterners. People from the heartland had fewer adjustment problems with the company's Midwestern way of thinking at its headquarters in downtown Peoria in central Illinois. Here was a global company run from a town in the heart of the Midwest that lacked a good airline link or any of the trappings of a world-savvy community. Being isolated was a problem, but Caterpillar's identity with mythical Midwestern values was just fine for the company. Caterpillar preferred loyal, hard-working people. People who would stay and live out a career. People who would travel the world for the company and then gladly come home to retire in Peoria. People who, it is said, bleed yellow, Caterpillar's color. Fites was one of these. He had joined the company after college and had never strayed. Nor do most Caterpillar executives.

But what set Fites apart from most other Caterpillar executives who rose to the top was his career trajectory. He did not climb the ladder of factory bosses and manufacturing gurus, some of whom had once risen from the blue-collar ranks. He was not, in the company's jargon, a factory man. He had spent most of his career abroad, working in South Africa, Brazil, Japan, Switzerland, all the time studying how companies operated in other cultures. His master's thesis at the Massachusetts Institute of Technology was on how U.S. firms could meet the challenge of the Japanese. His experience and thinking were tied to the firm's foreign existence, a significant factor inasmuch as Caterpillar was destined to become one of the nation's major exporters. Equally important, he did not have the same roots in the increasingly popular corporate culture of worker–management cooperation, a popular theme song of many American firms in the late 1980s.

By the time he took charge, Fites had little patience for the layers of company bureaucracy and the inertia it thrived on. In 1985 he became Caterpillar's president. When named CEO in 1990, he appeared impatient, decisive, and determined.

And he also had a ready instrument to put to work.

Shaken by its first losses in a decade, in the 1980s Caterpillar had undergone a metamorphosis. It had slashed its payroll in the United States and had begun producing far more of its products overseas. Worldwide, its workforce fell from 83,455 in 1981 to 55,950 in 1991, a

32 percent drop. It had taken on the challenge of its fast-growing Japanese competitor, Komatsu, and unlike other major U.S. firms had largely beaten the Japanese company in a fierce price war. It had modernized its plants. It created divisions and made them responsible for their profits and losses. The results: The company started outsourcing or building facilities in lower-wage areas to manufacture things once made by its major factories. It had opened its arms to its workers and set up employee-cooperation plans. And there was a payoff: Between 1987 and 1993, its workers' productivity grew by 30 percent.

After a 205-day strike in 1982–1983, the company had vowed to deal with the union in a different, more cooperative manner. For both the union and the company, the strike had had bitter results. The company lost over $500 million in 1982 and 1983. The union, which had gone on strike in 1982 amid widespread layoffs, a nearly suicidal gesture, stumbled badly. It had sought regular pay increases but wound up with only annual cost-of-living hikes. Over the decade, its workforce at Caterpillar tumbled from 20,000 workers to only 12,700 by 1991. Burned by the long strike and convinced that it had to work out its problems with the company, the union did not strike in 1986 or 1988 when its contracts expired.

Caterpillar had also battled with the U.S. government in a unique fashion: It assumed the pose of a righteous corporation. In the mid-1980s when it thought the U.S. dollar was too high, it lobbied the Reagan administration to bring down the dollar so that its products could sell better overseas. And it prevailed. When it thought that the U.S. steel industry no longer needed protection, it lobbied Washington again, challenging protective tariffs and claiming it should be allowed to buy less costly steel. No other major U.S. manufacturer had ever done that—publicly stubbed the toes of the nation's steel giants. But Caterpillar officials saw themselves as doing the right thing for their country and their company.

Yet one area remained largely unchanged when Fites took over: labor relations. To the circle of advisers gathered around him, it seemed possible to change this area as well. Fites's years in Japan had made him admire the dominant companies and docile Japanese unions. "In Japan," he said in 1992, "unions are deeply dedicated to the success of a company, and Japanese companies have been very successful."

To take on the union like never before was a "momentous decision," Walter Helmerich, a Caterpillar board member, told the Associated Press in 1997. "Year after year whenever the contract came due, we just knuckled under and paid the union whatever they demanded. That was an extremely dangerous move that he [Fites] had to get the directors on board. We talked about it for a year, maybe a year and a half."

While Fites and other Caterpillar officials talked about the need for UAW employees to step off the escalator that kept driving their wages up, another issue lurked in the recesses of their minds: the union's power. The company resented the union's ability under the contract to block and counter its decisions.

THE COMMANDMENT TO CHANGE

In late 1991, Caterpillar wanted to be able to slice wages for workers who were not on the factory floor making things. It saw no reason to pay guards and janitors and parts workers what it paid the blue-collar workers who built its giant machines. It wanted to untie itself from the annual raise given workers and replace it with productivity bonuses. It wanted to start new workers on a lower tier of wages. It wanted to undo what had taken the union 40 years to set down. It saw no reason that it should be tied to keeping a specific number of workers on the job. It wanted a six-year contract that would let it plan long-term and sit out any changes in the economy, not the three-year contract favored by the union.

The company didn't want a few changes. It wanted a whole new contract.

"I think the UAW leadership still thinks it is 1950," Fites would say at one point during the company's confrontation with the union. "Times have changed, and they haven't changed with the times."

As the confrontation grew and Fites became more of an emotional target for the union's distress, he stepped behind a virtual veil of corporate silence. For safety alone, he and other Caterpillar executives had reasons to worry. Every turn of the dispute twisted the tension higher. In the Peoria area, where most Caterpillar executives lived, local police soon became familiar with complaints about anonymous telephone threats and rocks or sharp objects left in company officials' driveways. Shots were fired at the homes of a Caterpillar executive and an office worker, but police could never find the culprits. The night the shots were fired at the home of the Caterpillar executive, the family was home. The bullets went through a window and hit a computer, police said. The probability of someone's getting hurt, the police said, had been high.

So Fites disappeared publicly, except for appearances at local business and charity events and nationally as the head of a very powerful global company. If he had any feelings about the showdown with the union, he no longer shared them publicly, and his company's public relations minions made sure that was so. Within corporate confines, however, Fites was still at the helm.

He was the architect of changes that would succeed miraculously in the company's terms. But Fites also became a national symbol of the new trend in corporate America in the 1990s, whereby companies made the claim that the only way to succeed was to keep labor costs low. Quickly and surely this trend overtook the upstart notion that Americans could compete worldwide by avoiding the low-wage route, that companies could afford to keep up workers' wages because they gained far more from them in terms productivity, innovations, and high-quality job performance. The trend left wages creeping along at miserly rates for most of the 1990s, even as corporate profits and CEOs' salaries ballooned. Essentially, workers were sacrificing their share of the corporate pie to enrich the executives and their companies' stockholders. Wall Street analysts regularly worried that one day pay-starved workers would realize the bad hand of cards they had been dealt and would rise up in protest and gum up the system, demanding pay increases. They didn't.

As strange as it seems, American workers seemed quite accepting of the argument that some had a greater claim on the fruits of the American dream than others. Then again, most workers probably didn't realize what was happening.

In November 1991, as the battle over wages and costs began with the UAW, Fites, who had earned $545,000 in wages and other benefits the previous year, offered a philosophy underlying the company's bargaining tactics. "A company like Caterpillar, which had not given up an inch of market share, has had to put some limits on how fast incomes can grow to stay competitive," he told the New York Times. Americans' incomes should tread water, he also suggested, while others' worldwide caught up. "There is a narrowing of the gap between the average American's income and that of the Mexicans. As a human being, I think what is going on is positive. I don't think it is realistic for 250 million Americans to control so much of the world's GNP."

Months before bargaining began between the company and the union, Fites had visited Detroit, at his own request, and told the union's two highest officials about his concerns. The company had to cut health care costs, he explained. And more important, it had to cut itself loose from the industry-wide bargaining that the union had historically used to link it to other major manufacturers. At the time, the company seemed headed into murky waters. For the first six months of 1991, it had sales and revenues of $5.37 billion, down 8 percent. It had posted a $49 million loss, and the company expected its first annual loss since 1984.

The UAW leaders were stunned at Fites's campaigning outside the arena of the bargaining table. After meeting with Fites, Bill Casstevens, the UAW official in charge of bargaining with Caterpillar, told his assistant that it looked as though there would trouble ahead with the company.

He hardly realized how much.

But Fites had not kept his ambitions secret. He was changing the company in a number of ways, and he broadcast the message for anyone in Detroit or Decatur to hear easily. "We're under tremendous competitive pressure," Fites said in May 1991. "We don't have time to take three years to change the culture of this company."

CHAPTER 5

An Honest-to-Goodness Hard-Liner

Bill Casstevens, Career UAW Man

At one time, nearly everyone got to the top of American unions in one way: from the bottom up. And those who rose from the job itself, from the factory or shop floor, from among the mythical rank and file, earned their credentials and gained allies among union colleagues for the political dealings ahead. That is the way they inherited a feeling about the work their fellow members did and an understanding of what the union meant to them.

It was a priceless education, and it seemed to work well at the time.

Later on, others began to come from outside the rank and file. They came from the university, which put them in the ranks of the better educated in unions of people who get paid for what they do largely with their arms and backs. Or they rose from the union's own bureaucracy. Or they made their name elsewhere, and the union was the second road they traveled.

And then there is another way, one that has persisted for years among a small group of unions. These are the unions that have held a monopoly on organized labor's deal with the devil. They share the same meeting room with less corrupt unions that have turned themselves into family businesses or fallen into a long, deep sleep and slowly shriveled away. People get to the top in these unions by belonging to the family of a union leader, by being friends of the family that runs the union, by being political allies of the union's leaders, or by being goons or bullies or being hand-picked by the mob.

In a mob-ridden union, you treat it like a family business. You drive a big car, earn a big salary, treat yourself and your cronies as though you own the place. You pick the pockets of people who can't afford to be stolen from. You make the rules. You have lawyers and others who will make it sound legitimate. The members are dealt with as employees, who are not to be heard from. Once you get to the top of a union like this, you normally make sure you stop anyone from following in your footsteps, because they too will one day want what you have claimed for yourself and your cronies. And if you are lucky, you can live very well for a very long time.

When unions were the darlings of workers' dreams and liberals' hopes, they drew bright young college graduates and others of their ilk to their ranks. Rather than go on to careers in law or business or social work, these Young Turks found a calling with the garment workers, miners, steelworkers, or auto workers. And, in turn, they helped to expand the unions' visions, to sharpen their strategies, to lay down a legacy of common thinking about what needed to be done to survive.

As corporations became more savvy and less willing to abide by the old bargaining rules, unions needed more than ever to rely on their brain trusts. But as unions shrank in size and imagination and their attraction waned, they lost the energy that had once driven them into new places. And as they lost this punch, they paid a price, a terrible price.

As American unions began to flounder, who got to rule and how they got there became more important than ever, because these factors turned into reliable early predictors of the unions' fate. Indeed, as the unions faced bargaining partners intent on changing basic contract assumptions, and as they dealt with far more savvy companies sprawled across the world, they had choices.

The choices were very simple.

One, either they learned new techniques of bargaining, of waging corporate campaigns, of using public relations as a tool for the union, and of organizing new members to give them more clout, or they got clobbered.

Two, either they made sure they had their smartest, best representatives at the top, or they let their old-guard leaders go about everything as if nothing had changed and they got smashed.

A number of American unions chose to do nothing, and, from the

1970s onward, they unwittingly helped arrange their own funerals as they clung to strategies and leaders that no longer looked ahead.

End of lesson.

A SOLDIER IN THE ARMY OF THE UAW

For years the UAW, like many other unions, had the career ladder of its leaders down pat. And it was unusually successful in churning out some of organized labor's best leaders. It was a union known for its honesty and progressive politics. Moreover, the UAW was a place where factory floor training was usually the only credential needed to climb to the top. It was good enough for Walter Reuther, who became a virtual eminence for his union, a legend that could never be equaled. Fiercely devoted to his job and the UAW, Reuther preached a philosophy that put the union in the heart of politics and the community. He was smart. He was progressive. He framed issues in ways that made him a states-man for labor, and labor had only a few of his ilk when he was alive. His inclination to protect the union was so strong that he didn't hesitate to drive out leftists at a time when they were under attack from right-wing politicians.

He was a man of sweeping social visions, whose words were weighed seriously by politicians and the news media. "The kind of labor movement we want," Reuther once said, "is not committed to a nickel-in-the-pay-envelope philosophy. We are building a labor movement not to patch up the old world so men can starve less often and less frequently, but a labor movement that will remake the world so that the working people will get the benefit of their labor."

His rapid rise in labor's hierarchy was almost mythical. At age 15 he left high school to go to work in a steel plant in Wheeling, West Virginia. But he was fired from his first job when he organized the workers in protest over mandatory work on Sundays and holidays. He went to Detroit, where young workers like him were being swallowed up by the thousands at the bustling auto factories. He shifted from one factory to another while finishing high school at night, as well as starting college. Let go from a job with the Ford Motor Company, for three years he traveled the world with his brother, Victor, developing a view about what made factory work tolerable. When he returned to Detroit, he threw himself into organizing auto workers. With a youthful interest in socialism behind him, a knack for public speaking, and a fervid appetite for organizing, he moved up the organizing and then union leadership, ladder. He was president of the United Automobile Workers from 1946 until his death in a plane crash in 1970. When he died, there were few union leaders who had drawn as much publicity and had had such an impact on American life.

Reuther's route to the top, from the factory floor to the important union office, remained open for years for people like Bill Casstevens.

Casstevens too rose from the factory floor to union headquarters. And in the union's way of thinking, he had well earned his right to make decisions for others' lives. In 1991 he was the second most powerful person in the UAW, its secretary-treasurer, and the man who oversaw negotiations with Caterpillar. The union's annual report, which he signed as secretary-treasurer, showed that in 1992 he had earned $92,865. Only the union's president earned more.

Casstevens was 61 years old and facing four more years on the job before hitting the union's mandatory retirement age, when the troubles with Caterpillar began. His handling of the Caterpillar contract was one of his last, a part of his legacy in the union. He seemed determined to go about it the way he had done before. It would be a battle that the UAW would take on by itself. Although he had a heap of doubts about what might be ahead, he viewed it as a showdown similar to others he had experienced.

There would be no fancy public relations war. No corporate strategies. Those steps may have been around the bend, but not when he first charted the route ahead. He would do it the way it had always been done, probably ever since the autoworkers' chest-beating, glory days in Flint, Michigan, in the 1930s: with union grit and gumption.

A modern-day campaign with all of the latest tactics was something he just didn't seem to think about, although somebody should have.

Besides being the boss of the Caterpillar workers within the realm of the UAW, Casstevens was very much like them. When a group of union leaders and members came streaming out of a meeting, it was hard to separate him from the rest. After meetings, he drank with them in hotel bars, standing off to the side, leaning indistinguishably at the bar. Like most of them, he disliked high-sounding speeches. Like most, he didn't measure his words.

Average height, thinning brown hair that had been receding for years, a small paunch, pale skin, and a slightly bulbous nose—he could have been any of the men who showed up for work one day in Decatur with a small cardboard suitcase after World War II. Yet while he was of them, of the same roots, and of same worldview, there was something within him that set Casstevens apart.

He was private, a solitary leader, someone who did not often share what was on his mind. But when he did so, he often did it with a fury. His face would redden, and he would let loose. He would vent his temper at the bargaining table and toward those union colleagues who disagreed with him—one reason that some feared him within the union.

At large union meetings he spoke with a soft Southern drawl and his few words were usually sharp, but he was a mediocre public speaker. In small meetings he preferred to be blunt, to the point, to show he was not someone to be fooled with. His stare was as sharp as his tongue. He didn't appreciate being misunderstood.

Once, at the start of his union career, Casstevens had challenged the union's one-party system, making him the first person ever, at that time, to run against a candidate chosen by the political institution created by Walter Reuther. He was snubbed by the leadership, but eventually he made peace with the union's Detroit-based leaders and climbed the ranks. As a UAW official in Cleveland, he had earned good points with the UAW's hierarchy as a political liberal, as someone who had worked with local Democrats, and as a union leader savvy to the ways of reconciling racial differences within the union. Years later those who had known him at the start said he had become like those he had initially opposed. Years later he was also deeply feared by union bureaucrats who didn't agree with him.

His hardscrabble ways and leaning toward liberal politics went over well with the union's leadership. But that was not enough to propel Bill Casstevens to the union's highest rank. He was not as flamboyant as others. He had made enemies among his union colleagues because of his temper. And some were not convinced that he had the foresight to run the union, especially with all of its problems as blue-collar jobs began disappearing in droves. So when the time came, as he neared his retirement days, he was dogged by an air of rejection: He was not in the running for the presidency.

Casstevens seemed to bargain by his own shorthand rule of conduct. If he trusted the company, he would take its word. But if he saw no way of making a deal, if he felt he was being set up and not given all of the details, he would not back down. He liked to believe that he could work things out, that he truly had a penchant for compromise. Pat Greathouse, his mentor within the UAW's hierarchy, was convinced that Casstevens would always look for a way to work out a deal. Some of those who faced him across the bargaining table saw him as a man who would make a deal. And yet some found him inflexible.

Casstevens's view of the world was from the bottom up, which somewhat explained his ability to shift from compromiser to hard-headed union man unwilling to give an inch. His thinking was like that of the low-level worker ever scrambling for a piece of dignity and full of doubts about what the boss really wanted. As the UAW leaned toward more cooperative ways to get along with corporations in the 1970s, as a way to survive the hefty workplace cutbacks facing the industry, the shift stirred great debate and deep divisions within the union. Casstevens had clear feelings about this shift, which had not really gained a solid footing within the leadership ranks. He was decidedly not on the side that urged the union to hold companies' hands and walk together with management toward greater cooperation. "I am not a great advocate myself of quality of work life [the UAW's term for labor–management cooperation]," Casstevens told the *Cleveland Plain Dealer* in 1981, when he was the head of the UAW's Cleveland-based regional office.

Throughout the 1980s he had urged the Caterpillar workers to be careful about the company's overtures toward workers, inviting them to sit down with their bosses and find ways of cooperating. Still, the union locals, trusting the company's words, agreed to make significant contract changes and to commit themselves to working hand in hand with management.

After their first few meetings, Larry Solomon thought Casstevens was fair and very strong willed. "When you start pushing him, he is going to push back," Solomon said. Casstevens struck Solomon as "just one of the guys from the old school." But he was sure that Casstevens understood "modern-day union busting." He would snap at a decision he seemed to grasp easily but take his time, Solomon recalled, on others. Yet, Solomon did not think he completely understood Casstevens.

Restless in school and feeling pressured to help his family financially, at age 14 Bill Casstevens had gone to work full-time on the night shift at a cotton mill in Erlanger, North Carolina. He was the third oldest of 10 children. His father, Lloyd, had been a textile mill supervisor, who had been let go when he was 55 years old without a pension. He was missing an arm that had been cut off years before by a textile machine. His father spent the rest of his life as a low-paid Methodist minister, traveling from one rural Southern church to another. Years later Casstevens told his dying father that he had lived up to his father's goal for him and had become a missionary too. "I told him that there was no greater calling than to serve one's fellow workers, and that was what I was doing," he remembered saying.

FINDING A CALLING, DOING THE UNION'S WORK

At age 16, Casstevens joined the Navy and served in the Pacific during World War II. After the war he finished high school in Low Moore, Virginia, tried a few jobs, and started college in Lynchburg, Virginia, where he sold hospital insurance on the side. He had an auto accident but couldn't afford to repair the car. So he dropped out for lack of money and by chance got a job at a General Motors' Coit Road Fisher Body plant in Cleveland, where his brother had worked. It was one of the last auto plants in Cleveland. He didn't plan on staying long. His thinking was to make enough money for the auto repairs and return to college.

The way his father had been abandoned had left him with a bitter feeling about companies. But he knew little about unions, coming from the South, and especially the textile towns where the companies fought union organizing.

"When I got involved in unions, I saw that the union did care about people and about their dignity. I kept thinking, 'What if my dad would've had a union? What if he had worked at those auto plants?" he recalled.

He was ambitious from the start, sometimes holding more than one union job at a time. On the factory floor, he had started at the bottom, carrying material to seamstresses. Within the union, he was considered more aggressive and more militant than most up-and-coming members. When he was elected to the union's executive board in 1972, he was 43 years old and one of the youngest on the board. He became a vice-president in 1983 and the union's secretary-treasurer in 1988. Another candidate for the secretary-treasurer's job was Stephen Yokich. But Yokich had not campaigned as strongly for the job as did Casstevens.

As he rose within the union as a bargainer, "Cass," as he was called, would shift between his two personas when dealing with companies:

the tough bargainer and the realist. He would often issue taunts from across the bargaining table: "I will be as nice as you let me be and as nasty as you make me be."

Those words, he had decided, would one day be his epitaph.

Cass's grit and tough outer layer marked him as quite different from Owen Bieber, the UAW's president. Bieber, elected in 1983, was not eloquent or original. He was aloof, shy, inclined to stick to the facts, and not willing to improvise. A massive, silver-haired man, he resembled a Hollywood version of a good union guy. He had arrived at his job by being a union politician, offering moderate views, not getting in anyone's way, and doing his job. The union's public relations office, which drummed out his strong-worded speeches, could never be on hand for all the times that he was forced to painfully spell out what he thought was best for the UAW.

As compared with his second in command, Casstevens, and his gritty ways, Bieber was almost a shadow of a leader. So when the time came to deal with Caterpillar, it was Cass's responsibility, and there was little second-guessing from the top.

PART II

A Blue-Collar Legacy: Working in History's Wake

C H A P T E R   6

On the Prairie's Terms

On Decatur:

> Prairie grasses and flowers push up against the doorsteps of the outermost houses and each spring brighten the vacant lots. The swell imparts to the streets a sense of affinity with the land; the blocks of low weathered buildings seem a part of the prairie; in no way foreign to it, having the horizontal line emphasized in Frank Lloyd Wright's conception of prairie architecture.
>
> —*The 1939 WPA Guide to Illinois*

Just as it fools the heart and soul, the prairie forever fools the eye.

From above, flying over, passing from one coast to another, it appears to be a monotonous, crumpled table cover, wrinkled here and there, bereft of majestic sights or compelling vistas. Straight roads that cut around square farm fields and an occasional blue-green shimmer from a river or lake. The sporadic blotches of greenery look as though they have pushed their way up through slits in the tablecloth.

From the ground it almost always is a visual distortion, the sky filling most of the eye's screen while the land takes up only a small part of the picture. Land stretches in all directions. Lush and green in summer, robust and then mellowed in the fall, it seems moldy, gray, naked, empty on a sunless winter day. After a fresh snowfall, it turns dazzling and sparklingly bright. After days and weeks of snow and cold, it is a bone-chilling blanket.

In the summer, you squint at the sun-baked horizon and the only discernible markings are way off in the distance. A silver-colored silo, a faded white-shingled shed, a timeworn red barn, a dark greenish clump of trees scattered around a solitary brown brick farmhouse, a tall line of telephone towers, or maybe, far, far off, a toy-like tractor. Off in the distance all of the prairie's signposts are reduced to miniatures.

At night the prairie is a vast, blackened board game, a few lights flickering at the edges of the sparsely lit board. In the dark, the board flashes with the staccato dance of lights from the lines of trucks barreling by on the interstates.

Fall is beguiling, enchanting. The fields are cleared of the brown, withered stalks of corn. But there is still a touch of green, and on bright, sunny days the red and white and silver farm buildings stand out, shimmering against the felt-like backdrop. The fall is when much of the year's gamble is measured and put on the table. It's the time when farmers' dreams are tallied on computer screens or spread out across kitchen tables after dinner in scribbled numbers on long pads. When the cost of the equipment and the supplies is subtracted from everything else, with any luck, there is something left over.

AT PLAY IN THE FIELDS OF CORN

The horizon in winter vanishes behind a curtain of rain, snow, or clouds. Then there is the wind, which sometimes roars like a fleet of rundown trucks rushing by. After a strong snowstorm, the wind can fill the air for hours with a fine white mist of snow that seems like a white bandage: It is almost impossible to see through. Nothing is more terrifying than being caught driving alone in a prairie whiteout. White on white on white on white.

Far from the Midwestern cities and Great Lakes, which act as buffers and insulators against the frigid thrusts of arctic waves of air that race across the flat land, a cold winter's day can be brutally punishing. As temperatures plummet below zero, the winds puff themselves into raging bullies, indifferent to strangers and hostile to everyone and everything in their way.

At peak strength, the winds bend back road signs, rip at the ground, hammer on walls, tap annoyingly on windows, and tear away at everything not stuck in place. Tornadoes spin across the land in the spring, gouging and pulling things apart like playful monsters. Droughts are the bane of the summers, when high temperatures and unrelenting sunshine crack the ground. Between winter and summer, between blistering cold and heat, the tortured land somehow adapts.

Adapting is the only route to survival on the prairie.

A TAMED LAND

Dissected by long and lonely treeless roads that cut across the land at straight angles, with few twists or turns, the prairie in central Illinois is not what it once was. It used to be a vast carpet of tall grass that nurtured numerous species of plants and animals. As they set foot upon this carpet, the first European travelers called it a *prairie,* borrowing from the French word for "meadow."

But the tall grass, reaching as much as 10 feet high, is long gone. So are the wildflowers.

Decatur sits on the eastern edge of this prairie, a typical central Illinois town. When the sky is clear, the prairie's legacy to the town fills the air for miles: plumes of smoke, pure white smoke, hot water escaping from the grain mills' tall smokestacks. These are the remnants of the water used to process soy or corn, and they fly straight up in the air, forming massive drapes of soft gray that sit high above the town on starry nights and blue-sky days. They are natural billboards for industrial Decatur.

The grains come from the nearby fields, some of the nation's richest farming soil, land enriched by the layers of black silt created as the glaciers retreated and the prairie evolved over centuries. In the mid-1990s an acre of good farmland was going for well over $3,000, twice what other Midwestern farmers were getting for their land. Land is a farmer's bottom-line collateral. If you have good, profitable land, then you can get a decent loan to buy equipment and materials. Without good land, you are forever scratching to exist. When farmland values plunged in the 1980s, even the farmers sitting on good land suffered greatly.

Few thought much of the land when the prairie around Decatur was settled at the start of the 19th century. The sod was too hard to break and plough. The prairie grass was as thick and strong as hair on a dog's back. Many came down with the "shakes," malaria, from the swampy stretches of land. But then the swamps were drained, a plough made of steel was made, and it was possible to work the black fields.

And so farming flourished. The land was so good, the farmers didn't have to worry about finding places to ship their crops. The big granaries came to Decatur to buy what they produced. Farmers in Iowa or Michigan or Ohio might have good years, and some might do well financially. But the farmers around Decatur were known to be far better off financially than most farmers elsewhere. That is how good the land was.

Yet despite the land's great value and productivity, it could no longer support people, a pattern repeated in farm communities across the United States. Where a farm family could once live on the income from 500 acres, it now needed 2,000 acres, even to get by on the rich land surrounding Decatur.

With vast acreage and investment in equipment and materials of well over $100,000, a typical family farm would generate a not-so-stellar income of about $37,000 a year—in the good years. Farming simply could not be a magnet, even with good conditions. Every year fewer graduating seniors return to family farms in the small farming towns around Decatur. The number of farms surrounding Decatur continuously shrank, and the acres owned by single farms grew, so that only several hundred farmers remained on the nearby land at the end of the 1990s.

However, the disappearance of family farms didn't matter, because the farms, now under much consolidated ownership, were still there and the mills were busier than ever, so the road signs welcoming visitors to Decatur were not misleading. "The Soy Capital of the World," read one. Another was more open to debate. "The Pride of the Prairie," it read.

Factory Town USA

Decatur is a blue-collar town. That makes Labor Day more
significant than it is in Springfield, Bloomington–Normal
or Champaign–Urbana. . . . When blue-collar prosperity
began to fray in the late 1970s, some said Decatur had not
done enough to diversify, to shield the local economy from
slumping auto sales, or slack housing starts or national
recession.

—GARY MINICH, *Decatur Herald &*
Review, Sunday, September 2, 1990

One hundred seventy-nine miles from Chicago. One hundred twenty
from St. Louis. Thirty-six from Springfield.

Here, beyond where the prairie roads widen and lonely gasoline
stations, fast-food stores, and windswept taverns begin cropping up, beyond the anonymous box-like moderately priced motels that surround
everywhere junction USA, sits Decatur, a factory town. Some say it's a
company town, and the meaning of the words depends on where you
work and what you do.

On the car radio's FM dial, light rock, classic rock, Christian rock,
country music, farm produce prices, high school sports scores, an-
nouncements of business group meetings: The town is sending out an
identifying beam.

Five public golf courses, two private. Six bowling alleys. Two public swimming pools. Two hospitals. One hundred forty-six Protestant
churches. Five Catholic churches. One synagogue.

Decatur is a fortress of blue- and pink- and white-collar jobs with a
handful of wealthy families and prosperous small businesses slapped

down on the edge of the prairie. It is a town like any other in the Midwest, where businesses and traditions found their roots amid the farmlands. It is like other towns that became hubs for turning out steel or rubber, car parts or electrical parts, or people who move to big cities.

A place where the values that people talk about are traditional ones, where hard work is theoretically rewarded, where the sore thumb sticks out, where hope is only downscaled, never abandoned, and where it is okay to look over someone's shoulder as he reads a newspaper at a diner.

"Hmmm. How do you like that?"

The only link between the surrounding land and the newborn industry was the indigenous labor force—once considered cheaper than could be found elsewhere, often made up of immigrants bestowed with special skills and endurances, looked upon as loyal and trusty. Sometime, somehow, a company had anchored its fate in the place.

It was this serendipitous nature of American industrial history that deposited farm equipment and auto factories up and down the spine of the Midwest and strung electrical parts plants, machine tool plants, furniture factories, steel plants, rubber making factories here and there. As the meat packing industry deserted Chicago's stockyards after the turn of the century in search of cheaper help, it settled in smaller Midwestern towns, and food processing plants were scattered like pins on a map of the nation's food chart. In Decatur, there were factories that had simply scratched out their roots and flourished. And then there were the mills that took the grains coming from the nearby farmers.

Whatever the case, Decatur and communities like it, communities that had lashed their fate to the future of the local industry, flourished when their factory paychecks were abundant. Later, their luck turned into a painful memory.

WHERE THE PRAIRIE ONCE STOOD

In the 1930s, patches of prairie grass still lapped up against doors on the outskirts of Decatur. If you look up at the walls of the post office on Franklin Street downtown, built in 1935, the history of the community stares down at you in somber seriousness from the WPA murals. Besides Abraham Lincoln's, these are the faces of the farmers and miners and railroad workers who gave life to the town. Nowadays the miles of farm fields that surround the town give way to gas stations, strip malls, and fast-food outlets on the edge of town.

The Sangamon, a slow-moving river that twists through central Illinois, winds through Decatur. To satisfy the thirst of the town's factories, especially the A. E. Staley Manufacturing Company, in the 1920s a dam was built across the river, creating 12-mile-long Lake Decatur, which curls through a large chunk of the community. Thanks to industrial pollution, swimming in the lake became less than desirable years ago. But people still swim in it.

On the banks of the river just west of town, Abraham Lincoln and his family came to Decatur in 1830. Decatur barely existed then, a near-town crisscrossed by footpaths. Thirty years later, Illinois Republicans met downtown and made Lincoln the state's choice for the presidential nomination.

Before long Decatur's farmers had given the town a reason for being. But it was the arrival of the railroads in the middle of the century that gave Decatur a reason to flourish. The railroads needed workers, as well as services. On the railroads, the workers wrote an enduring lesson in labor history about the price of all-out confrontations and the inherent weakness of the efforts of American unions.

PULLMAN: AN OMEN OF ROMANTIC DEFEATS

When newly organized railroad workers, led by Eugene V. Debs, the president of the American Railroad Union (ARU), staged the Pullman strike in 1894, the workers in Decatur's railroad yards answered the call. They walked out on behalf of the workers at the Pullman car factory on Chicago's far Southeast Side, whose ranks had once reached 20,000 but had dwindled to several thousand during the 1893–1894 Depression.

George M. Pullman, a self-made business tycoon and owner of the Pullman Palace Car Company, had cut back wages for his workers by up to 35 percent without trimming back the higher-than-average rents the workers paid in the town he had built for them on the South Side. Pullman had a reputation as a benevolent employer. The community he had built for the workers was considered an ideal. But Pullman's generosity also reflected his paternalistic belief that he had to insulate his workers from the radicalism and poor behavior to which, he was convinced, they were exposed.

When in May 1894 the workers complained about abusive foremen as well as the pay cuts and high rents, Pullman offered to consider their complaints about their bosses but immediately fired three of their leaders. The workers quickly decided to strike. Pullman, alerted to the walkout, closed his facility at once.

While the ARU was holding a convention in Chicago, the striking Pullman workers, who had just joined the one-year-old labor group, approached the union for help. The company had refused to budge, despite appeals from prominent Chicago leaders. Debs, who had gone to work on the railroads at age 14, had created the ARU as a way to bring together workers from across the railroad industry. Until then they had been badly divided by their different crafts. Debs saw that workers would remain weak unless they linked themselves in common causes, an idea that was not popular with more conservative union leaders. His vision was exactly what took place in the 1930s as unions signed thousands of workers according to their industries, rather than their narrow levels of crafts. Taking on the railroads was a risk for the young labor group, and Debs tried to find a way around putting his members into the heat of such a confrontation.

But the company showed no signs of retreating, and the convention's delegates were intent on taking up the challenge. Finally, the ARU ordered its members not to handle trains carrying Pullman railroad cars. In return, the heads of 26 Chicago-based railroads, who had formed their own industry group, readily agreed to fire any workers who went along with the Pullman strike.

The fury spread. Most of the nation's railroads soon ground to a halt. The United States was in the throes of one of its first national strikes. The *Chicago Tribune* said that the strike was an "insurrection" and that it needed to be crushed immediately.

Several thousand federal troops and state militiamen were sent to quash the strike. The federal government stepped in at the behest of the railroads because they argued that the trains carried the U.S. mails. In Chicago, when the federal troops faced the barricaded strikers, 13 people were killed and more than 1,000 railcars were destroyed. The railroads had hired several thousand strikebreakers, deputized numbers of them, and backed them up with private detectives.

As the violence swept across the country, the death toll reached 34. The ARU's appeal for support for a general strike from the American Federation of Labor was turned down, and as the strike fizzled, the AFL called on workers within its member unions to go back to their jobs. Debs finally called the strike off in August. Facing federal charges, Debs was given a six-month jail term following his defense by soon-to-be-famous Chicago lawyer Clarence Darrow.

A strike commission appointed by President Grover Cleveland came up with suggestions for avoiding such costly confrontations. It urged compulsory arbitration between the railroads and their workers, with a permanent strike commission overseeing the situation, and acceptance of the labor groups by the companies. Little came from the recommendations. Not only had the unions been badly defeated, but, with the strength of the courts behind them, companies relied more than ever on injunctions to halt unions from striking.

Railroad officials told strike activists in Decatur and elsewhere to look for other work in other towns. Officials at Pullman and several railroads said they would hire only those workers who signed a "yellow dog contract" promising that they would not join a union while they worked at Pullman.

In Decatur, the strikers had mostly abided by a vow of nonviolence. Now, however, many faced severe financial losses as they lost their jobs with the railroads and local businesses. They also carried with them a deep sense of defeat and the reality that they could not wield enough strength to counter the will of the large companies.

THE CHANGING ROOTS

As the railroads grew, so did Decatur. Factories followed, and one of them was founded by James Millikin, a businessman who set up the Millikin Bank and whose fortune was used to endow Millikin University. The school's first buildings were set among the low-rising hills on the west of town at the turn of the century. Theodore Roosevelt gave the school's dedicatory speech in 1903.

But competition from other towns, whose locations appealed more to the spreading railroad lines, drained away much of the work for the railroad yards. There was still railroad work, but Decatur was no longer the mecca for the railroads. Moreover, a handful of garment factories closed after a series of strikes in the 1950s. And so the large factories that had moved to Decatur for good Midwestern workers remained the core. Here and there disputes erupted and short strikes took place, but the feeling from the 1960s onward was that the businesses in town saw eye to eye with the unions.

North of Decatur the land runs flat, until broken by a handful of small farming communities and blue-collar towns. Then there are stretches of box-like suburban developments in one-time farm fields, then densely packed suburbs, and, finally, the Midwest's low-lying capital, Chicago, still a dazzling Oz for someone coming up from the prairie.

South of Decatur the flatlands turn hilly. The prairie yields to swamps and forests. Going all the way to the Illinois border takes you through an area known as Egypt, where once there were many working coal mines. Like the African country, this region contains a town called Cairo and features a delta, this one created by the convergence of the Ohio and Mississippi Rivers. In southern Illinois the country twang rolls with a longer drawl.

The hunger for coal in the growing Midwestern cities and the criss-crossing railroad lines to carry it there made the coal under the ground in southern Illinois a short-term warehouse of riches. Just before World War II, Illinois ranked third in coal mining in the United States, and John L. Lewis got his real boost in miners' union politics after working in a southern Illinois mine.

Mining life painted small southern Illinois communities with little houses and the slag of coal outcroppings. It tainted the miners with a tough, unforgiving view of the world, imbuing them with a sense of supreme loyalty to one another and a clannish distrust of the companies and others who made their hard-bitten lives more difficult.

In Herrin—a small town not far from Carbondale in the heart of southern Illinois, where the first mine shaft was drilled in 1895—in June 1922, hundreds of union coal miners beat, shot, stabbed, and strangled to death 19 strikebreakers, who had been promised safe conduct if they left the mines. The strikebreakers, mostly jobless men from Chicago, were buried in paupers' graves. And the townsfolk offered perfect alibis for the indicted killers. No one was ever convicted of the crimes. Illinois miners paid nearly $1 million to defend the miners charged in the attack and to cover the costs of the damages to the coal company's equipment.

Fortuitously, Herrin came to stand for something beside the bloody revenge wrought by unions against strikebreakers. "Labor," wrote the widely respected journalist William Allen White, editor of the *Emporia* [Kansas] *Gazette* and the voice of Midwestern conservatives, "is beginning to feel that skill has the same status as property. The right to apply their skills in the place where it will produce value, labor seems to regard as an essential human right. This is astonishing. But we cannot ignore it—this belief of the laborer in his right to what he calls his job. He feels that so long as the place he works is a 'going concern' his right to work is exactly upon the same footing as the owner's right to profit."

Mary Harris Jones, an Irish woman who had migrated to the United States and then to Chicago and worked as a dressmaker for wealthy Chicago families, became the miners' angel. They called her Mother Jones. She was a lecturer for the Socialist Party of America, organizer for the mine workers' union, and frequent witness at labor confrontations. Following her death at 100, she was buried in the miners' cemetery in Mount Olive, Illinois, not far from where she had rallied workers.

The mines succumbed to the same tragedy that overtook the miners' union, the shift of mining westward and declining demand for the high-sulfur coal found in southern Illinois. By 1991 there was not one town left with the kind of good-paying factory work that is still found in Decatur. And by the end of the 1990s, only a few mines were left open. Job-desperate towns in southern Illinois begged for the new black gold: state prisons.

WHERE IS THIS TOWN HEADED?

Lashed to the roots of a shrinking industrial network, Decatur's old world was ebbing away, but a new world was not filling in the void.

Once there had been large banks, all of them lined up on one major downtown street. By the 1990s, however, only one was locally owned. Here and there locally owned factories were closed, bought by outsiders, or shifted elsewhere. There was a shorthand explanation around town of what these changes meant to Decatur.

Decatur, it was said, was run, was watched over, was guided by a group of well-to-do businessmen who regularly met and set the tone for the town's doings. Some were among the town's founding financial giants, and they were generous.

When they met, they decided on a local project for that year, what would be done for the local charities, who would give what time and what money. Unions were not popular with these town leaders. Unions were organizations led by outsiders. They split workers from their companies. But the unions took off in the 1940s with a burst of popularity, and the companies learned to live with the unions.

When new companies came to town, they brought new and often tougher management strategies. They sidestepped the older family businesses that had a grip on the status quo. When Caterpillar Inc. came, it brought a rush of excitement, because it was a world-class company and its blue-collar wages were higher than anyone had ever received before.

When Erik Brechnitz arrived in Decatur from St. Louis in 1962, he quickly realized that a half dozen people made decisions for the community. "It was pretty much a closed club," recalled Brechnitz, who would come to represent the new rules, a new pragmatic business approach to solving Decatur's woes.

A stockbroker, he became a member of Decatur's city council in 1981, an unfortunate time: Decatur's problems were starting to balloon. "All of this business just happened," he said. One after another factory started cutting back. The downtown was suffering; stores were closing or moving to the outskirts of the city.

The national recession pushed Decatur's unemployment rate up to 14 percent, and factory after factory began laying off workers. Caterpillar, which had once employed 6,000 workers in Decatur, began scaling back, so that by the early 1990s it was down to just over 1,800 workers. In 1980, more than a third of Decatur's workers made their living in a factory. By 1991, it was a little over one-fourth. About 131,000 persons lived in the Decatur area in 1980. A decade later there were 117,000.

In the view of Brechnitz, a careful-speaking man of medium height who favors dark, conservative suits, the community was facing epic change. Over the years there had been classic miscalculations about the town's future and about its ability to rely on factory jobs, as he saw it. Now the question, he thought, was where the new jobs would come from.

The answer seemed clear: from small businesses, from warehouses, from new companies that did not pay as much as the older hemorrhaging factories, and from new factories that were not unionized. The old days were gone, Decatur's Chamber of Commerce officials declared with an increasingly authoritative air. And the town, they added, could no longer rely so strictly on its larger factories. The new jobs and new businesses might not make Decatur as rich as before, but they paid a salary.

Yet there were not enough salaries to go around. What came of these efforts? Modest successes, Brechnitz calculated. Modest gains. Not long after the strike started at Caterpillar and labor problems began brewing at Staley, Brechnitz, a Republican, was elected mayor. For over half a century, Decatur had been led by Republicans, and his coming to office was no change. The difference was that the background chorus of wealthy elites was largely gone. To the new mayor, there was something wrong with the way the unions were dealing with the town's companies. They did not realize, he thought, that times were different. He was sure they did not realize that they would not get as much support as they might have before.

Another change complicated things.

No longer did the *Decatur Herald & Review*, the town's only newspaper, speak with the conviction of a local product. That is what it had been for a long time, a feisty voice that echoed the whims of its Decatur-based owners. It had been owned by the Lindsay-Shaub company, a product of two Decatur-based newspapers that traced their history back to 1874. John Lindsay, a lawyer from Tennessee, had founded the *Decatur Review* in 1874, and then the *Decatur Labor Bulletin*, where he preached labor industrialism and the eight-hour day.

His son, Frank M. Lindsay, who was a boss at the Decatur newspapers for over 50 years, believed in having his newspapers speak their minds locally. As he grew older, he also became more concerned about management's inability to control labor. Lee Enterprises, an old, largely Midwestern chain, took over the Decatur newspapers in 1979 when they bought out the Lindsay-Shaub owners.

The new owners did not have the same determination to tell the rest of the state what they thought. Nor, some employees felt, were they as willing to embarrass local businesses. Bob Sampson had been a columnist until the early 1980s and then left town for a job in Washington. When he returned, the newspaper seemed even less likely to rile anyone and more likely to keep advertisers happy. The newspaper was selling just fewer than 50,000 copies a day, and a few more on Sundays.

A PATRON OF DECATUR'S NEEDS

Decatur had been known as a town where businesses had long opposed unions. Augustus Eugene Staley, founder of the large corn processing plant, had once threatened to close his factories if he were forced to deal with a union. He believed in nurturing his workers in a patronly way, but not hand in hand with the union.

How A. E. Staley came to reap entrepreneurial riches from the heartland would read, if it were written, like a Sinclair Lewis story about Midwestern businessmen: of tycoons and self-made men, of dreamers overflowing with zeal and confidence, of salesmen certain that they knew at the start of the 20th century the way the future was going.

Staley was a young, successful traveling salesman who had grown up in a North Carolina farm family. He set up a cornstarch company in Baltimore and then moved it to an empty factory in Decatur in 1906 so he could manufacture the product in the heart of corn country. The company profited unbelievably from processing corn, and then soybeans.

The company built a "castle in the cornfields," as its headquarters was called, and the building contained an elaborate lobby where farmers would feel like esteemed customers when picking up payments for their crops. In no time the company went from producing cornstarch to processing corn and then soybean products and high-fructose corn syrup, a product seized upon by soft drink makers. Founder Staley became recognized as a pioneer in soybean processing in the United States.

But it wasn't enough to succeed in the accounting book margins. Staley was a man of big visions, as a company-sponsored history of the firm repeatedly points out. He wanted to promote his company, so as a sports lover he set up a baseball team with top-notch players, which toured the Midwest. When the baseball team failed to achieve the fame he sought, he switched to football. He decided to hire the best athletes he could and work them in his factories while also letting them show off their football skills. In 1920 the company and town had a football team that would go on to fame. It was called then the Decatur Staleys. But the costs quickly proved too great, and Staley unloaded the team on its coach and manager, George Halas. Halas rooted the team in Chicago, where it quickly became known as the Chicago Bears.

Other companies nipped at the firm's heels. In the 1970s, the H. J. Heinz Company of Pittsburgh made an offer to buy Staley. But company executives flatly rejected the offer, and for the public the view was that the future would remain on an unbroken line with the past. The firm would remain in the close grip of the family, an important fact for

Decatur, because Staley was known around town as a company that provided for its workers and its roots.

By the 1980s, however, problems overcame the company. It bought a food service company in 1984 and soon after moved its headquarters to the Chicago area.

Its profits were down, its stock slumping, when Tate & Lyle PLC, a global giant in the food sweetener industry, began its determined pursuit of the firm. From the merger of two family-run refiners dating from the 19th century, London-based Tate & Lyle had become one of the world's largest refiners of corn and sugar. With foreign roots that went back to colonial England, its operations were spread across more than 50 countries.

Having fended off buyout offers before, company officials were not interested, but hostile takeovers were blossoming in the 1980s and Tate & Lyle officials were eager to gain access to the vast U.S. corn sweetener market. Undeterred, officials from the British company courted politicians in Decatur and Springfield, the Illinois state capital, telling them they had the highest intentions for the veteran company. In 1987, Tate & Lyle prevailed. It bought Staley for $1.48 billion, and its chairman, Neil Shaw, had plans for the company. Headquarters would be shifted back to Decatur. Research and development would be boosted.

"The old management took their eyes off the ball," said Shaw at the time. That would not happen again.

CHAPTER 8

The Great Industrial Slide and Washout

A Storm Cloud in American History?

> In Houston during the early 1980s, bumper stickers read,
> "Drive 90 and Freeze a Yankee." In part this exercise
> represented harmless interregional razzing, but it also
> expressed the contempt felt by cowboy entrepreneurs of
> the free-wheeling Southwest for the growing armies of
> jobless in the Rust Belt states.
> —JOHN HOERR, *And the Wolf Finally Came:*
> *The Decline of the American Steel Industry*, 1988

The wheels were spinning faster, dizzyingly faster, and each time unions and workers were coming up heavy losers in the game of industrial slots.

High wages—gone. Pay raises—put on hold, frozen. Pension plans—scrapped, abandoned, trimmed back. Company-paid health care plans—canceled, reduced, altered. Company job-training programs, the few that existed for blue-collar workers—also put on hold. Benefits—reduced. Even the smallest career protections were disappearing.

Before the nation's unions could muster any defense, plan any recovery, rally their forces, the legacies they had counted on were shattered and frayed, in some cases rendered worthless. The unions had pinned their futures to their blue-collar identities. A big mistake. They had grown careless, lazy, blinded by their onetime success, and too

70

weak to bend back the forces pushing them aside. Blue-collar workers had grown too reliant on their time-clock–driven lives. They believed too much in tradition. They counted too much on good faith and loyalty.

The world was changing, but the nation's Decaturs insisted on staying the way they were. And so the industrial slide that began in the United States in the early 1970s persisted without mercy through the 1980s and lurched forward in stops and starts throughout the 1990s.

THE END OF FACTORY LIFE AS WE KNEW IT

One day in 1977 a steel mill in Youngstown, Ohio, laid off 4,100 workers. The event soon became known in local history as Black Monday. By the mid-1980s steel making was only a cruel memory in Youngstown. Over 700 steel making and steel supply facilities shut down between January 1974 and June 1986.

In Akron, the tire factories essentially stopped making tires. In Pittsburgh, the steel mills stopped making steel. In the city of Detroit, most auto plants shut down forever. In Milwaukee, the epitome of an American factory town, a place where they made almost everything possible, one factory closed after another through the mid-1980s.

Factories and factory towns across the Midwest were falling like dominos, unable to compete with either the foreign steel mills and automakers whose products were appearing in the United States in new abundance or the foreign workers who worked for so much less pay than their American counterparts. These workers and communities were also second-hand victims of outdated technology. The firms that dominated their lives were competing against European and Japanese factories with the latest equipment and the latest thinking on how to get a job done. American manufacturers had either ignored the foreign threat or arrogantly plowed their profits into anything but their factories. They saw no need to change the way they dealt with their workers—people who had put widgets into holes for years without knowing what they were really doing—and that was it.

Worse than being victimized by global trade, these factory towns were caught in the stranglehold of a slumping U.S. economy. In the 1950s factory workers accounted for just over one out of three jobs in the United States. By the 1990s that number had been cut in half. On the surface, the recession of the early 1990s did not seem as severe as previous downturns—overall job losses were not as great and the rise in the jobless rate was not that marked—but among factory workers the silent earthquake was taking its toll. The permanent layoffs of the period took a far more severe toll than in any recent recession, the U.S. Labor Department said. At the same time, blue-collar wages plummeted at a rate unequaled in recent history.

As foreign products pushed aside U.S.-made goods, American manufacturers resorted to lowering their wages, saying that was the only way they could compete. For higher-skilled, better-trained workers there were some pay increases, but semiskilled workers only lost ground. With fewer workers represented by unions, there was little protection for those outside the union bargaining fence. Even for those inside, the protections were minimal at best as wage concessions and pay freeze mania spread throughout the blue-collar trades.

In 1982, 2,700 large-scale layoffs and plant closings wiped out more than 1.25 million blue-collar jobs across the United States. In Rockford, a longtime blue-collar town in northwest Illinois, when the jobless rate reached 19.2 percent in July 1982, giving it the nation's highest unemployment rate, Mayor John McNamara slapped a sticker on the front of his city council desk. "Keep the lights ON. I'M STAYING," it read.

The thinking was that the good times of the past would come back if everyone would show some patience. The assumption was that the world had not changed. But the world had changed, and the past did not repeat itself across the factory-rich Midwest. In the early 1950s, the Midwest had made up nearly 30 percent of the nation's factory workforce. That was the peak. By 1985, the number had fallen to just under 22 percent.

Youngstown, Akron, Detroit, Milwaukee—all changed, hollowed out. It was America's secret earthquake, unparalleled devastation that went largely unnoticed as the rest of the country daydreamed and looked the other away. Financially troubled companies turned their backs and fled communities in the middle of the night. Corporate headquarters were shifted, squeezed, erased. Communities that had counted on their corporate patrons to watch over them suddenly found themselves orphaned.

As the companies shrank or moved on, so did community life. Downtowns slowly faded away, withered. People picked up and moved elsewhere, looking for jobs, new lives, new illusions. Workers used to assume they would return to the job one day following layoffs. Not any more. From the 1970s onward, layoffs were more and more likely to be permanent. Of the factory layoffs experienced between 1990 and 1992, 90 percent turned into permanent job losses.

Even those who still had jobs did not have the earnings they had once enjoyed. In 1975, America's factory workers were the third highest paid in the developed world. By 1991, they ranked thirteenth. Between 1985 and 1990, factory workers' wages and benefits increased by only 14 percent, the lowest such change in the industrialized world. Between 1973 and 1990, the average earnings of those who had graduated from high school but not gone on to college, when adjusted for inflation, actually fell by 30 percent. During the 1980s, the average blue-collar worker's wages, when inflation adjusted, dropped by nearly 10 percent.

The humiliations and indignities were enormous for the unprepared and unsuspecting.

When the UAW struck Caterpillar in 1982, it was several years after the end of the 205-day strike before many workers went back to their jobs. The company, suffering from the downward spiral of the recession, said it did not have enough work to call the workers back to their jobs. One of the Caterpillar workers in Decatur, Randy Morrell, lost nearly all of his savings while out of work. Thrown into a new job pool, the formerly well-paid UAW workers in Decatur and elsewhere throughout Caterpillar's system were stunned. They struggled and stumbled for the next few years, rarely reaching the same pay levels.

Meanwhile, the unions, the communities, and the U.S. government threw up their hands and wanly said there was little they could do to staunch the flow of disappearing jobs. The unions said retraining was not their job. The government said it did not have the money for retraining. Few companies said it was their duty to retrain and redeploy their workers in the midst of shifting markets. Operating with reduced budgets, federal and local job retraining efforts skimmed the best candidates from the laid-off workers for their programs, and the rest of the displaced workers had to make do for themselves. But they barely knew where to find help, and what they found was a maze of government programs that often didn't meet their needs. "American manufacturing and service workers have the skills for yesterday's routine jobs," concluded a 1990 study of worker training by the Office of Technology Assessment, a former research arm of Congress.

Financially strapped states tightened the rules for their unemployment benefits, and the ranks of jobless qualified for the handouts steadily declined. A social Darwinism set in just as the workers' problems mounted in the early 1980s.

Under Ronald Reagan and the new political conservatives in Washington and across the country, laid-off factory workers were given the option of picking up and moving elsewhere or accepting their bad luck. Some moved. Many swallowed their bad luck.

In 1986, I came across a 33-year-old laid-off worker in a small southeastern Michigan town who was considering taking his life because everything had fallen apart.

No matter how he tried, he could not support his family the way he once had. The crowning blow came when he was hired back at the auto parts factory where he had once worked. Under the new ownership, he was getting two-thirds of his old pay. He had washed dishes for medicine for his family. He had taken Christmas baskets to feed his family. But he was not prepared to do the same work and receive one-third less.

I had spent over a year tracking down all of the workers at this plant for a series of articles about the nation's blue-collar casualties. Before long, I knew them like relatives and neighbors. Sometimes when I went to visit with them, it was more to keep in touch, to check in on them, than to do any reporting. When the young laid-off worker told me that he wanted to kill himself and that he had a place picked out where he might do it, we drove out to a field so his wife would not hear us talk. I slowly told him about how his former colleagues were also facing tough times, but that they were dealing with it. They were moving on with their lives.

We stood alone in that cold, windy field without saying anything for a while, and I remember his face when he said he would not use the rifle he had set aside and he would try to get on with his life too.

"I didn't foresee these times coming," he said.

THE LEGION OF THE UNWANTED

If you were middle-aged and poorly educated, your chances of starting again were dim. If you waited for the past to miraculously return, you were likely to drop out of the job market and disappear into the world of handouts and makeshift jobs. If you were an African American factory worker, your chances of holding onto the same economic rung were even more dismal. In the mid-1980s, the Bureau of Labor Statistics compared white and African American workers who been let go by their companies. The African American workers went longer before finding a new job, were rehired at a much lower rate, and after finally finding a new job, more frequently dropped out of the job market than their white counterparts.

Years later, the impact of the loss of these jobs would grow. Young African American workers would no longer have a foothold in the factory workplace as others still did. And that foothold had lasted, sadly enough, for barely one generation for most African American workers. Big-city African American neighborhoods that were anchored by factories were devastated when the jobs disappeared. In the small towns, African American workers, who had only recently won a place in the factory, and often doing the dirtiest, toughest jobs—working in the forge or the body shop, the places that smelled and were dangerous—were likely never to be seen again on the factory floor.

For most of the nation's blue-collar casualties, the losses were so sudden they barely had time to think. A survey by the government's General Accounting Office, a congressional watchdog agency, found that more than one-fourth of the factories that closed had given no warning to their workers. The day the plant closing came, the company shut the door, and that was it. The average warning time for a plant closing was seven days. Union workers were no better off than others. Just 10 percent of the union contracts in the 1980s required employers to give warnings of shutdowns. Once the plants closed, only one-third of the factories gave their workers severance pay, the government agency discovered when it examined plant closings in the mid-1980s.

In Mount Pleasant, a working-class town in central Michigan, the Ferro Manufacturing Company put up a sign in July 1983 telling its workers to have a "safe July Fourth." Without giving any warning, and working behind windows covered with canvas, the company stripped the auto parts factory clean. None of the 130 workers at the plant, many of them middle-aged veterans, suspected that they would lose their jobs during their annual summer leave. Two months after the plant's abrupt closing, the 55-year-old shop chairman of the local, a man who had taken much of the burden on himself for helping others, died of a heart attack.

"We really had nothing to live on but our little savings. I knew it did have an effect on him. He held it inside," recalled the shop steward's widow at the shuttered factory. He had put in 37 years at the same factory.

Complaining was not the way these former union leaders were accustomed to facing up to a crisis. The problem was that most didn't know what to do, and they had little help. Many went back to work on the line, or doing anything available, and the work was harder than they had done in years.

As companies bailed out of pension plans, leaving workers financially stranded, the unions fought for laws to help them at least prepare for funerals. They also sought plant closing laws, but none went into effect until February 1989, as Southern Democrats teamed up with the Republicans to prevent anything from standing in the way of manufacturers closing northern plants and moving the work to the less expensive and union-free South. The law required companies with 100 or more workers to give 60 days' notice of large-scale layoffs, but it was a dubious victory. Employers learned that they could empty a plant slowly without giving any notice, and the only recourse workers had when a company broke the law was to take the company to court, a wait that many did not have patience for. Even then they could get paid only for the days they had gone without notice.

Gains won by blood years before were vanishing day by day.

WHAT UNIONS WROUGHT

After the 1930s, after unions' rise to power via a bloody and often unpredictable number of trench-warfare–like campaigns, a different system had fallen into place. A loose sort of grand design worked out between organized labor and business soon turned into a tradition of mutual acceptance and collective bargaining.

Slowly the tradition ground forward, stumbling here and there, setting precedents along the way. Innovations were digested and institutionalized into thickening contracts. Nuances crusted over and became "the way things have always been done around here"—at least since the last contract.

Annual raises. Vacation pay. Company-paid health care. Pensions. Seniority. Rules for who does what job for how long and on what shift and at what extra pay and on which days. Rules for what the union could do and where it could stick its nose and for what the company had to do.

What unions achieved benefited not only their workers but others in firms that competed with organized companies. As long as unions operated as effective lobbies for worker-related issues such as pensions and on-the-job safety controls, they were a counterbalance to business. The government did not have to speak up, did not have to act as an artificial voice for workers. Pressure was already on the government. That was the role of organized labor.

As contract traditions developed, so did hundreds of rules governing the way things were done outside the contracts themselves. There were, for example, rules for how contract fights would be waged: They would not be all-out, knock-down, drag-out wars. Disputes would not turn into fights without a safety valve, a way to reach a deal that both sides could live with.

These traditions thrived because most of the competition in the large blue-collar industries abided by the ground rules. Contracts were industry-wide, so there was little room for variance, little incentive to go against the tide. Soon there were also laws protecting workers' bargaining rights.

All of this was suddenly at stake.

BLUE-COLLAR UNIONS IN RETREAT: WHEN MOTOWN BECAME A GHOST TOWN

As the work vanished, the unions began to implode. Before the slide commenced, the membership of the UAW, the union that had pioneered cost-of-living raises, health benefits, and pensions after 30 years on the job as basic contract ingredients, numbered 1.5 million, its peak. By 1992, its membership had tumbled by more than 40 percent.

During those years, the auto industry cut 30 percent of its workforce. And the steel industry faced an even worse decimation. From 650,000 workers in 1953, it fell to 178,000 by 1992. As the steel industry evaporated, the United Steel Workers union shrank. So, too, as the American tire industry shriveled away and most of the firms were bought by foreign companies, the membership of the once proud rubber workers union, the United Rubber Workers, fell to 100,000, less than half of its peak size.

Each time the nation slid into an economic downturn in the 1980s, the number of factory workers dropped. In the electronics industry alone, 15 percent of the workforce (238,000 jobs) was let go between 1988 and 1992. During the 1980s, General Electric Company cut loose 120,000 workers. USX let go 94,600. Ford Motor Company eliminated 72,000 jobs. Bethlehem Steel wiped out 56,000. Navistar International erased 52,000 jobs.

Desperate autoworkers would write to Doug Fraser in the early 1980s, telling the former president of the UAW about their plight, and he would reply that he had been there. He meant the Depression, when his father had been laid off in Detroit and his family had been evicted from their house.

Faced by a worsening crisis, shrinking membership and financial roots, the unions lashed out at foreign imports and fumed about technological changes that had put thousands out of work. Beyond barring foreign imports, however, they had few solutions for their problems. Nor did they find salvation in organizing new members, because few unions had thought out their strategies, let alone spent the money to organize new members.

They were boxed in. The excitement, the hunger, the momentum that had once inflated their ranks had left them. American business, aware of the weakened state of its bargaining partners, became more aggressive. Their backs against a wall, unions played out different strategies to survive. A handful stuck by the old ways, the long grueling strikes, but they rarely won. Some sought out a compromise, a partnership of sorts with business, saying they could exist only if they had a foot in management's door.

Among the large blue-collar unions, another mindset took hold. They were driven by a furious fear of escalating job losses and a fierce determination to cling to what they had in hand: their workers, their members, their jobs. This meant sometimes accepting concessions that tended to divide old and new workers—accepting a lower pay scale for new workers while protecting the older ones, accepting a pay scale that would never reach the current high, consigning future generations to lower pay and benefits.

By accepting wage deals that set the salaries for new workers below those of veteran employees, unions thought that they were buying time and that such deals would vanish when the good times returned. But companies were not eager to give up the newfound savings. The unions were then stuck with contracts that essentially pitted one generation of workers against another. When the nation's economic recovery arrived by the mid-1980s, the flight of blue-collar workers did not end. Nor did the two-tier wages, nor any of the new pressures that companies pointed to as the reasons for declining wages and declining workforces.

LOOKING FOR SOLACE

When middle age overtook them, many of those who had gone to work in the factories in the 1960s and early 1970s were certified comfortable middle-income Americans. They were comfortable enough to some-times vote Republican and often grouse about the way regular American values had been forgotten. But then the blue-collar job drain began to worsen in the 1980s, and their view of the world changed. So did the way their neighbors looked at them.

Blue-collar workers became more frightened and less sure of the world ahead. They felt vulnerable to foreign trade and to factories that seemed to desert them for nothing other than lower wages. Their visions of passing on their blue-collar inheritance to their children suddenly was wiped away.

Meanwhile their next-door neighbors had grown envious of the good fortune that they were not sharing. They did not work in the factories that still had good-paying jobs. They did not belong to unions that still guaranteed a decent salary, albeit without raises or even with pay cuts. They were blue-collar workers too, but they did not have the same breaks as their neighbors who belonged to unions and did the factory work. They considered their neighbors whiners when they talked about hard times. They looked at them, with all their benefits and protections, as pampered babies. The nonunion neighbors would be happy to have the job at two-thirds the union pay.

And as the ranks of union blue-collar workers continued to decline, this type of envy inched upward toward those with the better-than-average wages, workers with union contracts like many of Decatur's factory workers. The disgruntled nonunion workers were surrounded by others with the same skills and similar jobs, but those workers were getting higher wages, driving nicer pickup trucks, going on better vacations. And as the drain of good-paying jobs increased throughout the 1980s, the jealousy also increased because there were more in their ranks.

Some of the high-wage union workers in Decatur sensed the resentment that surrounded them. But most were surprised when they tried to make their case for public support and it was not there. Class loyalty could not be found among neighbors, who either signed up to take their jobs at the factories locked in disputes or turned their backs on their struggles.

It was hard for them to deal with this resentment because they had nursed their own anger for years. Many still viewed themselves as victims of a war they did not fully understand, the Vietnam War. They had gone to school, joined the military, and then returned home to no welcome. They resented the time that they were made to feel had been wasted. They resented their images as losers, and they resented feeling like losers. As the years went by, they were able to put aside the dreams and feelings linked to the war. But when their problems recurred, they found themselves coping again, and their resentment returned.

They were not the only ones who believed that America had slipped into a mysterious, inexplicable decline. There was a feeling shared more broadly among Americans that something had gone wrong, and whether the demon was global economics or another force, the economy surely seemed to be wobbling in a different orbit.

How could this be?

They were true believers, these factory workers, in an America that had been framed for them as adolescents in Vietnam, an America etched in childhood memories of victory marches after World War II, an America that had rewarded them every day when they drove up to the factory.

They were nurtured by an incredibly enduring faith that as long as you worked hard you could get a job, a good job in a factory, and good pay, and, thank God, a good life too. And that made it all the harder for them to fathom what was taking place.

Cut loose from their factory moorings, blue-collar workers fell back down the wage ladder. They were among the growing ranks of low-income workers. From 1979 to 1990, according to the U.S. Census Bureau, the percentage of full-time workers with low-paying jobs climbed from 12 to 18 percent of the workforce.

The bigger picture was even more disheartening. If you were poor in 1960, you were likely to be poorer, as compared with the rest of society, in the 1990s. At the other end of the scale, the rich were doing much better than they had years before. The inescapable fact was that America was becoming more unequal.

As winter set in soon after the Caterpillar strike began, Decatur seemed stuck away on a shelf of joblessness. One of every ten workers in town was unemployed in January 1992, and local relief agencies were scrambling to help those in need. The jobless rate in Illinois was 9.3 percent, the highest among the nation's 11 industrial states. The nation's unemployment figure was lower, 7.1 percent. There was a foreboding gloom about the economy. Help-wanted ads were down. Consumer confidence was slumping too.

Amid a fierce winter storm that raged one day outside the Knights of Columbus Hall just off Eldorado, where Decatur's Catholic Charities held its bimonthly food giveaways, Jerry Newingham, a middle-aged factory worker without a job, grumbled as he waited his turn in line.

"I always had a job before. I never went without a job like this before," he said as he moved along the line that had been formed outside the building in the frigid dawn before the doors had opened. By the time he got his turn, the people in line had scooped up most of the five-pound bags of flour and cans of peanut butter.

Beside him, looking down at the slim pickings, were several striking Caterpillar workers.

The prairie slept that night under another snowy whiteout, a fierce, swirling winter storm that blinded anyone on the highways leading out of town and covered over almost everything for miles around with a deceptive white blanket: the old, the new, and scars of the old.

The Scab Ascendancy

How Weakened Unions Got Even Weaker

In the 1980s, labor took a detour. A major one. Instead of rising up in-domitably as it had done following numerous beatings of the past, orga-nized labor was pulled into the maelstrom at the bottom of the indus-trial slide. There it foundered in dizzying confusion. Preoccupied with keeping its head above water, it largely forgot about everything that made it more than a bargaining agent for its workers.

A PRIMER IN SURVIVAL TACTICS

The nation's big unions tried one strategy after another to stay afloat. One, aimed at the modest goal of mere survival, was simply to hold on through the terrible times, to make deals, to offer concessions in the hope of at least keeping a foot in the door. In two rounds of contracts in the late 1980s, for example, the United Automobile Workers union backed down on a number of contract issues with Caterpillar. It agreed to drastically reduce the number of job classifications. It gave Caterpil-lar more freedom in subcontracting work and organizing jobs. As a sign of its faith in the company's word, it also encouraged its members to put their hearts into the company's employee participation plan. By helping the company make changes, many in the union were convinced, they could avoid the old battles and work out a new partnership.

Another popular strategy was to go to war, to wage a fight, to show the union's grit, to put a stake in the ground and vow not to retreat beyond that point. The rationale was to strike, to push the company as far as possible and maybe, with luck, to make an honorable deal. That approach sounded great but was largely a dud in the 1980s because of a major shift in the way companies did battle.

In the past companies might have kept their plants open and run them with a skeleton crew of white-collar workers and others on hand. No matter how bitter the negotiators sounded, the company might keep paying its workers' health care benefits.

But in the 1980s, American companies showed a greater willingness to set aside the unwritten rules of combat of the past. They were quite willing to replace strikers with scabs—permanently.

Using scabs had been legal since a 1938 United States Supreme Court ruling made the United States one of the few industrialized democracies where companies had the right to throw out their striking workers on the spot and eliminate their jobs. It was, however, not a popular tactic.

When a company replaces it striking workers, it is resorting to the harshest weapon in the hands of management. Taking this step marks an absolute breakdown in trust between the company and its workers. In an instant, the company sweeps aside years of seniority, in one smooth motion negating everything that has gone before. For workers who frame their lives within their jobs, it is as if they no longer exist.

The use of strikebreakers is a tool of destruction, not construction. It leaves behind fear and anger and elicits calls for revenge. In small towns it is not uncommon for violence to break out as the company brings in the new hires.

In the 1980s a handful of companies began to realize they could unleash this ultimate weapon and nothing horrible would come flying back their way. The communities that were the battlefields were too weak, the voters disinterested. Eventually a flurry of large-scale incidents led the way for yet more businesses to replace striking workers, or at least threaten to do so. Between 1985 and 1989, companies threatened to replace workers in nearly one-third of all major strikes, according to a survey by the U.S. General Accounting Office. About half the time, the company actually went ahead and replaced its striking workers. Eastern Airlines, Greyhound Lines, and Continental Airlines all ended up replacing their striking union workers during the 1980s and

early 1990s. But the transformation was so great in the paper industry
that organized labor should have swallowed its pride and taken notice:
A sacrosanct tradition had truly been undone.

WAYNE GLENN'S LESSON IN COMPANY LOYALTY: HOW INTERNATIONAL PAPER TURNED HIM INTO A CRUSADER AGAINST SCABS

In the 1970s the members of the paper industry's major union, the
United Paperworkers International Union (UPIU), benefited from contracts that were often far better than those won by other blue-collar unions. By the 1980s, however, the union was largely on the run from
companies seeking cutbacks at the bargaining table. As it retreated, it
left concessions and small pay increases, if any, in its trail. In 1987 its
membership stood at 236,000, down by about 35,000 members since
1981. And its ranks kept shrinking through the decade.

The paper industry's bargaining style had changed. Its financial position was not as strong as before. Growing foreign competition and the
high price of the dollar raised new challenges for the industry. Bad investments added to the problem. A wave of mergers led to increased
corporate debt for some firms. Still, despite short-term downturns, the
industry was prosperous, and companies took an increasingly hard line
with the union. In the mid-1980s paper companies hired permanent replacements in the midst of at least three strikes, and that buoyed the industry's confidence that it could broadly whittle away long-term contract terms with the union.

One company led the way. International Paper (IP) aggressively
sought contract changes, wage cutbacks, and greater power for management. Then, in 1987, UPIU locals at plants in Jay, Maine, Lockhaven,
Pennsylvania, and De Pere, Wisconsin, struck IP.

Only a few years earlier the union had reluctantly agreed to go
along with IP, bowing to the company's pleas about financial problems
and banking on the company's vows to reward it in future negotiations
for helping out.

But in 1987, amid record profits and hefty bonuses for its top executives, the nation's richest paper company and largest landowner
wanted its workers to accept a sizable pay cut, to face the loss of hundreds of jobs, and to give up their holiday pay on Christmas. It had
earned $305 million on sales of $5.5 billion in 1986.

When the locals struck, it stirred a sadness in Wayne Glenn, a tall, thin, silver-haired man who had been president of the UPIU since the late 1970s. The son of a sawmill worker, he had grown up in logging camps and was familiar with the tough breaks life handed to those who work with their arms and backs. He had gone to work for IP almost 40 years earlier in Camden, Arkansas, starting out as a pulp tester.

Years later Glenn remembered how fair-minded the company had been. If it couldn't talk the local union representative out of responding to a worker's grievance, it would concede and agree to do so. He also remembered how IP had gone from being a company that listened to the union to one "that dictated."

Convinced the company was not going to pay much attention to the union, he cautioned the three locals against striking. He had a reputation within the union as a pragmatist, as a feisty, powerful orator and a very politically savvy union leader. Wayne Glenn prided himself on not being a rebel or a troublemaker. He was not the kind of man inclined to declare open warfare on companies that betrayed his union. In the back of his mind was the possibility that IP would replace the workers. So he advised them instead to refuse to work weekends.

The union locals didn't see much sense in staying off the job on Sundays, so for 16 months the three paper workers locals struck. The union spent over $16 million on strike pay and other costs to support the strikers. "We went broke doing that," Glenn recalled. And union officials found themselves stunned when the strike, launched as a grand battle, a highly publicized, highly emotional showdown with the company, dragged on. Only once before, in 1921, had there been a strike that long against IP.

The union's campaign to embarrass and shame IP into a settlement went nowhere. With the union's treasury nearly empty, with barely nothing left to support the strikers, the union's leaders sought to end the debacle. And so the locals admitted defeat and made an offer of unconditional surrender. But the company had already replaced them with 2,250 workers.

Not only had most of the workers lost their jobs, but in years to come the newly hired workers would vote the union out.

The failed strike was a stinging defeat that provoked unending fury among the striking workers, especially for some of those in Jay, Maine, who were not convinced that Glenn had done his best to bring IP to its knees. They felt abandoned by the union, certain that it had backed down just when they were gaining steam and exerting pressure on the company with their campaign. For its part, the union had to tighten its belt and cut costs to get by. The country's other big unions could not avoid noticing the devastation. But the sight was so gruesome that many seemed to turn away.

HOW THE GAME HAS CHANGED

The lesson that should have been learned was this: From then on, whenever the possibility of industrial warfare arose, the potential for ultimate kill would come along with it. Organized labor's response should have been a communal decision to disarm the weapon.

Wayne Glenn thought he understood why his labor brethren had failed to read the writing on the wall or help erase the precedent IP had set. All of them had their problems, he reasoned. They were fighting for their lives daily. But he wouldn't forget or forgive. "When I brought up the issue of striker replacements, the bigger unions said, 'We are so big they can't replace us.' I couldn't get anywhere. I couldn't get enough interested people," he recalled.

Nor did the anger subside among those workers who cursed and resented Glenn and the workers who had replaced them at the paper mills. They did not bury their sense that the union had been too passive, too cooperative with IP, and too willing to abandon their strike and their cause for the sake of greater union goals.

Their fury remained with them. In a collection of memories put out by the workers in Jay, Maine, years after their strike had collapsed, anger seethed through their words.

"I was very arrogant and outspoken in the mill, willing to challenge management at the drop of a hat, and treating scabs like the dirt they were," said Maurice Metivier. Maurice Poulin, a third-generation worker, counted up all the time that he and his relatives had put into the paper mill—379 years—and swore his undying disgust toward the company.

"I am emphasizing this great number of years of faithful service," said Poulin, "to show that it is unbelievable that a company would forget all of this service and dedication and, in 1987, would replace all of us with one sweep of their greedy corporate hand. How heartless, how cruel can a company be? It is almost like we had our own Holocaust at the hands of the IP thugs."

PART III

A Call to Arms

Sizing Up the Enemy

December 1991

No progress. Each side is holding its cards, watching the other's moves.

As the company shuffles and studies its hand, Casstevens is convinced he is playing both roles, the tough guy and the conciliator. Caterpillar officials think they have seen only one: the unbending tough guy with a foul mouth and mean disposition. Casstevens has a strategy, but he is keeping it to himself until the very last minute. He is worried that it will get out in the small Illinois towns, where families are both union and management at Caterpillar, where gossip travels fast, and that will mess up his plotting. He thinks he has a new wrinkle that will throw off the tough guys at Caterpillar.

Caterpillar officials had approached the union months before the contract expired, indicating they were seeking something different in the coming contract. They were indeed. The company was determined to put an end to the kind of year-after-year bargaining whereby the same contract grew thicker, with more pay and power for the union's members. And the union was determined to stand its ground.

Casstevens balked at the company's early overtures, suspecting something was afoot. When someone from inside the company smuggled him a copy of an advertisement that the company was going to put in local newspapers, he was furious. The ad stated the company's position to the workers directly, bypassing—and, as he saw it, snubbing—the union.

"Don't do this," he told Wayne Zimmerman, Caterpillar's vice-president for human resources in Peoria. "Wayne, you are going down the wrong path again. How in the heck can you forget the 205-day strike? I am pleading with you not to go down that road. It will make matters 10 times worse."

But the company went ahead with its unprecedented publicity campaign.

As Casstevens weighed the company's offer just before the contract expired, it was clear that Caterpillar was not bending from its effort to extract pay cuts from some workers and concessions overall. More important for the union, the company had made a point of saying it would not accept a contract patterned on those reached between the UAW and its competitors. Casstevens insisted the union was not demanding a "cookie-cutter deal," but the company insisted that was the case.

To make his point, he handed the company a copy of the contract the union had reached with John Deere & Company. He said the point was to show them that there were differences. The company insisted that the union was brazen enough to issue its demands as a carbon copy of the Deere agreement. There was no seeing eye to eye.

IN SEARCH OF A STRATEGY

Although the company had shown a new toughness, the scenario hadn't seemed much different to Casstevens. It was a route he had taken many times before. He knew the union would have to strike once he stood up to the company. But he was leery about an all-out confrontation at the start, fearing a backlash locally among the membership and local communities because of the burdens they had suffered in the 1982 205-day walkout.

The union was no newcomer in dealing with Caterpillar.

When the labor earthquake shook the American landscape in 1937, Caterpillar was not exempt. In April, amid the wave of sit-down strikes, 11,500 workers at Caterpillar's tractor assembly plant, the nation's biggest at the time, sat down for two days and refused to work. The result was a loose agreement with a small union that lasted until 1941, when the company signed its first formal agreement with United Farm Equipment and Metal Workers of America, a union tied to the CIO.

In 1948, when the farm equipment union refused to sign the anti-

Communist loyalty pledge required by the Taft–Hartley Act, the landmark law that imposed regulations on unions, Caterpillar refused to deal with the union, and the union struck. Two months later, Caterpillar recognized the UAW. But the first years of bargaining with the company were not easy. It wasn't until 1958 that the union and the company bargained for the entire workforce rather than plant by plant.

By the 1960s, the UAW had replicated what it had done in the auto industry, creating a pattern of similar agreements linking Caterpillar and its competitors in the heavy equipment, earth moving, and farm machinery industries. It would become a golden link for the union. Eventually the companies outside the world of the big three automakers went along with the practice and even quietly coordinated their bargaining. For the UAW, this was a great victory because the union could peg its contracts with the ring of companies like Caterpillar to the high-paying deals it had reached with the automakers.

As much as Caterpillar and the union fought—the union struck eight times between 1948 and 1980—these were gentlemanly bouts, and union negotiator Pat Greathouse had never had bad relations with his Caterpillar counterparts. In fact, the company officials with whom he had bargained for years eventually became his friends. When he retired in 1980, the company negotiators and others gave him a dinner in a downtown Peoria restaurant and handed him a toy tractor, which he valued for years after in his home in the Detroit suburbs. Written on the tractor were the words "Pat Greathouse, Cat Skinner."

Between 1979 and 1991, the UAW's ranks at Caterpillar tumbled from 40,500 to just over 15,000. Showing its toughest face ever with Caterpillar, the UAW struck for 205 days in 1982–1983. Never before had there been such a long strike for Caterpillar. Never before had a UAW unit at a major company been out for such a period. And in the end, the union had hardly anything to show for its effort. Amid a job-chilling recession, the workers turned their backs on their UAW bargainers' suggestion to turn down the contract. They returned to their jobs empty-handed. They agreed to freeze their wages. But this was all a part of the times. An unusual time, people said, a very different time. Yet neither the union nor most workers could truly forget how things had once been.

As Caterpillar slowly recovered in the 1980s, it began to spread out its production, beyond its UAW plants in the United States to smaller, nonunion contractors, and beyond the United States to other plants worldwide. Still, its Midwestern plants were its production core, and the company relied on them to meet its customers' needs. These were things Casstevens mulled over. And so he decided to be cautious. He thought a gesture would be enough to get the company moving.

Before any threat of a strike loomed, however, it was clear that Caterpillar had a new agenda. Convinced it could reach its workers with a different message than the union's, Caterpillar had kept up its advertisements in Illinois newspapers, giving its take on basic contract issues.

It was the start of a campaign that had a common theme: The company aligned with its workers against the union. It was a new tactic designed by the company to appeal to the small-town Midwestern sentiments of the workers.

The company's publicity viewed the UAW as a distant operation run out of Detroit, a union interested mostly in the auto industry, not one linked to its Midwestern members at Caterpillar. This was a new public relations strategy, making the workers feel that the company was more on their side than the union, run by uncaring leaders far away. It was a stretch, however, to portray Detroit as a place with interests very different from those in Decatur, Peoria, or any number of other Midwestern towns. And the union leaders from Detroit who descended on Decatur hardly looked or acted differently from anyone else on the street. At its core, however, Caterpillar's slant had some logic. The company was appealing to the notion that unions had lost touch with their roots, something that could not be denied for most American unions.

The union was outraged by the company's tactics and called off early bargaining. As a result, the talks started in late September, only days before the contract expired. As the union pressed for a pattern contract, a contract along the same lines it had reached with other companies in the same industry, the company firmly resisted. As the company asked for federal mediation, the union resisted.

Smack up against the union's deadline, the company would not budge. Theoretically, when a contract expires, the union can call all of its workers out on strike. If the company can prove that it has bargained to a deadlock, it can impose changes in the contract.

The union stuck to the pattern it had established with Caterpillar and its competitors. It was convinced that the company was out to break the union's power, not just to win the concessions. Casstevens, fearing a backlash from a widespread strike, called out the 1,800 workers in Decatur and another 1,000 at one major building in Peoria, where the bulk of Caterpillar's workers were located. Both facilities churned out products not made elsewhere, which made the company more vulnerable to a strike because it needed the products. He felt he knew Caterpillar after dealing with its leaders for nearly 20 years. He thought they would bargain hard but then give in. Still, he had a number of doubts.

"In the back of my mind, I was wondering," he recalled, "would they use permanent replacements?"

Larry Solomon understood the strategy: Put pressure on the company by striking the facilities that are busy, and keep the workers on the job at the other places so they will continue to earn a salary. But this plan was not very popular in Decatur. Within a short while Solomon wanted to see the entire UAW workforce out on strike. He was itchy to see a full-blown battle. He feared that Caterpillar would simply ship whatever work it could from one factory to another. He was growing impatient with Detroit and with Casstevens.

A new game had begun, indeed, for the UAW, for its workers in Decatur, and soon, for Decatur's other major factories. Traditions were about to be undone.

THE BATTLE BEGINS

So much began to change so fast. Within three days after the Caterpillar strike began, the company punched back harder than ever before. It locked out 5,600 workers at its factories in Peoria and Aurora, a small community on the far suburban ring of Chicago. That negated Casstevens's hope of limiting the strike. The company had never before locked out workers.

As the strike inched forward, Casstevens made no plans at first for a news media battle with the company. The union did not set up a war room that blitzed the news media with its views. It relied on the union's public relations staff in Detroit to crank out the union's word. Casstevens was convinced that the union would not get a fair shake from the press. Gradually, however, the union began sending out pamphlets and answering Caterpillar's newspaper advertisements. It realized it was in a battle for its members' minds. Caterpillar had made a clear decision to use advertisements in the local newspapers where its plants were located to give its side of the battle.

Nor did Casstevens plan for any pressure from those still working within the Caterpillar plants. If the union did not show the way, the locals didn't know what to do either. The local leaders did not know much about strategies that slowed the work inside the plant, or ways to put pressure on Caterpillar to deal with them. The union asked its members not to work overtime while the strike was under way, but a number of workers ignored the union's pleas. In East Peoria, where there were the largest number of UAW workers, fewer than half of those not striking were contributing the $35 per paycheck that the union had sought for help for the strike.

Casstevens thought Caterpillar would soon bend, pressured by the production slowdown, a tried and tested maneuver. But he had made a tactical error. The company had stockpiled equipment, planning ahead for the strike. And it began to look into ways that it could ship equipment to the United States from its overseas plants.

At the Decatur plant Caterpillar custom-built certain tractors, items it could not easily supply from elsewhere in its sprawling production empire in the United States or overseas. Casstevens was counting on Caterpillar's running short of equipment there and coming back to the bargaining table. He was also hesitant to stir the wrath of union members who had suffered through the long strike in the early 1980s. His strategy: Apply direct pressure in certain spots, avoid a massive blow. "If we all would have gone out, they would have just waited us out," he explained.

But the gamble didn't work. For the first three months, there were no talks.

The New Paladins

Guardians at the Gates

February 1992

Still cold. Gunmetal gray skies. The UAW regularly stocks the picket lines' barrels with wood for fires. Day and night, around the clock they are there. Among some of the older workers, the ones staring ahead at retirement, there's a wave of anxious talk. Maybe, they think, this is a good time to get out before it gets worse.

Nothing doing at the bargaining table. Larry Solomon wonders what the union's strategy is, but he doesn't raise his doubts much with the others. Grumbling grows on the picket lines: Where is this thing going?

Local UAW leaders do not want other unions' help. They fear violence if there are any massive street demonstrations. That's not their way of doing things. Not the UAW. After avoiding a media war, the UAW begins sending out pamphlets and putting ads in newspapers. Twenty thousand show up for a union solidarity rally in Pontiac.

Still no progress.

Then Caterpillar makes a move that breaks the stalemate.

They were dressed in dark blue jumpsuits, dark blue baseball caps, and knee-high military boots. They looked tough, seriously tough. They seemed to be some sort of flashy paramilitary group, and they were suddenly all over the Caterpillar plant, standing at the gates and on top of

95

the factories, wielding cameras and binoculars and other fancy equipment.

The minute they showed up, people got on their phones and called the UAW's union halls. Word spreads fast in towns where outsiders rarely come wandering through.

"What's going on?" the UAW workers asked with a pitch of panic in their voices. "Who are these goons?"

Even the plant's regular guards were surprised.

Bill Casstevens was furious. At a negotiations session in mid-February, he angrily asked why the company had hired a "rent-a-thug" operation. Company officials merely shrugged off his question.

Local union leaders were troubled. Was this the prelude to bringing in strikebreakers? The end of any chance for making a deal? Privately, they said they couldn't believe this kind of thinking would come from the company executives they had known for years, from people they had hunted with or gone to church with, people they had even once known on the factory floor as bosses or fellow workers. They had been counting on these people to show reason and to bring the standoff to an end.

A CORPORATE WAKE-UP CALL

Calling in outside security guards was indeed an unprecedented step for Caterpillar. But the tactic was hardly a new one. Beset by angry unions holding losing hands in their bargaining, American companies were increasingly calling on security services to protect their facilities, outside firms that stood sentry-like between companies and unions that seemed on the edge of war.

Caterpillar had hired the Asset Protection Team of Vance International Protection Services of Oakton, Virginia, because, as Charles F. "Chuck" Vance, president and founder of the security firm, recalled, Caterpillar officials feared that there was "great potential for violence" and his company would not make things any worse. Caterpillar officials were concerned that thousands of autoworkers from Detroit and throughout the Midwest, workers enraged over the company's embarrassing rebuff of their union, infuriated by an arrogance that the auto companies had not dared show since the bloody organizing days of the 1930s, might descend on their plants. Company officials thought that the UAW would surely show its fury, because, as they reportedly explained to Vance, "the UAW had a lot to lose."

It was, as Vance later recalled, "a pretty easy sell" for him. Violence seemed imminent.

In the mythology of union struggles, few company gestures have been more detested by unions than the hiring of spies, detectives, and goon squads to quash strikes or put down confrontations. As far back as the 19th century, companies had been using this great unequalizer to neutralize union efforts.

In 1889 steel magnate Andrew Carnegie had decided that the union was too strong, and Henry Clay Frick, the president of Carnegie's steel company, decided not to bargain with the union that represented the workers at the steel plant in Homestead, Pennsylvania.

To show the company's grit, it hired the Pinkerton National Detective Agency of Chicago. Allen Pinkerton, a Scottish immigrant who had been an intelligence officer for the Union army in the Civil War, was the company's founder. From protecting the railroads, the company had branched out and soon become the muscle used by companies in coal, steel, and lumber strikes.

The Pinkerton Agency dispatched 300 detectives to secure the Homestead steelworks, round up the strikers, and hold them inside. But when the strikers heard that the detectives were headed their way south from Pittsburgh on two barges, they stormed the steel mill.

As the Pinkertons arrived, gunfire erupted and an unprecedented battle took place for the next few hours. At last the outnumbered detectives gave up and surrendered to the strikers, who marched them through town, where they were attacked and beaten. Seven strikers and three Pinkertons were killed in the showdown. Dozens were injured in the confrontation, which ended when the state militia regained control of the steelworks and escorted strikebreakers to work.

In the fallout from the brutal experience, a number of states passed laws barring companies from bringing armed mercenaries across state lines, but the Pinkertons and other detectives continued to be hired to deal with union outbursts. In Illinois such a law is still on the books. But it is a legal relic that does not apply to guard services or to replacement workers who are hired from out of state. No confrontation was as rancorous as the one that sprang forth in Matewan, West Virginia, in 1920. At the time, it was considered one of the deadliest gunfights in American history. And it took place in a community ripe for an explosion, a tightly knit, isolated mining town surrounded by hills and hollows, newly caught up in the fervor of union organizing and long smothered in anger over the way the coal companies ran the miners' lives.

The miners had gone on strike when the coal companies fired a number of miners who had joined the union. As a dozen detectives, hired by the coal companies and wearing deputy sheriff badges, arrived in the small southwest West Virginia town to evict the fired miners and their families from the company-owned houses and tent colonies, they were confronted by local officials. Fighting broke out as the detectives confronted Sid Hatfield, the town's chief of police, who had urged the townsfolk to arm themselves in advance and who challenged the authority of the detectives. Seven detectives and four local residents were killed.

A year later, Hatfield, who had been acquitted for his role in the confrontation in Matewan, was on trial for another shooting in a coal camp. As he and another defendant in the case climbed the steps of a county courthouse, they were shot down, allegedly by detectives seeking revenge. The two were unarmed.

Outraged miners rose up and swore that they would march from Charleston to Logan County and show their support for the organizing there. Some counseled calm, saying the march would lead only to violence and play into the hands of the coal companies, which had the police and government officials on their side. But there was little will for restraint as they headed for the mostly nonunion counties.

During the previous year, 1919, numerous confrontations between the miners and companies' detectives or local police had taken place. The mood in the minefields was explosive. Unemployment was rampant, and the union was facing stiff resistance from coal operators across the state's southern region. The miners seethed with fury over the unchecked clout wielded by the detectives and guards hired by the coal companies.

As they began to march across West Virginia, armed with weapons, hundreds joined them. A long line of miners, wearing red bandanas, formed as if in a military campaign. They became the small army that finally clashed with groups of police. In an unusual show of force by the government, federal troops brought the uprising to an end after the Battle of Blair Mountain, in which 16 persons were killed, most of them miners.

The miners' uprising may have ended, but the use of security forces by employers did not. Between 1933 and 1937, the major detective agencies hired out 3,871 detectives to companies, and the companies spent over $9.4 million for spies, scabs, weapons, and arms. They bought machine guns, rifles, gas guns. General Motors Corporation, which operated a small army of industrial snitches, had spent over $800,000.

In the 1920s, American unions, which had been struggling for decades, were in full retreat. When the Great Depression spread across the land, it was as if labor had been put under sedation. Here and there, jobless and destitute workers rose up. Rent strikes, sit-ins at relief offices, and hunger marches spread across the country. Desperate for solutions, some workers thought the answers were in self-help efforts and organized around various schemes. But there was no fury, no anger, no organized drive from union leaders that showed they could do anything about the workers' fate. Organized labor was tongue-tied, baffled, empty-handed.

A turning point came with the 1933 National Industrial Recovery Act (NIRA), Franklin D. Roosevelt's fulfillment of his campaign promise to protect workers beaten down by the nation's economic disarray. In Section 7a of the Act, workers were guaranteed the right to bargain collectively with companies through their own unions. Workers rushed to join unions, but found many of the first organizing efforts were shams set up by employers to siphon off the drive for unionism. Unions called the National Recovery Administraion (NRA) the "National Run Around."

Undeterred by such challenges, more militant union leaders were gaining control, and they led their unions into strikes. Daily the number of workers on the picket lines grew. They were striking for better wages or simply for recognition of their unions. But the first waves of strikes led nowhere, and union activists looked for new leadership outside the conservative, politically timid American Federation of Labor. The AFL had failed to eliminate onerous company practices like the line speedup, an incredible cost cutter that squeezed more work out of the same number of workers, and had proved powerless against employers' relentless rebuffs of unions.

The AFL's philosophy was to organize workers along craft lines, but other labor leaders wanted to organize whole industries. Led by mine workers' union president John L. Lewis, in 1935 they created the

Committee for Industrial Organization, which later became the Congress of Industrial Organizations. The old-line AFL leaders deeply resented the CIO and the recent immigrants and northern-bound minorities who worked in the nation's factories and made up the future pool of CIO union members.

"Already the AFL has begun waving the red shirt and yelling 'Bolshevik' and in a few localities their less responsible representatives have tried Jew-baiting to stop the C.I.O. They may make a few hits, but they are throwing boomerangs," wrote J. Raymond Walsh, a Harvard University economist, in 1937.

Despite labor's own squabbles and employers' stepped-up resistance, the unions pressed ahead. They struck again and again, facing stiff legal and financial penalties. But they persisted, going outside the law and beyond their own expectations about what they were likely to achieve. They were affirming their existence with each sit-down and strike.

Big business gradually abandoned its brute opposition and hamhanded techniques as it settled into a pattern of more mature dealings with unions. But it never forgot the inclination to protect itself or to be ready to defend its interests. That instinct was awakened in the 1980s, and weakened unions thrashed about in fury as they faced challenges they had not encountered in years.

HAVE CAMERA AND JUMPSUIT, WILL TRAVEL

By the time Caterpillar hired them, Vance's workers had become the largest army of a new breed of corporate paladins. Dubbed the "Pinkertons of the late 20th century," Vance's guards had a 40 percent share of a growing market of corporate protectors. West Virginia coal miners had called them worse things, accusing them of taunting and tempting them into violence, charges Vance officials heatedly rejected.

The company had gained a reputation in the 1980s in the West Virginia and Kentucky mine fields in a bitter face-off between the United Mine Workers union and the A. T. Massey Coal Company. But its workers had also faced strikers at Southern paper mills and an Arizona coal mine as it built its fame. There was work, Vance said, because companies "were taking a strong stance" and were "no longer abdicating to the unions."

A medium-sized man with a powerful build and a frank way of talking, Vance had been a cop in Oakland, California, and a U.S. Secret Service agent. A physical fitness buff, he did hundreds of sit-ups daily. His firm had not started out providing guards for strikes, but it took part in one dispute and the work blossomed. As it did, Vance developed a philosophy about how this work had to be done.

The rules were simple. His guards had to have at least two years of police or military training. Some had come with Special Forces military training. They wore dark blue jumpsuits, dark blue baseball caps, and black leather military-like boots. They were given four days of training before being sent out to work 12-hour shifts for up to 45 days. They earned from $120 to $200 a day, depending on their expertise.

The guards were ordered to remain nonviolent, recording on film any violence or infractions of court orders as evidence that companies could take to court. His photographer-guards needed good lighting day and night, and that meant high-tech equipment. In one case, Vance hired a helicopter to photograph a miners' rally in West Virginia.

But gathering evidence against the unions was only one goal. The other was to deter aggression. The guards' very presence was meant to deliver the message "These are not people you want to mess with." His people were not to have or make any local ties. They would not come from the community, and they would leave town after the dispute was over. When they left, even the plant's security staff was supposed to be able to say, "Yeah, I didn't like those guys either."

Collapse and Surrender

April 1992

If ever violence seemed likely, the moment had come. This was it. Showdown time. Who was going to back down? Larry Solomon had long suspected that the company was going to replace everyone, and when it actually made the threat, he had no doubt it would do so. Five months after the strike began, Caterpillar sent letters to its striking UAW workers, saying they had a week to return to their jobs or the company would replace them.

As the deadline neared, workers searched their souls: What should they do?

So far, in Decatur only 11 had crossed the picket lines.

On April 6, 1992, at Decatur and other Caterpillar factories, increasing numbers of workers began to buckle under to Caterpillar's threat by showing up for work. The company had placed advertisements in local newspapers, saying it was hiring workers at wages ranging from $16.12 to $17.85 an hour.

Caterpillar was no longer waiting for the union to bend. It had begun the battle, determined to write a new kind of contract, a contract that took away much of the clout that the union had commanded over the years, and now it was not going to back down.

In February 1992 the union had walked out of bargaining sessions, saying the company was not budging. The company said it was getting nowhere with the union but made another contract offer in March.

It offered no wage increases for the one-quarter of the workers at the bottom of the pay scale. They would receive cost-of-living boosts only. Others would get 4 or 3 percent increases for the first year of a three-year contract, followed by cost-of-living pay hikes for the next two years. The company said average hourly wages would come up to $19.19 an hour.

The UAW was not interested. It had 10,600 Caterpillar workers on strike, and they were getting $100 a week from the union. Soon it bumped up the number of workers on strike to 12,400.

On February 17, 1992, pickets lined one of the gates to the Caterpillar factory in Decatur and partially blocked it with their cars. City, county, and state police had to escort trades workers in and out of the building. The striking UAW workers were furious that fellow union members were crossing their lines and working inside the plants.

Where was this thing called union solidarity?

The company had just put large metal fences at the entranceway to the Decatur factory, making it more difficult for the workers to get close to the plant with their picket lines.

And union solidarity was crumbling left and right.

The least number of workers crossed the UAW's picket lines in Decatur, where 2,000 workers had lined the long road leading up to the plant to show their solidarity every day.

"We made them wealthy, and now they're done with us," grumbled Mike Whittington, one of the strikers in Decatur, as fellow workers and UAW members streamed by the pickets.

Altogether, about 1,000 union members had crossed the union's picket lines at all of Caterpillar's factories. When Caterpillar officials realized that the union had not collapsed, it issued another warning. Within weeks, it would hire a new workforce to replace the one on strike.

On the first day that Caterpillar put out the word that it was hiring, it received more than 40,000 calls from people all across the United States asking for the jobs. Its telephones were so clogged that the company urged people to mail their résumés. The story raced across the news wires and was echoed widely by the news media.

"This is not the Peoria those who love this community know," read an editorial on April 7, 1992, in the *Peoria Journal Star*. "This is not the Peoria they want their children to inherit. And this is not the Peoria we want to sell to the folks in Buffalo or Atlanta or Denver. This is not what people put on economic development brochures.

"We cannot believe anyone here wanted what has been described as one of the great showdowns in the history of labor and management to take place in our town. If Peoria had its way, this contract would be settled by now, and the big yellow symbols of a healthy community would be rolling out as they always have. Frankly, we think most Caterpillar people—labor or management—feel the same."

On April 9, Arkansas Governor Bill Clinton, hungry for union support in his campaign to become president, visited UAW strikers and company officials in Peoria and urged the company not to fire the striking workers.

Working-class Americans showed little concern about the strikers who were making $17 an hour. They did not seem to care much about the picket lines or the possibility of workers taking jobs away from their neighbors.

The union had no plan, no escape route, no comeback. No one was riding to its rescue. Organized labor watched from the sidelines.

A narrow opening for the union came from federal mediators. Bernard Delury, the head of the Federal Mediation and Conciliation Service, had recommended that Owen Bieber meet with Don Fites at Chicago's O'Hare airport. Fites flatly refused to meet with Casstevens. Bieber, in turn, said he would not go there without Bill Casstevens, his specialist on the dispute. But Casstevens urged him to go alone. Out of that meeting came an agreement for negotiating teams from both sides to talk once again. The idea, put on the table by the federal mediators, was for the UAW workers to go back to their jobs and Caterpillar to call off its hiring of replacement workers.

The 33 members of the union's bargaining committee, meeting in an anonymous-looking office building used by the Federal Mediation and Conciliation Service in suburban Chicago, had to make a decision. They talked among themselves and then waited as Casstevens left to meet with the Caterpillar people. It was a chilly, overcast day.

When he came back, Casstevens explained the situation and asked what should be done.

Jerry Baker, a local official from East Peoria and the chairman of the bargaining committee, which represented the various Caterpillar locals, felt immediate anger at the idea that he had to make a decision because of the scabs. Then a sense of hurt and defeat came over him. Otha Boyd, another local official from Peoria, did not want to give in to Caterpillar but accepted the idea that there was no choice. That was what most felt. They had been backed to the wall.

Without any declaration, the choice ultimately fell to Casstevens. He had been their leader, and they turned to him to make the critical decision. Casstevens did not think the company could bring in replacement workers that fast, but he did expect replacement office workers to snap up the higher-paying factory jobs that belonged to his union's members. His bottom line was that he was not going to expose his union's members to any more sacrifices.

And he feared what would happen to the union if there were scabs in the plants. That would change the whole workplace dynamic within the plants and the negotiations. It would stoke up the tension in the plants, and the union would have to fight at the bargaining table to get the scabs out.

So he made a motion, using only a few words. "We're going back to work," he said.

No vote was taken. They would go back to work. Nobody said the strike should go on. Nobody made any speeches about winning or how long they had held out. A mood of exhaustion and defeat filled the room.

It was the right decision, Larry Solomon figured. The union needed to regain its footing, and it couldn't do that if its jobs were being filled by scabs. Untypically, he didn't speak up.

In less than an hour, the group walked away. The UAW's five-and-a-half-month strike was over. The once mighty UAW—the union that had seized control of General Motors factories in Flint, Michigan, in the 1930s and dared the company and the government to do something—had surrendered, very publicly. For the first time in recent American history a major manufacturer that was not teetering on the brink of financial collapse had handed a crushing ultimatum to its veteran workers and their union and walked away without a worried glance backward. From a manufacturer that had sworn allegiance to honest-to-goodness heartland values and heartland roots, it was a blistering slap in the face.

Fearing any greater losses, Casstevens had decided to send the strikers back to work under the company's rules. But as he walked away from the meeting, he refused to acknowledge the depth of the setback.

"There are no replacement workers that will be hired," he said. "We're not going to be negotiating on the company's last offer. We're going to negotiate on our own offer."

"I've never seen an issue that is hotter in this plant," said Bernie Rickie, an officer of the late Mr. Reuther's local 600 in Dearborn, Mich. . . . Al Puma, a fellow officer, asked, "Who's next? If they can do it at Caterpillar, what's going to stop Ford, General Motors and Chrysler from doing it to us."
—*New York Times*, April 16, 1992

The UAW has long needed a reality check.
—EDITORIAL, *Wall Street Journal*, April 16, 1992

Caterpillar's Success in Ending Strikes May Curtail Unions' Use of Walkouts
—*Wall Street Journal*, April 20, 1992

CHAPTER 1 3

A Historical Question

What If . . . ?

What if the union had given up its givens? What if it had not buckled under?

What would have happened?

What if the workers had not been bulldozed by Caterpillar and had not been betrayed by their own?

Would Caterpillar have taken the unprecedented step of replacing its entire workforce?

A decade earlier President Ronald Reagan had fired striking air traffic controllers, giving a powerful sense of legitimacy to an action that had been used by several large companies facing dire financial straits, but more often by small, struggling businesses. But Caterpillar changed the formula. Never before had a powerful, mainstream manufacturer like Caterpillar threatened to toss out its striking workers. This was a nuance of a significance as great as Reagan's move. It raised the stakes. It made available the most powerful weapon in an employer's arsenal in cases where the company simply didn't want to deal with the union anymore.

The people whom Caterpillar was prepared to throw onto the street were middle-aged veteran employees. In most cases, they had spent their adult lives working for the company. As middle-class as anyone on their blocks, they embraced most of the middle-class values about work, including especially a sense of loyalty to their employer.

Caterpillar spoke up once again, as it had in battles with the government over trade and other policies, in Washington as well as across the country, to make sure it kept this right to replace its striking employees. Caterpillar and 200 other companies had formed the Alliance to Keep Americans Working, a lobby based in Washington, to fight a bill that would ban striker replacements. With the Caterpillar–UAW debacle in the background, organized labor had struggled to bring a vote on the bill in the U.S. Senate. It had succeeded in passing the bill in the House, but the margin was not big enough for it to survive a threatened veto from President George Bush.

Within the AFL-CIO, serious misgivings had been expressed about risking organized labor's already beaten-down image in another losing battle. Organized labor did not do well in Congress, and had not won a major legislative battle in years. In fact, it had barely raised its voice for years. Stuck in its downward spiral, it was no threat to big business, and it acted accordingly. Its defeat was a self-fulfilled prophecy.

Two months after the Caterpillar workers returned to their jobs, fearful of being replaced, the union effort to deal with strikebreakers in Congress came to a head. But even though the union leaders had bowed and made a historic concession—they agreed to limit workers' right to strike in some cases—they could not muster enough votes. Twice they failed to defeat a Republican filibuster, and the effort died in Congress. The defeat would haunt the leaders of the AFL-CIO.

And what about the Caterpillar workers?

If they had stood tall and not crawled back to their jobs, if the union had stayed outside the gates as hundreds of its members turned their backs on the union and streamed back to their jobs, joined by their neighbors and others hungry for the high-paying factory work, it is not hard to figure what would have happened.

What if they had stood their ground?

The answer is simple. The company would have gone ahead, and they would have been out in the cold for good.

> At the risk of administering a small shock here, let me just confess that I'm getting a little sick of hearing the word "global." I'm sick of "global competitiveness." . . . Simply put, Caterpillar's anti-worker, anti-union takeaway strategy is a crime of domestic opportunity—not a legitimate struggle over global economic survival.
> —UAW PRESIDENT OWEN BIEBER,
> speaking at the Economic Club of Detroit, May 4, 1992

Forming a Second Front
The Staley Workers Join the Fray

June 1993

He lectured on intensely, spinning theories and appearing much like a crew-cut, healthy, middle-aged Midwestern professor. But he had the arms of a wrestler and the gut inclinations of a true-believing factory troublemaker. And when he talked, it was as if he were reciting from a religious text. His words were, indeed, important, because that was how he had made his name. He was a strategist, an idea man in a community desperate for new ideas, an outsider peddling ideas that were as old as a picket line.

The slowdown. The stall. The rebellion from within, from the line, from a place where the company would have to work harder to put its thumb on the problem and the workers behind it.

From the beginning of the century, workers had tried it out, and in the 1930s it was a popular tactic of union organizers.

The strategy is hardly complex. You gum up the works, but you do it carefully so you don't break any laws, don't get fired, and you force the company to deal with what's driving you to cause such trouble. You work to rule. That is, you work exactly by the company's rule books, no faster or slower, just going through every nitpicking detail, every safety-required action, every step in the small-minded manual to get the job done. You don't volunteer any help. You don't offer to shoulder any overtime. You don't do what you are not supposed to. That slows things down, for sure.

This was a major part of Jerry Tucker's antidote for unions in trouble with management. And by the time the Staley workers met him, they were more than eager to embrace someone who seemed to offer a way out of their plight. His ideas were perhaps one of the few innovations organized labor had added to its meager arsenal as it realized, late in the 20th century, that striking usually meant carrying out a death wish. Tucker had tweaked an old tactic so as to strengthen the union's bargaining power. But for leftists and union activists, his way of doing things also appealed to their hopes of draining away the massive power held by union leaders.

Tucker's method of attack on a company was based on rank-and-file organizing, linking as many workers as possible to confront the company. It meant that a worker would have to take a stance while working on the line or at the machine. And this, theoretically, gave the average worker a sense of power and involvement. Thus, the workers could clearly see that it was their jobs they were putting on the line. It was a far more personal act than marching out the front gates like sheep along with the rest of the flock.

AN END RUN AROUND A STRIKE

Convinced that A. E. Staley was going to make a tough contract offer, Dave Watts and the other leaders of the Decatur local had balked at early negotiations. In October 1992, the local had voted overwhelmingly against the company's contract offer. Within days, the company had imposed most of the contract and within months installed 12-hour rotating shifts. The workers had no real choice. If they did not want to work under the company's new contract, they could strike and most likely lose their jobs. Or they could quit. They lost out no matter what they did. Fearful of being replaced, the union chose not to strike. The Staley workers had already engaged Ray Rogers, who had begun to devise an attack on the company's financial network. Instead, the union took another tack, one it had only recently set out to learn. Tucker would be the local's other punch. He would teach the local how to put pressure on the company while on the job, and Rogers would show them how to exert pressure publicly. Watts and the local's leaders were convinced that the company was going to goad them into a strike, which they figured would be suicidal leap. So they wanted a way to stay on the job while putting up a fight. Tucker was their man. On the advice of Larry Solomon, Watts called him in late July 1992. Within two months, he had come to work for the local as a part-time consultant.

Tucker, a one-time high-ranking UAW official, had been building a very small niche for himself in his hometown of St. Louis by helping locals from any union that would hire him run in-plant strategies. In 1981 he had made his name by forcing a St. Louis company, Moog Automotive Inc., to bargain with the workers after it had handed them a contract riddled with pay cuts and other concessions. In most cases the workers would have struck and the company would have handed their jobs to replacement workers. Under Tucker's guidance, however, the workers slowed the production line as they did their jobs exactly according to the company's instructions. They filed one grievance report after another, forcing the company to deal with the stream of complaints. And they met during their lunch breaks to plan their strategy. In the end, they got a contract without the pay cuts.

But Tucker's strategic skills were lost to the UAW because he had run afoul of the political system. So he became a consultant, an independent troublemaker, some would say. His eagerness to move up within the union's ranks had brought him down. He ran against an incumbent candidate for a regional union job in St. Louis, challenging the party apparatus that had ruled the UAW since Walter Reuther came to power in the late 1940s. Detroit was furious with his rule breaking. He won the election. But the union leadership fought him furiously the next time and beat him, freezing his career plans within the union.

Within the UAW, Tucker became a political pariah, a leader of a very small group of dissidents who openly challenged the union's cooperation with management and who bemoaned the lack of militancy. He cut a different image from that of many local leaders. Middle-aged, stocky, broad-shouldered, with a broad Midwestern smile, he seemed almost like an academic expert on unions, not a street-level organizer. When he spoke, he drew pictures of the long term. In small meetings, he would quiet down his listeners, nod at them, and then explain, usually in minute detail, how his plan was going and how this played out against the big picture. He was not a mesmerizing, born-to-rally speaker, not an arm-twisting screamer. He was a college graduate, a wrestler and a football player at Southern Illinois University, who once dreamily thought about becoming a poet.

His father was a tool and die maker, his mother a seamstress in a St. Louis factory, and he became a UAW committeeman at a factory when he was 22 years old. He flew upward within the UAW's ranks, taking a job as a lobbyist in Washington and then as assistant director of its regional office in St. Louis. After his fatal clash with the union's hierarchy, he formed New Directions, a tiny dissident movement within the UAW, and he was its sole employee. Despite much grumbling from UAW workers about the way the union was being run, few joined the dissidents. The group sent up more sparks than serious warnings to the leadership. It sputtered for years. Tucker, who had tasted the social justice campaigns of the 1960s, and felt strongly about workers' issues, had stumbled, unfortunately, on his way up the UAW ladder.

At the UAW's convention in San Diego a few months earlier, in the summer of 1992, Larry Solomon had incurred the wrath of the union's leadership by standing up and publicly supporting Tucker for the union's presidency. It a was fantasy campaign, easily put down by the union's leaders. The rebels had only a handful of votes, and it was painful for them to realize how weak they were. "To those of us who have been trying to reform this union for the last 10 to 15 years it is a real question if there is any space for us in this union," said Eric Mann, a UAW activist from California, on the floor of the crowded convention center in San Diego.

Yet the UAW's leaders had indulged in their own fantasy, thundering about the beating they would one day administer to Caterpillar without any acknowledgment of the pain the union had suffered at the hands of the giant manufacturer. It seemed almost delusional. But the union leaders apparently felt they needed the bravado—the kind of lament you hear from long-time politicians who do not want to admit they have been whipped by their opponents—to keep the faith and stir the troops.

When Dave Watts asked whether he would help out with the struggle in Decatur, Tucker said he was interested, but he had some conditions. It could not be a top-down, leaders-led operation, he said. It would have to be based on rank-and-file solidarity. He would have to feel comfortable with the effort. "They had to convince me that the struggle was something I wanted to be associated with," he recalled. He didn't ask for much financially, $100 a day for two days a week. He later learned that the local was paying Ray Rogers $20,000 a month. To pay Rogers's fee, the local had upped its monthly dues from $22 to $100 a member.

Rogers said he needed the money for the small office he ran in New York. The office churned out the pamphlets, did the corporate research, raised funds, sought alliances, and backstopped him. But that still seemed like a lot of money to Tucker.

MOBILIZING THE MEMBERSHIP

Although the local had been gearing up for the confrontation with the company, when Tucker arrived on the scene in the fall of 1992, fewer than one of every ten members came to the local's regular meetings. His goal then became to have them meet weekly and recruit as many members as possible to take part in planning what would be coming up. Eventually, two of every three of the local's 800 members were attending the meetings. His goal shifted again. Now he was going to get them to focus on a few main ideas, one of them their fight with the company. And they grew increasingly angry at the company.

"You will have to change your normal way of doing things," Tucker told the local's executive board. "The idea of the leadership speaking for the workers, filling them in on everything, is not enough. My approach is very solidarity based."

They said they accepted that. Still, Tucker had his own doubts about where the effort was headed. He got along "fairly well" with Rogers, the two dividing their tasks. Rogers was to put the local struggle on the map, and Tucker was to mobilize the workers. Privately, Tucker had some misgivings about Rogers's strategy. He thought, for example, that Rogers might have played down his publicity efforts and gone after more support from labor groups at the start.

At one meeting, a veteran worker stood up to say that they all had been corks bobbing on the water, victims of the way things had changed. "There was this romantic sense that the old Staley would not have treated them this way," Tucker recalled. At the meetings and within the plant, the workers were coached by Tucker and those at the local who worked with him on how they should work to rule, doing only what they were supposed to and not offering any extra efforts. With the local's approval, Tucker also began to take part at bargaining sessions.

From the first day of the contract's rejection, the work to rule campaign had an effect. Production dropped markedly. But company officials said they were also witnessing increasing sabotage: Brooms and boots were found in starch bins; a client reportedly found a headless canary in a starch shipment. The union adamantly denied any sabotage. And although the company disciplined several workers for not doing their jobs, it could not point to anyone who had carried out an act of sabotage.

In a fury over a worker who was disciplined, the union staged a 32-hour walkout in early June 1993. Tension had been building. But this was a tactical blunder, and a serious one.

Ray Rogers did not know about the decision to walk out. Neither did Dave Watts, who was out of town, talking to workers in Peoria. The news reached him after the walkout had already begun. "People were just 100 percent fed up, and they thought they had a right to do what they did," Watts recalled.

Pat Mohan became the company's unruffled representative during its dispute with the union. As the fury mounted, he still talked about what was happening as if it were a chapter in a modern management textbook. It was the local, he said, that had failed to see the bigger picture, that was trapped in another time, that had read all of the signals wrongly, that was paranoid when it shouldn't have been, that escalated the battle when it did not have to, and that had wrongly assumed the marching orders had come from London.

At the peak of the conflict, when the union plastered Mohan's face on posters that labeled him a corporate criminal, he kept a collection of them sitting in the corner of his office, next to the door. He kept his phone listed and answered it personally, even when the callers were furious and indignant, to show that he was not afraid. He would speak proudly about how his children attended the Decatur schools, even when the workers' rage had spread to their children and the fury had engulfed neighbors and families. He liked to talk about the dispute as a matter that involved only the company and its workers and did not draw much attention in town.

But he knew that wasn't the case. His family was often the target of marches and picketers, and he had at least one security guard posted at his house when the dispute with the local widened. When the marchers drew too close to his house, he took them to court, saying they had violated a ban on residential picketing. He limited the places he visited in Decatur, hoping to avoid uncomfortable confrontations.

Middle-aged, slightly balding, speaking with a slight Central Ohio twang, he could get lost in a lunchtime crowd of Midwestern businessmen. His specialty was not dealing with unions. He was a tax law expert with a master's degree in tax law, who had earlier worked with the U.S. Securities and Exchange Commission and had been in private practice in Columbus, Ohio. When Mohan joined Staley in 1979, the company was still on a quest to find its business niche.

LEAVING CERTAINTY BEHIND

After months of the local's training its members not to be tripped up by the company, not to be forced off the job, the decision to walk out came impulsively. The local had been fighting with the company over the way it was reassigning workers. The company saw no reason that workers could not take on more tasks going beyond their traditional job classifications. But the local balked. Its members would do the work, but only after the company taught them how to do it safely and properly.

Talking over their on-the-job walkie-talkies, workers spread the word through the large, rambling facility that another worker had been laid off. Then telephone calls went out to the local's leaders who were available. It was a spontaneous decision. Nobody said, "Stay on the job." And so they walked away from their jobs in bigger and bigger groups.

Up until then, the company was not convinced that it could run the sprawling 400-acre facility without its union workers. But it quickly learned that it could, and that triggered the decision that came within two weeks. A day after 5,000 persons marched through Decatur, forming a three-mile-long human billboard and linking the Staley and Caterpillar plants, the company acted. Staley locked out the workers, for the first time in its history.

A dark cloud hovers over the use of lockouts in American labor history. Unlike the United States, few countries recognize the lockout as a basic right of employers, and a number ban the use of lockouts.

A lockout is a small bomb that is more lethal than a million threats. It is the weapon employers call on when they theoretically have no other choice, when their bargaining with the union hits an impasse. It is their match for a strike. It pushes the workers out the door whether or not they want to go, whether or not they have truly brought the situation to a boil.

American companies locked out their workers with impunity. They locked out the workers at the Homestead steelworks in 1892. They used lockouts against the miners and cigar workers and laundry workers at the turn of the century. And they locked out the garment workers at one factory after another across the United States in the 1920s. Lockouts were poison to union efforts until the National Labor Relations Act in 1935 limited their use to cases in which the company could show that the two sides were deadlocked. Unions try to bar companies resorting to such steps by writing a ban on their use into their contracts.

Within two months of locking out their workers, company officials made another discovery within the large facility that they now had on their hands. To run the plant, production managers took over day-to-day operations with temporary workers at their side. The managers quickly realized that they could immediately eliminate 200 hourly jobs and a number of managers' positions. For the first time, company executives had a chance to find out whether they could get by without many of the existing jobs. They could. With the use of white-collar and clerical workers and temporary employees, production was not only on a par with its former level but quickly setting a record at the factory.

Never before had the union and the company stumbled into such a bitter showdown.

> It is so serious that picket headquarters, a brick garage set far back behind a dirt parking lot of Eldorado Street, is nicknamed "The War Room." In the War Room, the word Staley is seldom spoken. On the company calendar used to mark the days of the lockout, the words A. E. Staley Mfg. Co. have been crossed out with a pencil. Written underneath, in screaming red marker, is "Take & Lie," a popular variation of Tate & Lyle [the name of Staley's parent company].
> —*Decatur Herald & Review*, July 26, 1993

A Third Flank

The Tire Workers Go on Strike and the Beginning of the End of a Longtime Union

July 1994

Halfway between the Staley and Caterpillar plants is Bridgestone/ Firestone's Decatur tire factory, a half-century-old brown brick relic set off from a heavily traveled road by chain fences, squat, timeworn guardposts, a string of large parking lots, and a neatly kept athletic field. On the inside, it is dark, brooding, and smoky in places, a noisy monument to the almost unchanging way most tires are still made: with much reaching and lifting and cutting, a lot of human muscle power, and an endless demand for unflinching robot-like concentration.

Here Caterpillar built large engines for the U.S. military all during World War II. The facility was a U.S. Army Signal Depot until 1961; in 1962, Firestone, the old Akron-based tire making company, bought the 160-acre site for $2 million. The first day the plant made a tire, Local 713 of the United Rubber Workers union of Akron was chartered in Decatur. A year later, Illinois governor Otto Kerner dedicated the plant and proclaimed Firestone Day across the state.

Vast changes were in store for the company, for the U.S. tire industry, and for the union, a gritty survivor from the 1930s that had been

117

one of the first to wield the raw power of the sit-down strike to get its way with company officials.

By the 1990s, however, the union was barely able to get its way with its contract partners. It had become a relic, an industrial discard like a handful of blue-collar unions that could not resurrect themselves as their members' jobs slipped away.

Sweeping technological advancement, the globalization of the tire industry, the takeover of nearly all of the major U.S. tire companies by foreign firms, the flight of companies to nonunion plants, and unrelenting pressure for bargaining changes had been met by the union with militancy and concessions—mostly concessions. The union faced an even greater round of concessions when it encountered Bridgestone/Firestone. For like Caterpillar and Staley, the tire maker wanted to remake the rules, to change the boilerplate workplace conditions that the union had gotten accustomed to over the years.

A FEEBLE EXIT

By 1994 the rubber workers union had shrunk to just under 100,000 members, half of its size only 20 years earlier. It was no longer organizing. Instead, it was trying to survive, to hold onto what jobs its members had as the tire makers closed old plants and built new ones. It barely had the staff to help its locals keep their heads above water. Whereas richer, more powerful unions could dispatch attorneys and experts to negotiations to help out local officials, the rubber workers couldn't. A sad end was fast closing in on a union that had come to life with a glorious burst of energy and guts.

Born in the 1930s in Akron after decades of disastrous strikes and failed attempts to organize tire workers in the United States, the union had shown imagination and grit. Its politics were progressive. It gave African American workers a voice in small mid-South communities. It had pioneered the sit-down strike and used it like a ready club in its hand. An idea that began as a fluke, dozens of workers sitting down on the job, blossomed into a powerful tool.

In the mid-1930s, rubber workers sat down countless times, protesting line speed-ups, wage cutbacks, the beating of workers by company toughs, racist intimidations. But a sit-down was not enough to get the workers what they wanted, and it wasn't clear that the United Rubber Workers union had the leadership talent to get the union off the ground.

In February 1936, the Goodyear Tire & Rubber Company had laid off a group of workers after a recently enforced pay cut. The workers quickly voted to strike. The day they walked out and set up their picket lines, the temperature in Akron had fallen to nine degrees below zero. Snow filled the factory town's streets, and a fierce wind bore down on the city. Expecting the company to rush in replacements, the workers circled the world's largest rubber plant with a picket line of 10,000 persons, a number of them workers in Akron with little to do with the tire factories.

Their picket line sprawled for 11 miles and blocked the 45 gates to the company's plants. The strikers threw up shanties and shared food and clothing with each other. What had begun as a wildcat strike without the union's approval was quickly supported by the heads of the United Rubber Workers union. When the strike ended more than a month later, the workers had won a number of demands. The company balked at signing a contract with the union, but it was clear that the union had the mettle to endure. It was definitely clear that the rubber workers union was not going to vanish.

When veteran journalist Ernie Pyle visited Akron in 1937, the odor of burning rubber filled the air, and one-fifth of the city was shut down with strikes that seemed to pop up almost daily. But unlike the UAW, the United Rubber Workers union lacked a Walter Reuther to help give it a giant image as the working person's savior. It lacked a philosophy to propel it through difficult times. Its voice within organized labor became muffled as it stumbled through the years. And it dwindled just as the tire industry dwindled. It clung to its dreams in Akron, where the last major tire plant was built before 1920.

Milan Stone, president of the rubber workers union during most of the 1980s, didn't think the union could long stand on its own. He was sure it would have to merge with another union. "We had lost half of our membership," he recalled. "We didn't have the wherewithal to grow. We were not organizing very much." For years there had been talk of mergers with unions such as the UAW and the Oil, Chemical and Atomic Workers union. But the talks went nowhere. Why? Union politics, more than anything else, Stone said. "The feeling was that we would lose our identity, and for the union officers, they feared losing their jobs."

Besides dealing with disappearing jobs, the union faced another challenge. In one of the largest rushes to buy up American businesses, the tire industry was nearly snapped up entirely by foreign firms. And the foreign firms had different ideas than the American owners about unions.

By the 1990s only one major tire maker in the United States— Goodyear Tire & Rubber—was American-owned. Sumitomo Rubber Industries, a major Japanese manufacturer, had bought formerly British-owned Dunlop Tire Company, thereby taking over its plants in the United States. Yokohama Rubber Company of Japan bought Mohawk Rubber Company. Germany's Continental Tire AG had bought General Tire. Italy's leading tire maker, Pirelli, had bought Armstrong Tire and Rubber. France's major tire maker, Group Michelin, had bought Uniroyal-Goodrich. And the world's largest tire maker, the Japanese-owned Bridgestone Corporation, had bought Firestone in 1988.

AN AMERICAN COLONY FOR THE WORLD'S TIRE MAKERS

The arrival of Michelin in the United States was devastating to the union. Not only did the French company set up nonunion operations, but it ran its facilities around the clock, seven days a week. The 24-hour tire factory was a reality that the union had staved off. "I always said in hindsight, if we had negotiated just one of their plants, . . ." said Milan Stone. If it had, the union would have eliminated the pressure that Michelin suddenly created for it. With a major nonunion competitor, the union's bargaining partners were able to point to Michelin as the spoiler, as the company that was forcing the other tire makers to keep their wage costs down, and to mirror the work rules in Michelin's plants. If Michelin had gone union, the other tire makers would not have been able to use it as a club against the union for contracts more to their liking. But as the union lost its dominance over the industry, it lost its bargaining clout. Looking back, one problem Stone never figured on was Bridgestone, because, upon its arrival in the mid-1980s, "we seemed to get off on the right foot," he recalled.

Among all of the tire makers at the time, Stone considered the new Japanese company the best to deal with in the industry. The company and the union had so much in common that Bridgestone agreed to let the union organize a new plant in Warren, Tennessee, with member-ship cards signed by a majority of the plant's workers. It did not require the union to go through a secret ballot, a procedure that often results in lengthy court challenges by employers to union organizing drives. In-stead, it allowed the union to survey the workers. With more than half of them willing to join the union, the union became their voice. That was an astounding gesture in an era when companies fought like cats and dogs to keep organizers out. The Japanese had also returned the $1-an-hour cuts Firestone had won at two plants. Indeed, in 1991, Bridgestone reached a deal with the union that became the pattern for the rest of the industry.

Three years earlier, under the prior management, Firestone had gone through a one-week strike because it would not accept a pattern agreement. But now things had changed. Now management gurus lauded Bridgestone's Japanese bosses for breathing new life into Fire-stone plants suffocating under old ways of leadership. The company was a "poster child" for recalcitrant American firms, which had yet to learn how to trust and empower their workers. The Federal Mediation and Conciliation Service gave the company and the union its partner-ship award.

Faced with companies complaining about the terrible competition in the tire industry, the union under Ken Coss, Stone's successor, con-tinued to make concessions, continued to try to prop up the companies so that it could hang onto long-term jobs. At the same time, however, it struggled to maintain the integrity of its industry-wide contracts. But Coss, who had defeated Stone by a comfortable margin, had waged a campaign that promised to put an end to concession bargaining.

So he, too, was under pressure to show his mettle, although there was little about Coss that marked him as a hot-blooded hard-liner. He was too soft-spoken, too cautious for some of the union's local leaders, who would soon have an opportunity to show their militancy.

In 1994, Coss got his chance to prove that he was not one to back down when four companies, all foreign owned, balked at the union's proposal and the industry pattern agreement it had laid down with Goodyear. At best, it was a modestly improved contract that called for no permanent wage increases but only cost-of-living raises. The compa-nies balked, and the union struck them. In almost every case, the com-panies were making the same argument. Coss furiously accused them of making a war pact, a charge that Bridgestone/Firestone officials strongly denied. At one point, more than 7,300 tire workers were on strike.

A sign of the tire makers' willingness to toss tradition aside came in June, when Sumitomo, Japan's third largest tire maker and the owner of Dunlop, permanently replaced 1,600 workers at a plant in Huntsville, Alabama. Only a month after the union struck, the company wiped away their jobs. Since the union had begun bargaining in the 1930s, that had never happened, and it was a foreign firm that took the step.

BRIDGESTONE HOLDS ITS OWN

The union's biggest problem was now with Bridgestone. Coss had had a premonition that Bridgestone would present a problem. The year before a local at a Bridgestone plant had struck in La Vergne, Tennessee, against Coss's advice. The company closed the plant and refused to let the workers return until they agreed to come back on the company's terms, which they did. That, Coss recalled, "was an omen."

What marked the difference was the elevation of Yoichiro Kaizaki to the head of Bridgestone/Firestone in 1992. "He immediately told us he didn't want close relations," Coss said. "He refused to speak English. He would just sneer at us." An internal company document, one of a number that Coss said the union received anonymously over the years, explained that "while it was nice to share a good relationship, it would no longer be in the company's interest," Coss said.

A July 1993 memo sent out by the company and circulated a year later by the union to its locals, including the local in Decatur, said that the company's Japanese parent would provide support during a strike by supplying 3 million tires. It also said the company would demand revisions of the master contract and, it added, "Mr. Kaizaki expects us to be firm and avoid unnecessary compromise." It praised the company's recovery and warned about a potentially destructive price competition to come.

Coss had another inkling of what might be ahead. He was close friends with Sam Torrance, Bridgestone/Firestone's human resources director. In early 1994, Torrance left the company, and before he did, Coss said he gave him a warning that "things are going to be different." Torrance, he claimed, had "quit his job over the moral aspect of not being able to do what Bridgestone required." Torrance would not confirm the conversation.

Things were indeed about to change.

BRIDGESTONE REWRITES ITS SCRIPT

From the moment Kaizaki took over, the company was on notice that it had to stem its losses and improve the bottom line. Kaizaki wanted problems fixed, said company officials. Before contract time, the company sought out the union and described its concerns. "We said we had no secrets. Nothing to hide," recalled Peter Scofield, one of the Bridgestone/Firestone negotiators. The union, however, "went on radio silence," said Scofield; it perceived the company's gesture as a pressure tactic.

"We had given them so much information, I thought a reasonable man could see what was going to happen," Scofield said.

What the company wanted was to end years of negotiated precedents and to sidestep the industry-wide pattern that the union had struggled to keep in place.

The company wanted to go from 8-hour to 12-hour shifts that would rotate between days and nights, to run the plants for seven days, not five, to replace cost-of-living wage increases with pay hikes linked to productivity, to start new hires at 30 percent below other workers' wages, to require hourly workers to begin contributing to their health care benefits—a perk preserved by only a few blue-collar workers—and to trim vacation time for senior workers from six to four weeks.

At a meeting in Akron in January 1994, the company laid out its new contract scenario. John Sellers, the union's highest-ranking non-elected official, was indignant. He told the visiting Bridgestone/Firestone officials that if they persisted with such a broad makeover of the union contract they would push the union into a fight. But the company did not back down. It kept giving the union a metaphorical warning, saying that "the train was leaving the station." The company complained about spending too much to buy the plants, its losses over the years, and dismal profits in 1993. It said it needed an overall fix, not a piecemeal solution.

On some issues, the union was willing to give ground. It was agreeable to accepting seven-day-a-week operations, but it did not want to go to 12-hour shifts. Sellers, however, was firmly against letting the company rewrite its contract.

What was the gamble for the company? If the union struck, the company figured it would wait a month or so and then start talking. In a few months, the union would come around and work out a deal. There was no bending on the basic issues: The company wanted things to change—it wanted control over its factories.

WHAT CAN THE UNION DO?

As the company stood its ground, Coss faced a quandary: to strike or not. He thought the company's contract was terrible. Yet he didn't think that the union's 4,200 workers would bring Bridgestone/Firestone to its knees. He didn't see a strike turning around a company so large. He got the same advice from federal mediators. But he saw how the union local leaders had been whipped up, how their emotions were on high alert, and how the union had almost no choice but to strike. He, personally, didn't call for a strike. The local union heads along with other union officials, meeting as a policy committee, took that step.

So the union sent its workers out in July 1994. It was the last strike in the history of the URW.

PART IV

Skirmishes and Sieges

Living amid Fear and Hatred

The Strikebreakers

November 1994

The Caterpillar workers had trudged back to work, their tails between their legs. Staley's workers were locked out and forced to watch untrained office workers streaming through the plant gates to do the jobs they had performed for decades. The rubber workers had been on strike for four months.

On a wall of the URW local, under a large label that said "The Hall of Shame," the names of all of those who had crossed its picket lines were listed in dark-colored letters. One of them was a former president of the rubber workers local.

Decatur's UAW local had put together its own less public list of its renegades. In Decatur, the 11 UAW defections numbered far fewer than elsewhere, though the totals were always in dispute. Caterpillar counted 1,000 line crossers in 1992 and claimed the figure reached 5,200, or more than one in three, at its peak in 1995. The union never agreed with that figure, claiming it was lower but never offering any details.

But the numbers were almost insignificant as compared with the larger trend they reflected. For years American unions had been retreating, like soldiers fleeing from a battlefield, scurrying from one place to another, almost as if they were racing to avoid being caught in house-

127

to-house searches by corporate America. But U.S. unions had almost always also carried their wounded with them to safety. And from the 1930s onward, they had rarely turned on each other when pinned down and stuck in a losing battle.

In those earlier times, scabs and strikebreakers would have had a hard time finding refuge in most blue-collar communities. In the long history of American labor disputes, no other event so set off the potential for violence as the arrival of strikebreakers along with scabs from within the union's own ranks. When shoemakers struck in Philadelphia in the 19th century and strikebreakers tried to fill their jobs, crowds descended on the strikebreakers. In the 1920s, steel and mining companies used African American workers as strikebreakers, carelessly exposing the picket line crossers to repeated violence.

When the Hormel Company hired permanent replacements at its plant in Austin, Minnesota, in 1985, the violence and vandalism were so dramatic that Governor Rudy Perpich called out the National Guard. When Greyhound Lines decided to hand its striking workers' jobs to permanent replacements, starting in 1990, a furious reaction followed. There were 52 sniper attacks against the buses driven by the newly hired replacement workers.

But the strikers' wrath has always been greatest toward their own who turn on them. And this truth was reconfirmed in Decatur.

The rift within the unions' ranks came first for the UAW: Only a handful of workers at first and then by the thousands across Illinois, they defected. Later, the same process afflicted the rubber workers. Despite the fact that neither union had ever suffered such desertions, the unions' national leaders were largely silent, furious and dismayed but not at all eager to put any more light on the splintering of their members' loyalties. At the local level, however, there was great fury.

That was what the line crossers quickly discovered.

Once they had taken the step to defect, some of those who had flaunted the authority of their unions were terrified by what they had done. They didn't realize that the unions could fine them and then expel them and that they would face the unions' taunts for some time to come. And although Caterpillar officials had praised them as heroes, some of the line crossers still felt abandoned As time passed, some sensed that they were resented even by Caterpillar's managers.

For most, their biggest concern was safety. Some feared for their lives.

In Decatur and at the company's other large Illinois facilities, the workers who crossed their union's picket lines said dead animals had been left on their doorsteps, death threats made over the phone, tire tracks gouged in their yards right up to their front doors. Bullets had shattered the window of a line crosser as he was driving his truck one day. Line crossers began to meet at one another's homes for support and to plot ways of defending themselves.

Daniel (not his real name) ordinarily wouldn't have crossed. But Caterpillar's threat to replace workers convinced him he had to save his job and break with the union.

The Decatur plant was the only real long-term job he had ever had, having been hired after high school. And when the factory was hit by massive layoffs in the early 1980s, he went four years on the outside, scraping by on unemployment benefits and low-paying jobs. He was mostly out of work, however. It terrified him. He discovered there was nothing in the small Illinois towns that paid as well as a factory job at Caterpillar.

During his long layoff, he had also grown furious that some of the Caterpillar workers were putting in overtime while he was barely getting by. He swore he would do something about a union that ignored its members, and so got elected as a union steward as soon as he was hired back at Caterpillar in the late 1980s. Daniel liked being a steward, telling himself that was making a difference on the factory floor for some fellow workers, and vowed to run again after being defeated in a 1991 election. Then came the strike and the company's warning in April 1992 that workers would be without jobs if they did not march to work. He had no doubt that Caterpillar would get rid of its union workers if it could. So he showed up at 5:00 A.M. at the factory's gates, counseled by the company to come in at such an early hour to avoid facing the pickets. But they were still there.

> "The first day I crossed the picket line, I had never seen people with expressions like that on their faces," he said. "They looked wild. I was kind of amazed, but I expected it. Then I looked over and there were these state troopers with dogs and there were these Vance people in paramiliatry outfits, and I thought, 'What the hell is going on?' We walked in, me and another guy, and we were the only two there. I thought there would have been a lot more coming. I knew there were a lot who wanted to come. That's when I pretty well made up my mind and said I wouldn't go back the next day.
>
> "But the next morning a pal called and said 'Let's go in,' and I did. I don't know why I did. I thought somebody was going to hurt you,

and I realized there was nobody to protect you. That night I got a call from a friend who said somebody from the union had asked if I had any guns or dogs and how to get onto my property. I asked him who it was, and he wouldn't tell. He was just trying to give me a heads up. Somebody in one of the company offices must have given the union that day our badge numbers and that is how they must have learned about us. I moved my wife and kids out of the house, and they were out for about a week."

A few months later, Daniel took a medical leave for a back operation. He needed the operation, but he also felt that he really had to get away from the factory. His nerves were on edge. He had been deluged at home with calls with nobody on the other end of the phone, and his name had been put on lists posted everywhere for miles around as one of the few line crossers at the Caterpillar plant. His first day home from the hospital after surgery, he was lying in bed when he suddenly felt that he couldn't breathe. It was a heart attack, he was sure, but it went away. Again and again, for the next three months, he had the same brief terrifying experience, until he sought help from the employee assistance office at the factory. He was directed to a psychiatrist, who prescribed medicine for his anxiety attacks.

But the medication and the company's shifting him around within the plant, moving him from job to job, did not change the uneasiness and emotional, physical tightness he felt at work. It did not restore his lost sense of security. Every time a car drove by his house, set back on a lonely road near a small farm town far from Decatur, he would sit and carefully watch it pass. Every time he was driving home from work, he would study the car lights behind him, prepared always for trouble. "You lose that sense of security and you don't know who you can trust. You are always in a state of heightened awareness."

The violence wasn't aimed at line crossers alone, however. The homes of a Caterpillar official in Peoria and a secretary for the company's top officials were also fired on. Nobody was hurt, but the potential for personal harm was great.

One of the workers who crossed the UAW picket line had, by chance, tuned to a Court Television production that had great resonance for him. It took place in Cleveland, and it involved a group of workers who were suing the UAW and the local involved in a labor dispute, for violence against them because they had crossed the union's picket line. The outcome of the case was even more interesting. The four workers won damages totaling $2 million from the union and the local. The line crossers decided to talk with the attorney who had just won the case against the UAW before the Cleveland jury.

Edward W. Miller was in his late thirties and had been handling a regular stream of cases that he felt matched his desire to do good deeds—*zadaka* in Hebrew. He called them instances of institutional violence: credit companies abusing debtors, banks and businesses that took advantage of consumers. An orthodox Jew who had spent some time studying to be a rabbi, Miller mixed his law practice with his religious convictions and an interest in standing up for people who had been abused.

In his first case against the UAW, he decided that he was also up against a political issue—the power of unions—and he could use all the publicity he could garner for his side. That is why he had contacted Court Television. And that was how he was invited to Peoria in March 1993 to meet with Caterpillar workers who had drawn their union's deep scorn. They wanted to meet with him and talk about their strategy.

As the meeting began, Miller asked David Webb, one of the organizers of the effort, to address the gathering. From then on, the meeting became a riveting experience for Miller, something he had never before encountered and something he thought had been far more redemptive for those attending, almost a catharsis for their fears. Webb, a decorated Vietnam veteran, talked about how his children slept on the floors at night, fearful of something being thrown into the house, and how difficult his life had become. He was on the verge of tears.

From the audience came cheers and hollers, words of support. People called out and told Webb to stand firm. They said they would fight back and that if they didn't fight back their days would only get worse. It was the closest, Miller thought, that he had ever come to a Baptist revival meeting. It was even better, he later told himself, than winning a trial, because the workers had felt defenseless and vulnerable prior to the meeting. Afterward, however, it seemed to Miller that they had a new will to go on.

In the lawsuits against the UAW locals in Illinois, which Miller filed within weeks, the line crossers said that the union had set up an "Adopt a Scab" list that gave their names and addresses, and union members were assigned to each scab. They told of being stalked after work at their homes and being told on the job that they faced trouble ahead. They said gunshots had been fired at their houses and their trucks and cars had been vandalized. Besides the abuse they faced when they crossed the UAW's picket lines, they said they were isolated, harassed, and made victims of vandalism by the returning UAW workers after they gave up their strike in April 1992. They were asking the courts for $15,000 damages individually for their suffering from the local and $4 million each in punitive damages.

Asked to help support the lawsuits, Caterpillar's initial public reaction was uncertainty. Its decision eventually to provide support for the lawsuits had little precedent among corporations. In addition to a fund that Caterpillar set up to support the lawsuits, another was created to accept outside donations.

Altogether about 29 workers at Caterpillar facilities filed lawsuits making similar charges against the union. Outraged, convinced it was another ploy in the company's battle with the workers and union, the UAW threw itself into fighting the lawsuits.

The New Law of a Larger Land

The Gladiator Companies

July 1994

Only a couple of years before the strike began, Bridgestone/Firestone seemed like the model on which all the myths about the new Japanese bosses in American business were based:

That American managers live largely according to short-term goals, whereas newly arrived Japanese managers in the United States focus on long-term goals.

That American firms are out of touch with their workers, whereas Japanese firms know how to tap their energies.

That American firms are autocratic and slow moving, whereas Japanese firms are innovative and open to new risks.

That Americans throw aside their workers in tough times, whereas the Japanese respect and nurture them.

That corporate America is long-suffering, but the Japanese have arrived to show the way to the future.

And on and on.

This was the sense about Bridgestone/Firestone—at least at first. Some of the company's workers, wearied by a decade of corporate job slicing that had cut their ranks in half, viewed their new Japanese bosses as saviors because of their willingness to give them a voice. The new Japanese ownership did not fight organized labor but worked hand in hand with the rubber workers union. The level of worker participation in the company became a business management guru's dream to hold high in the academic journals. Like other global companies, Bridgestone/Firestone stirred hopes because it forced daylight to shine on economies and industries that had slumbered under the control of national cartels or had been insulated by protectionist laws or had dozed off simply because of their isolation.

Then there was the company's headquarters in Nashville, a model of the global corporate stronghold.

Bland, so bland it was almost anonymous. Four stories of glass windows reflecting back a world of wispy clouds and a bright blue sky. The building was covered with subdued gray cement and surrounded by a carpet of thick grass, manicured greenery, a hushed parking lot, and a duck-filled pond. It sat at the bottom of a sloping hill in a corporate warren of similarly bland façades. Nashville's airport was a brief hop away; Opryland, the country-and-western mecca, was a tad farther.

No massive signs out front. No banners. No flags. No imperial-sounding corporate statements covered the entranceway. No elaborate security or fawning greeting staff awaited visitors downstairs. Nothing screamed out that this was the headquarters of Bridgestone/Firestone, one of the largest tire makers in the United States and an important arm of the Tokyo-based industrial Goliath, Bridgestone, the largest tire maker in the world.

Frugal, efficient, businesslike. It was the kind of headquarters created by hundreds of Japanese firms since the early 1980s, when they began digging in from coast to U.S. coast, planting roots in major American businesses and industries. Following in the deep footprints of the Japanese auto giants, smaller and medium-sized Japanese companies too were eager to find their American niches. And many settled in the industrial heartland.

Once they did, they established a corporate regimen.

They were loath to draw attention to themselves. They preferred to avoid conflict and controversy. They were mindful of the resentment some Americans had shown toward Japanese firms and their victories over American competitors. They were not blind to the fury that in the 1980s had driven jobless autoworkers in Detroit to publicly demolish Japanese-made cars as a sign of their economic despair. Inclined to stay away from long-established U.S. businesses, fearing they would be caught up in problems of meshing the two cultures, Japanese firms leaned heavily toward forming new ones, so-called greenfield operations. That way they would also not inherit any problems handed down by the Americans. And Japanese manufacturing firms, especially in the auto industry, preferred doing business without American unions. Not one independent Japanese automaker that set up shop in the United States agreed to a contract with the UAW. The only contracts the UAW has ever signed with Japanese auto companies have been with those that began their operations in partnerships with American automakers.

Finally, there were the unarguable successes of many of the newly arrived Japanese firms. When faced with no alternative, the Japanese often showed American managers that they knew how to boost hopes as well as production in union shops. Pushed by the unions, they tended to acquiesce, to back off from confrontations. And they were quickly lauded for showing how to efficiently run large factories once condemned to the scrap heap by cynical American bosses.

No wonder one myth after another developed about the new Japanese bosses. As time would prove, however, most were indeed myths, and the image of the ideal quickly developed cracks in its façade.

First there was the 1992 move to Nashville, a move that did not please Akron officials, who were already sensitive about the corporate flight from their city. The company had given Akron officials only one hour's notice of its decision. City officials were furious, feeling blindsided and abandoned, but the tire maker saw nothing wrong with what it had done. The move was symbolic of the company's quest for a new face. It showed the firm's ambition to leave behind the old ways of tire making and the traditional industrial thinking of Akron, to abandon its historic links with the Rubber City and its leftover headquarters of long-departed tire making companies. It wanted to cut a new image, one closer to Bridgestone's way of thinking,

By 1994, however, Bridgestone/Firestone had truly broken the mold.

THE COMPANY TAKES ON THE U.S. GOVERNMENT

A tire making machine is a complex metal contraption that has not benefited much from 20th-century technology's ability to ease the burden of the person using it. Making tires is still tedious, time-consuming, and sometimes dangerous. The tire making machine must be checked and adjusted when shifting from constructing a tire of one size to another. And whenever it is being worked on, the machine should be shut off. If it is not, the belts, pulleys, and arms that move the rubber along can suddenly turn into lethal weapons.

Bob Julian, a veteran worker at the Oklahoma City plant of Dayton Tire, a division of Bridgestone/Firestone, was setting up a tire making machine in October 1993, leaning over it as he worked, adjusting it from one tire size to another, when it snapped into action. He may have hit a lever with his wrench and set off the machine.

It is not clear what happened.

The tire making machines were set far from each other, and nobody was near him when the accident happened. Nobody heard any screams or noises when the 53-year-old worker, a medium-sized man, was caught between two parts and yanked forward. His head was crushed by the machine. He may have fought the machine for his life for 30 or 40 minutes. That is how long it was between the time he was last noticed and the time a passing supervisor found him. A set of false teeth was found caught inside the machine. A few days later Julian died of head injuries.

The URW local was outraged. Its safety officials had been talking with company officials in Oklahoma City for some time about enforcing a procedure that would have made sure such machines are locked and turned off. This is a procedure that the union's safety officials said would have saved Julian's life. But the company had balked, according to union officials, saying that such procedures should be limited to maintenance workers, who work for a company contracted to work at the plant. The company did not want the machine operators doing such a task.

When the report about Julian's death and numerous other industrial accidents at Bridgestone/Firestone landed on the desk of U.S. Labor Department secretary Robert Reich in April 1994, the feisty labor secretary was outraged too.

The U.S. Occupational Safety and Health Administration was proposing a $7.5 million fine, the maximum possible, and Reich decided to fly out to Oklahoma City for a well-publicized confrontation with the company at its factory doorstep. Seeing himself as a champion against "industrial evil" before his arrival, Reich showed up at the plant armed with notice of the hefty fine and an order for the company to immediately equip the facility with the required safety devices.

Much to Reich's surprise, Bridgestone/Firestone punched back and announced the next day that it would shut the 1,100-worker plant because, it explained, it could not comply with the government order.

But the company's decision to close the factory was unnecessary inasmuch as a federal judge in Oklahoma City quickly rejected the government's emergency order. A month later a federal judge ruled that the company had not violated federal standards requiring it to give locks to workers when they are servicing equipment.

Almost everyone was unhappy.

Although members of the union local had gladly stood beside Reich and applauded the gumption demonstrated by the cabinet member in publicly upbraiding the corporate giant, union safety officials more expert on the problems inside the plant had a different view. They were furious over the failure of the government's bureaucracy to act fast enough.

If the plant truly faced imminent danger, they asked, why hadn't the government done something six months ago, right after Julian's death? As for the company's threat to shut the plant, they had witnessed such theatrics with other companies and were hardly shocked by Bridgestone/Firestone's maneuver.

Nonetheless, the union local's members saw Reich as a hero. Tony Carr, a long-term rubber worker who was the local's head of safety and health, made sure to save his cassette copy of the press conference that Reich held during his visit to Oklahoma City. "He said this company was sacrificing its workers on the altar of profit. I'll never forget that," Carr recalled.

As Carr pieced the situation together, the fatal incident was yet another reflection of the company's ever-growing effort to speed up production and take the power of controlling the flow of tires out of workers' hands.

Giving production workers the right to shut down their machines during servicing—the issue that the union had wanted resolved months ago—would have meant adding only moments here and there to production time. But the plant was under great pressure to keep cutting away more costly production time. Carr was furious and totally in agreement with Reich.

So, too, were Bridgestone/Firestone officials furious.

After several months of dismal negotiations with the URW and five days before the contract was set to expire, the labor secretary had shown up outside the Oklahoma City facility, attacking the company. The event had to be a ruse set up by the union. The company was convinced it was merely a negotiating tool used by the union. And it was clear to the company from its experience at the bargaining table that the union was not going to give in easily. The company officials saw through Reich's speech. They were sure he was going against the advice of his OSHA bureaucrats. They would just have to stand up for their rights. If there was going to be a strike, and there had been many before, they thought it would not be long. But they were ready for one.

A CHART OF THE COLLISION
BETWEEN THE UNION AND THE COMPANY

So when July rolled around, the union didn't trust the company, and the company didn't trust the union. The union felt that it was backed up against a wall, and so did the company. The union couldn't believe how stubborn the company officials had become, and the company had the same view of the people on the other side of the table.

This is the way two sides grow apart, grow embittered, and pump themselves up for an all-out clash. It is the basic anatomy of a labor–management dispute in the United States, which has been studied to death by experts of all sorts. Management gurus have offered countless prescriptions for avoiding or controlling it. Lawyers grow even richer advising their clients on the steps to avoid in this dance.

But it happens again and again. This is the reality of labor–management relations in the United States, despite the myriad business school courses on human relations and the uplifting workshops held by private think tanks sponsoring workplace peace.

Consider the case of Bridgestone/Firestone versus the URW.

The company had been a very good partner with the URW, right? When Bridgestone first took over the old Firestone network of plants, it had been extremely cooperative with the union's health and safety officials. Yes indeed. The same was true for the way it dealt with problems on the factory floor and at the bargaining table.

So what changed, turning two partners into foes almost overnight?

No longer was the company unexpectedly cooperative in the union's eyes. It began disputing the union over safety and health procedures here and there, like other companies that try to cut costs and keep the union out of their business. It began shunting aside middle-level managers who were doing things the old ways. It began tinkering with production, shifting it more to the Japanese way of continuous improvement and high production.

A new way of thinking was pushing the company. The union saw this as clearly as a new clock on the factory floor with a different time setting.

For all of the money Bridgestone had paid for its new American outlet, $2.6 billion in 1988, and the added money it poured into tire making, the U.S. operation was not measuring up to expectations. The company had been caught up in a bidding war with Pirelli S.p.A. to take control of Firestone. And it markedly topped Pirelli's offer because it wanted a foot in the United States as the beginning of its global growth. With Firestone, the company would be locked into dealing with the big three automakers and the Japanese transplant automakers. It would have the nationwide sprawl of tire stores, and it would reach overseas on the backs of Firestone's foreign links. Bridgestone officials toyed with the idea of building their own plants, but they were in a hurry.

The company had traveled far from its turn-of-the-century roots.

In 1906, on the Japanese island of Kyushu, Shojiro Ishibashi and his brother Tokujiro had taken control of their family's clothing business. They soon began making the *tabi*, the traditional Japanese footwear, and eventually branched out into using rubber as soles for their shoes. In 1931, Shojiro Ishibashi formed a tire company, and he wanted to give it a special name. *Ishibashi* means "stone bridge" in Japanese, so he reversed the words in English. Thus, "Bridgestone" was born. In 1942 the company changed its name to Nippon Company but went back to Bridgestone in 1951 and was on its way to dominating Japan's tire industry.

TREADING MIGHTILY AMONG THE GIANTS

From 1988 to 1991, Bridgestone/Firestone, which had not made money for most of the 1980s, lost a total of $1 billion in the United States. It was losing $1 million a day in 1990 and 1991. The company was stunned by the unrelenting losses. "They knew they had been dragged around, taken for a ride," said Yoshi Tsurumi, a professor of management at Baruch College of the City University of New York, who often talked with Bridgestone officials as they shaped the firm's comeback policy. From the moment Bridgestone had made its U.S. extension, its rivals were skeptical. Outside Japan, they predicted that Bridgestone would not fare as well. It would not have the same advantages of workers willing to put in long hours, the shorter vacation periods, and easier financing as in Japan.

The company moved to make the change in 1991 with the arrival of Yoichiro Kaizaki, the high-level Bridgestone official, to replace chairman George Aucott. Firestone's success was important to the Japanese parent. Within no time, Kaizaki instituted steps to cut production costs and to set aside the old ways of doing things. Most of the Firestone managers were replaced. It also sidestepped Teiji Eguchi, an older Japanese executive who had been the company's chairman, a position with little clout. But change was not coming fast enough. Nor was the union bending as much as the company wanted. By 1993, the company had stemmed the losses. Yet its earnings were $6 million out of sales of $5 billion, still not what the company had expected.

By 1994, however, its earnings jumped to $29 million, and a year later, in the heat of its confrontation with the union, earnings quadrupled. At home, Bridgestone Corporation was on the beginning of a roll too. Between 1993 and 1995, when it ordered the cost cutting at its American subsidiary, its largest arm, its profits more than doubled.

But the company had already done the math and made its decision before its bottom line starting growing by leaps and bounds. "Kaizaki decided he would rather take a long strike and no more incremental changes. They were prepared to shut down things," Tsurumi said. Kaizaki returned to Tokyo after two years to head Bridgestone, and his place was taken in 1993 by Masatoshi Ono, someone with the same passion for a fight.

When the union struck in July 1994, the company vowed to keep the plants going, and within a month it began hiring temporary workers at wages 30 percent lower than those paid to the union. By January, it had already hired 2,300 workers. Company officials were convinced the union was not going to return to work in the short term, and they needed to get production going. So they notified the union that its members had been permanently replaced.

Roger Gates, a tall, hefty, unusually soft-spoken man with a droopy moustache and somber smile, president of the URW local in Decatur, was in Akron at a high-level union strategy session when the announcement was made. He had been hoping a breakthrough would end the strike. Many of his members back home in Decatur had not really been prepared for the walkout. It was almost as if they had stumbled into a nightmare. Nor had they considered the company likely to bring in temporary workers. Then the fax came in at union headquarters where Gates was meeting with other local officials: The company was permanently replacing the workers.

Gates felt as if the world had ended. He called back to Decatur to learn how the news was being taken by the members. Fear filled the long, narrow union hall built of concrete block that sits just around the corner from a busy gas station that flies one of the biggest American flags in all of south central Illinois. Randy Gordon, the local's no-nonsense vice-president, a wiry Vietnam veteran who always made sure the local flew the black-and-white veterans' MIA and POW flag, told him that the union hall was full of people and a wild sense of panic was in the air.

Fearful of losing their jobs, about 1,000 URW members had already returned to work.

Never before had a private company permanently wiped out the jobs of so many strikers in the United States. It was only the second time a Japanese company had come even close to taking such an action in this country.

THIS IS THE UNITED STATES. THIS IS NOT JAPAN

Replying to angry complaints that Japanese firms do not replace their own workers in Japan, Bridgestone/Firestone officials explained that in Japan companies have the right to replace strikers. In America, they said, American firms not only have the right, but they use it. Amid denials from Bridgestone/Firestone officials that the company was suffering, Kaizaki told reporters in Tokyo that the striking plants were costing the firm $10 million monthly.

Global companies, operating at home or abroad, rewrite long-time rules of behavior, long-time social contracts, and long-time expectations of them. They rip up contracts and demand wage cutbacks or workplace changes, such as a longer workday. They set in place a cascading descaling of wages in industries where agreements once protected the lifestyles of blue-collar workers.

Why? Global competition, they explain. They have no choice, they say.

How dare they take steps they would never take at home? How dare they hire scabs or shut down the only factory for miles, a source of livelihood in the community for generations?

They are doing it in the name of global competition, they say.

Anyway, that's the law of the land where they are now operating. They are not back home. What's good for the people back home is not always good for those abroad.

Not all global competitors align themselves with such ways of thinking. Not every company that goes beyond its home is an uninhibited swashbuckler.

But some are. They are the gladiator companies, and they represent what goes wrong when companies compete like foreign armies. These companies travel the globe with several commandments as their guide. Their most important mandates are to expand the company's reach, to do the best for their shareholders and the core company and to protect them above all else. The mindset of the gladiator company is that the company is right, not just in the narrow, protective sense, but right in the sense that it has an enlightened, liberating vision. This allows it to brush aside the talk about broken social contracts and shortsighted planning. It allows it to invoke the holy name of its investors and shareholders, even though it rarely asks them what they think.

Much of the work of a gladiator company at home and abroad is to make sure that this vision becomes real. Gladiator companies are flush with righteousness.

Gladiator companies like Bridgestone/Firestone did not come out of nowhere. Global companies arrived with the wheel and the sail. They organized the ledgers and collected the profits for the ancient warlords. They dreamt up new deals and underwrote the long march of empires and colonialist nations up until the end of the 19th century. They did the same in the 20th century, but not on behalf of their national masters. Rather, as the century waned, they took the risks increasingly on behalf of themselves and at their own will. And once again they organized the world, column by column. This time, though, they did it on a scale never before seen and with the biggest spreadsheet ever.

After World War II, American companies terrified the Europeans with their power and sprawl. But in no time the Americans were fretting about the Europeans grabbing up their best business possessions. In the Third World, the newly independent and poor former colonies in Africa, Asia, Latin America, and the Middle East threw up barriers to keep out the handful of truly global companies with the power to wheel and deal there. But then they too unlocked their doors and waited to cash in on the deals to be made. Some were able to take advantage of such opportunities, but many Third World countries are still waiting for the foreign firms to show up at their doors.

In the 20th century few could stay the power of the global companies. Nor could the membership in the club remain exclusive. In the early 1970s, as authors Richard Barnet and John Cavanaugh point out, the world had about 7,000 multinational firms, mainly American or British. Twenty years later, such firms had multiplied fivefold, and membership no longer was limited to elite American or European enterprises.

Just as the Americans had stalked the world for markets and places to churn out their goods at better prices, so had the Japanese and others. When Japanese and German automakers opened new plants across the United States, it was the same deal. They came seeking lower wages, fleeing the higher rates they paid at home.

From the 1980s onward, the rise of the global company engendered new fears in addition to the hopes that some, like the Bridgestone/Firestone workers of the merger's early days, started out with. There were fears because global companies swept aside older, more established local firms with their power, their financial clout, and their ability to link up markets as easily as putting out clothes to dry on a clothesline. They shook up the business elite and uprooted the thinking of the control-minded government bureaucracy. Moreover, as global companies traveled farther, so did global investors, and their ability to whip in and out of insecure industries was devastating to some countries' economies.

At Bridgestone/Firestone, some of these fears were being realized as the myths were disintegrating into dust.

Baffled by such anti-labor behavior by a Japanese firm, and angry over the widespread replacement of workers, Secretary of Labor Reich tried to reach Bridgestone's CEO, but he could not get through. He complained to President Clinton, and at a White House luncheon a few days later Walter Mondale, the U.S. ambassador to Japan, told the visiting Japanese foreign minister that Ono, the tire maker's CEO, should meet with Reich. When the two met several days later in Washington, Ono would not budge on the company's tactics.

With Reich pushing for it, Vice-President Al Gore handed the nation's union leaders, who were holding their annual winter bash in Miami in February, a gift.

He announced a federal ban on contracts for firms that had replaced striking workers, clearly a blow at Bridgestone/Firestone. It was estimated that the tire maker could have lost $12 million in business because of the order. When the company received notice from the Labor Department soon after that the government order was going to be carried out, it understood that the White House was not bluffing. It realized that there was money at stake. In no time the company challenged the order in federal court, and it was joined by the U.S. Chamber of Commerce, the American Trucking Association, the National Association of Manufacturers, and the Labor Policy Association.

A year later the company won its case in a federal appeals court in Washington, and the government let the case die there.

Bridgestone/Firestone had been a good gladiator.

So had Staley and Caterpillar, in their own ways.

When Bridgestone/Firestone confronted the URW in 1994, it was driven by a straight-backed determination to carry out its visions. It took on the U.S. government, the unions, and the communities where it was doing business because it had a goal to serve. This was not the communal-minded Japanese firm so firmly tied to its rightful role as a corporation. This was a company on its own.

For some time before its showdown with the UAW, Caterpillar had been a righteous American company, making its voice heard and asserting its independence to U.S. officials and even to some in the corporate world, who questioned its determination to put down the union so strongly. But as its confrontation with the UAW escalated, it was consumed by an ever greater determination not to waver from its vision, not to surrender after waging such a struggle.

How could the union challenge Caterpillar's loyalty to the United States? company officials asked. It had not fled the United States to build foreign factories. It had not deserted the United States, to be sure. But it had begun to invest more overseas. From 1979 to 1992, the percentage of its total hourly workforce that was located overseas grew from 20 to 30 percent.

As for Tate & Lyle, the British parents of Staley, it was less engaged in a moral quest. Its vision was to extend and compound its grasp. The firm's expansion in the United States with the purchase of Staley represented growing control over the U.S. market and a new overall global expansion by the company. Along with the rest of its broadening global base, its new American portfolio, Staley, a company nurtured for decades by indulgent owners, had to fall in line with London's vision. Within a few years Staley's presence as a corporate voice in Decatur's community life had withered and shrunk. This was not a high priority in London.

Each of the companies pleaded that it had no choice but was forced to take such steps because of the pressure of global competition. Yet these three were the giants in their industries. They were not being squeezed by outsiders or pressed to the wall by a gang of bully competitors. They were firms that stood atop their industries.

As the 1990s began, Caterpillar was driven by its global vision. The company could not cite its export sales numbers often enough. In 1991, as company officials pointed out, nearly 60 percent of Caterpillar's sales came from outside the United States. This became the core of a theme the company would regularly recite as it joined one business lobbying group after another that matched its belief in free trade with few restraints.

Caterpillar didn't believe in letting the United States punish countries that had violated human rights by cutting off trade with them. Rather, its solution was to engage them in business and to draw them closer to United States values. And closer, too, to business with the solid Midwestern manufacturer from Peoria. If the country was South Africa at the peak of its apartheid rule, or a rogue nation that had broken most rules of international decency, Caterpillar created its own set of corporate morals and rationale.

WHERE DID THIS THINKING COME FROM?

Caterpillar had been burned financially in the 1980s when the United States had imposed an embargo on the Soviet Union and the firm lost out on a major contract. Caterpillar swore it would not suffer such a financial setback again. So, bit by bit, it cobbled together a normal-sounding platform to hide behind. By advancing this new form of internationalism, it said, it was merely protecting its workers and shareholders. It didn't matter that shareholders increasingly protested such actions, or at least the small number who had the grit to raise the issue at the company's annual meetings. The company knew better about such things than these shareholders or the U.S. government or most world organizations that struggle to enforce human rights.

As Caterpillar increasingly portrayed itself as a loyal American company that still built most of its products in the United States, its view was also pragmatic because the company determined it was most competitive if it didn't move its base of operations out of the United States. This allowed it to stand up to the U.S. government when it thought the government was hindering it, and to reach out for the government's help when it needed it.

For instance, whenever there was talk of imposing pressure on Japan to open its market to other U.S. firms, Caterpillar complained loudly, saying it was already a major competitor in Japan and would suffer. Therefore, its interests came before those of the other American firms clamoring for a foothold in the Japanese market.

When American steel companies pressed for a long-term extension of steel quotas in the late 1980s, Caterpillar was the largest single manufacturer to stand up in opposition. It did not want to see the American steel industry bathed in protectionism.

Never before had a major U.S. company taken on the steel industry, but Caterpillar saw itself as a unique breed of world competitor. After waging a successful lobbying campaign, it was able to steer the Bush administration into making a decision that it liked.

But Caterpillar did not mind taking the government's help in some of its overseas business.

GLADIATORS KNOW ALL OF THE DEALS

For much of the 1980s, Caterpillar was one of the large U.S. firms that benefited from loans to foreign purchasers of its products or insurance on its sales through the Export-Import Bank. And when there were complaints from unions and taxpayer groups about the corporate welfare doled out by the government to companies through agencies like the Export-Import Bank and the Overseas Private Investment Corporation, Caterpillar only spoke out louder.

If any businesses worldwide got better deals because their governments gave them a financial boost, company officials said, American firms should have the U.S. government match them dollar for dollar.

Caterpillar had no intention of losing out. Gladiator companies don't.

> Some would call the Caterpillar I just described a "stateless" or "borderless" company. We disagree. We're still very much an American company. . . . In fact, we are one of America's largest exporters. But we recognize that globalization isn't a passing fad.
> —DON FITES, June 6, 1990

> As I see it, there is no question about which paths to follow if we as a nation are to be successful global players. We must discard patterns that have worked in the past and look instead to new business models, new ways of thinking, that allow us to unshackle the American creative genius that got us where we are: the world's most powerful economy.
> —DON FITES, Foreign Trade Association
> of Southern California, May 1992

No Help Here

The Trade Union Workers

1994

Across the United States, organized labor looks as if it must be a vital presence everywhere. Councils exist in the big cities, states, and local communities. You can imagine union leaders and their lobbyists speaking out in the state capitals, hanging around city halls to make sure labor gets its share. You can picture local union officials banding together to lend a hand with a strike that goes sour on the other end of town.

It's a system as old as most of the railroads tracks that cross the United States. It goes back to when workers first organized themselves into professions in the 19th century.

When the AFL merged with the CIO, the two groups melded their local organizations. But the whole was an underfunded and uncoordinated operation and often didn't matter much. There were exceptions, but they were few. Nearly half of the member unions by the early 1990s were not contributing to the state federations, for example. And the AFL-CIO wielded little real power over these groups.

Getting a job in the local or state office was often the reward handed union officials after they had climbed the ladder. They wound up with cushy jobs and nothing much else to do. In towns where there once had been thriving industries, the local labor council was still there even though the work wasn't. Time had passed, but the local councils had not kept up. There were more than 600 local councils and a labor federation in every state.

By the 1990s this network had become a façade of itself. At best, it was still alive only in certain places. State capitals? More than likely. Big cities like Chicago or Detroit or Pittsburgh, where unions still carried some clout? Probably. But when it came to small towns like Decatur and festering disputes like the one the Decatur workers faced, the organized labor system seemed to have dried up, atrophied to the point of uselessness.

In the 1990s this system operated across the United States like hundreds of small businesses. Some cooperated with one another, some took directions from those higher up the ladder, and some even tried to work toward the same goal. But many lived in their own worlds, isolated from doings even miles away. And what was going on in Washington might as well have been a matter of foreign affairs.

When Decatur's troubled locals began searching for help, they turned to the bottom rung of this system.

THE LIMITS OF SOLIDARITY

This was a kingdom long ruled by William H. "Skip" Dempsey, whose titles included head of Decatur's Central Labor organization, its Building Trades Council, and head of Local 65 of the Plumbers and Pipefitters Union. The three unions caught up in disputes wanted him to order the construction and building trades workers to stop working at the three plants. Most of the workers were going and coming without paying any heed to the unions' picket lines. And some of those were running equipment inside the plants, jobs that had been done by the workers outside on the picket lines.

Yet there were some of these workers who refused to cross the lines and thereby do the work that would be a setback to the unions picketing outside. They stopped by the UAW hall to share with Larry Solomon their feelings about being caught in a bad situation between the striking workers and the trade unions.

Dempsey, a veteran union man who rarely minced words, didn't see the situation the same way as the three unions. He was sympathetic to the workers' plight, especially those at Staley. "I blame the Staley management," he said. "It was unthinkable to ask for everything. They [the company] put them in a bad situation." But he refused the unions' request, for several reasons.

First, he insisted, the trade union workers were not running any equipment within the plants. Second, in the past the same type of loyalty being requested now had not been available to the builders. Years earlier, the autoworkers and rubber workers had ignored picket lines put up by the building trade unions and wound up taking their jobs away. Because the industrial unions in Decatur, he explained, had not honored the unions of the building trades, there would be no deals. Even if the trade unions would have wanted to join with the striking unions, he said, their hands were tied by their own contracts, blocking them from honoring any other strikes.

Finally, Dempsey didn't like what he had been hearing—union people making statements he had never heard before in Decatur. They sounded like 1930s radicals. The only thing they didn't do, it seemed to him, was stage a massive sit-down strike. The radicalism had started, he figured, after Ray Rogers came to Decatur, and it had kept growing. But there were others the unions had brought in who were also not friendly toward the AFL-CIO.

Dempsey was convinced that the local union leaders had tunnel vision and didn't realize they were headed for trouble. And he was tired of their demands for support. Always they wanted more. And they rarely offered any thank-yous.

Finally the three unions demanded a show of support, and Dempsey flatly replied that the other unions in town would not take part, would not walk away from their jobs at the three factories.

Threatening calls to his home began, calls that made him check his driveway regularly for rocks and broken glass. His response to one union leader in the heat of the conflict was that they were asking for too much. Get the UAW people and everyone else out in a field, he grumbled one day, letting his temper flare. He would bring all of the construction people, and they would settle it once and for all.

"I asked them a couple of times if they thought they were going in the right direction," he said. "I wasn't sure they were headed in the right direction. They had tunnel vision. And you couldn't do enough for them."

Lost in a Maze

The NLRB

1994

Let us now consider some basic facts from National Labor Relations Board cases 33-CA-10559 and 33-CA-10563, as reported and decided by Stephen J. Gross, administrative law judge, Washington, D.C. These cases involve Randy Morrell, an assembler in the Mining Vehicle Center in Building D of the Decatur, Illinois, facility of Caterpillar Inc. The company is based in Peoria, Illinois. Morrell has complained about being harassed by the company in violation of the nation's labor law amid the long-term dispute between his union, the United Automobile Workers, and the company.

In his ruling on these cases, the judge writes that Morrell is intelligent and articulate, has been praised for being cooperative, and was considered safety-minded by his superiors. He was also, says the judge, a strong supporter of the union, and his supervisors knew that. Morrell wrote a number of letters to the local newspaper criticizing Caterpillar management and at one point was chastised by his boss.

Between December 1993 and March 1994, employee Morrell took part in a series of squabbles with his supervisor about safety problems with the equipment on his job, his need for a union safety representative to help him deal with the problem, and his on-the-job breaks. He felt his rights had been violated.

The issues involving Morrell are not earth-shattering. They are nitty-gritty questions about what the company can and cannot do in the midst of an uprising within its plants. Sounds as if they could be answered quickly. But it will take years before the government agency, the NLRB, will hand down a ruling.

When the ruling was finally made in June 1997, the judge wrote that the supervisor was not off base in raising questions about Morrell's behavior because of the way Morrell had handled several incidents. (He seemed to be asking for trouble, the judge suggested.) But he did rule that the company supervisor had no right to order Morrell to take off some union materials that he had taped onto a company toolbox and onto an empty cardboard box where he works. A small victory for Morrell, for the UAW, and for workers across the land on the right to slap union stickers on their toolboxes.

That was not, of course, how it always went.

A VICTIM OF THE BATTLE OF THE YELLOW PADS

Richard Zerfowski's legal problems started early one day on the job at Caterpillar. He was driving a small gas-driven cart. Another worker, who had previously crossed the picket lines during the strike, passed by him. The man passed by again; they talked. Zerfowski's supervisor came by soon after and said Zerfowski had called the other worker a "scab." No, Zerfowski denied saying that, but the supervisor was insistent that he leave the factory floor.

Zerfowski called for his union shop steward and told him that he was being walked out of the factory and that he had not done what he was being accused of.

After a hearing, he was suspended a month later. That, he fumed, was not justice. Zerfowski had gone to work at Caterpillar at age 18, right out of high school, and never strayed except for his two years in the military during the Vietnam war. Blue-collar work seemed to be in his blood. He never considered what other work he would do, only that he did not want to work on the railroads.

To be cut loose by Caterpillar, whether temporarily or forever, was job death. In Decatur and Peoria and the other blue-collar towns where Caterpillar jobs were the dream jobs, high-wage tickets to a good living, a disciplined worker became a pariah, somebody who had clearly violated sacred corporate rules and could not be trusted.

Few other companies wanted to hire them, and if they were hired there was a feeling that they would not stay around for long. As soon as they won their battle with Caterpillar, it was assumed, they would be headed back. With few employers paying wages as high as those at Caterpillar, why would these workers serve any other master?

When it was clear that nobody else would hire him, not even for a part-time job parking cars for an auto dealer, and that his battle with the company through the NLRB could languish for years, labor history buff Richard Zerfowski began writing letters.

He wrote to every politician he could think of. "When my case has gone completely through the court system, and is settled, the most I can receive is full back pay," wrote Zerfowski. A tall, somber, slow-moving man who had been on the job for 31½ years when he was fired from his job as a tool and die maker, he could not believe that he had been cut loose from Caterpillar. "There is no penalty for Caterpillar for illegally discharging me," he wrote.

He kept copies of all of his letters. Zero, as he was called by the others at the Caterpillar plant in Decatur, was an unusually meticulous person who kept copies of nearly everything. His wife hounded him about his files, but he insisted that someday somebody would find them and consider them a treasure. Maybe the University of Illinois would want them, he said. He was serious, too. He kept notes about what happened every day at Caterpillar after the strikers went back to work, recording his thoughts and impressions. He kept his personnel reports year after year, the documents in which his supervisors had described him as a team player and dependable, as someone who never called in sick and who was an outstanding worker. Does more than asked. Rarely misses work. Gold star accolades.

THE AMAZING LABOR RELATIONS LEGAL MAZE

This is how the UAW and Caterpillar ultimately fought out their war, within the legal maze of the National Labor Relations Board. This is an infinitely slow-moving, procedure-laden world in which cases normally slumber for years while companies stave off any legal pressure to change their ways and lawyers run up larger fees. In the end, nobody gets hurt, one side eventually gives up, and the other side takes some ineffectual action out of frustration. Unions and companies might as well stand in the middle of a field for several years and then pelt each other with flowers.

This is the system that was meant to bring reason and order to the chaos of American industrial warfare. It was a solution born of the labor tumult of the 1930s and Franklin D. Roosevelt's unprecedented decision to give organized labor legal support from the government. With the passage in 1935 of the Wagner Act, or the National Labor Relations Act as it was known, the government finally turned a steady gaze on the brutal combat waged between unions and companies and laid down rules that were meant to help workers organize.

Roosevelt's goals were strictly economic. Initially cool to the law proposed by the liberal Democrat from New York, Robert F. Wagner, he ultimately saw a system of labor laws as stabilizing the still very troubled U.S. economy. In the process, of course, labor laws would help American workers, and the NLRB, charged with the task of administering the law, would guarantee a basic democratic right to workers to organize, an idea that was not even universally supported by liberal Democrats at the time.

The business community of the late 1930s was up in arms, declaring the law unconstitutional and a "dangerous weapon of social coercion" and vowing not to comply with it. And they didn't. As companies regularly rejected the law, the number of strikes grew.

In 1937, as the annual strike toll grew to over 4,700, the U.S. Supreme Court turned aside the business community's complaints against the Wagner Act in a case involving the once powerful steel maker, Jones & Laughlin Steel Company. By a five-to-four vote, the Court laid down historic doctrine for the American workplace. Chief Justice Charles Evans Hughes, writing for the majority, said that the law was proper inasmuch as it went no further than safeguarding employees' rights to self-organization and to take part in collective bargaining without restraint or coercion by their employers. "That," he wrote, "is a fundamental right."

Years later, not all companies in the United States agree that there is fundamental right to belong to a union. And if corporate America were honest, it would also admit what a deal it has with the NLRB. But it gripes more than ever, which is good strategy for its lobbyists and business groups to use to ensure that little will change.

I have heard business people and their lawyers complain endlessly about being victims of the NLRB. But I have never once heard anyone from a union openly rejoice in the system meant to protect the workers.

A BLACK HOLE FOR THE UNIONS' LEGAL BATTLES

By the early 1990s, unions looked on the NLRB as a dark hole, a wasteland where their legal battles languished or died. Either they were lost to the costly legal defenses mounted by companies, or they were killed by the board's unhurried approach to deciding cases. Long-delayed decisions read more like epitaphs.

A union might win a drive to organize new workers. It might win the secret ballot supervised by the NLRB, or win the card check process whereby it showed that more than half its members were willing to join the union. And then it most likely would be stopped dead in its tracks. That's because the company would drag the issue out in the courts, picking apart the union election with one challenge after another. It does not matter whether a company has a strong case to stand on. It needs time to kill the union's effort, and the legal system provides that. The NLRB cannot enforce its own rulings but must go to the federal courts for enforcement of its decision. A company that wants to stand up to the NLRB can go through all of its appeals with the government agency and then slog its way onward through the federal courts, fighting the agency's ruling. Meanwhile, the union organizing effort is frozen. The longer this battle drags on, the more likely it is that the pro-union spirit within the factory will fizzle or that the workers most committed to the union will find work elsewhere. Some will also pass away. The smaller the union, the more likely it is to lose heart somewhere down the road, realizing that it will be stuck with an enormous legal bill. From the perspective of cold-blooded economics, it is smart for a company, that expects to lose, to wait out a long legal battle, because it knows that the court-ordered fines or back payments will never total what it might have had to pay in union-negotiated salaries and benefits. Furthermore, it has kept the union out, an action upon which no price can be set. The winner is the last one standing, not the one who was in the right.

Many union leaders claimed the nation's labor laws were more foe than friend, and they hoped desperately that the laws would be reformed: If employers faced heavy fines for illegally derailing union elections or faced the prospect of damages, unions would have a better chance of organizing workers and standing up to companies. If time lines were set, the battles over union elections would not drag on. If companies faced heavy penalties, or even had to pay the legal costs for the cases they lost, the law would have more impact.

American workers have good reason to expect the courts and government to defend them if they have been discriminated against because of their race, religion, sex, or disability. Ironically, however, they have little hope of the government's rushing to their rescue if they are unfairly fired or punished or simply deprived of basic workplace rights.

Nevertheless, some union officials and legal experts doubt that the labor laws are the real problem. In the 1930s, they claim, before there were any real labor laws, unions flourished and signed up millions, but now the unions have lost their initiative, their spirit, their ability to innovate. Ignoring the NLRB and fighting their battles in other ways, they suggest, would get the unions greater results.

But those urging the alternate path outside the NLRB have not discovered organizing nirvana either, nor do the workers seem fired up and willing to seize their factories as they did in the 1930s.

The government's numbers show what has happened to unions over the years as their organizing pace has slowed drastically. In the early 1950s, unions won nearly three-fourths of the organizing elections supervised by the NLRB. By 1990, they won just less than half. That was not the only shrinkage. By the 1990s, unions held less than half as many elections as in the 1950s. And the number of members in the newly organized units was minuscule as compared with the number in the unions' heyday in the 1950s.

MEDIEVAL FEUDS AND LEGAL JOUSTS
IN MODERN-DAY AMERICA

After casting its lot with President Clinton, organized labor hoped that perceived flaws in the legal setup would at last be corrected by changes in the labor laws. It pinned its hopes on the commission headed by former labor secretary John Dunlop. It was the nation's first official look at labor–management relations since the Great Depression, and it came close to meeting the unions' expectations.

The fact-finding report, issued in May 1994, talked of workers trapped in the "dark ages of labor management antagonism," and of the United States as the only major democracy with such a confrontational relationship between unions and companies.

By most of its calculations, the commission said that companies were breaking the labor laws more often than before and that the number of rulings the NLRB handed down against businesses easily dwarfed those made against labor organizations. Between 1950 and the late 1980s, the commission said, for example, the incidence of companies illegally firing workers for participation in union activity rose from one in every twenty union organizing elections to one in four. Even more stunning, the commission said that when the NLRB orders a company to stop bargaining in bad faith, most of the time the union cannot get the company to agree to a contract. It is simply stymied. But if it is successful, then it is usually unable to follow up with a second contract. Harvard law professor Paul Weiler has estimated that between 10 and 20 percent of the workers who voted for unions in NLRB elections were fired for backing unions.

Business groups liked the report's criticism of the federal bureaucracy and the explosion of job-related lawsuits, but that was all they responded to. But the glimmer of hope the commission had instilled in union leaders was extinguished when the final report came out in January 1995. Organized labor didn't think the report went far enough, although it urged more power for the NLRB to protect workers' interests in organizing elections.

The unions felt let down again. For all of the hopes labor pinned on the commission's hearings, it was another empty dream. Nothing ever came of the commission's recommendations.

PART V

Rallying

Hit and Run at Caterpillar

June 1994

In a way, Larry Solomon's dream was at last coming true.

Before, some of his members had suffered from a moral rigor mortis, as he called it. They had gotten lazy. They didn't show the spirit he thought unions needed. They weren't willing to stand up to the company, let alone shoulder more of the burden at their union hall.

Now he had the core of an angry workforce at his disposal. But it was not just in Decatur. A seething unrest was showing up almost daily wherever the union faced Caterpillar. It was as if the workers were spitting in the company's face: these middle-class, middle-aged workers from all over the Midwest and beyond, all fired up and furious as they drove to and from work in their pickups and vans.

The union struggle had started to mutate, slowly but surely, on the day the workers returned to their jobs in April 1992 under threat of replacement. Now the talk was not about getting a decent contract but about saving the American dream. Now the gripes were not about the losses the union had suffered but the arrogance of the company to think it could do without its union help. Now the union was able to duel with the company inside its plants. And it did.

Throughout the Caterpillar system, as the union cranked up its campaign, it transformed its largely conservative Midwestern members into disgruntled protesters.

In East Peoria, at Caterpillar's largest complex, workers would unfurl a large American flag and parade through a factory at the end of

161

their shift, chanting loudly until they reached the parking lot. It was a stunning spectacle of defiance. They didn't seem to worry about what would happen to them. In Decatur, they blew whistles at shift change. They held meetings on their lunch hour. They were pushing the company's managers to the limit. Those who had turned their backs on the union and crossed the union's picket lines were openly shunned and rebuked.

Workers covered themselves with buttons and shirts bearing messages, letting the company know about their discontent. The company did not hesitate. It reacted by disciplining workers, firing a growing number and briefly suspending hundreds. Its great increasing fear was that it would lose control of the plants. And those who felt torn between the union and the company simply tried to stay clear of both sides. In time, there were more who sought refuge by withdrawing, by holding back their emotions, by trying to go to work and imagine that they could somehow stay uninvolved. They were tired of the feuding and wanted to abstain from it. That was impossible. Even to abstain was a step in one direction or the other.

One after another, the union called hit-and-run strikes, infuriating the company by demonstrating how little real strength it had over the union. The pressure kept building. At his work site, Randy Morrell, who had become entangled in the union's legal battles with Caterpillar, defiantly held union meetings during his lunch period. He wanted the union to show its grit once again and strike the company. We should be out, he told the others. We should be on strike.

As time went by, Morrell, tall, blond, and in good shape, would become more of a presence at the local's offices. Like at least half of the local's members, he came from a small town outside Decatur. So he knew all the loyalties and traditions of places such as Vandalia and Effingham, Clinton and Bethany, where people are, as he said, "very strong, loyal people, the kind of people who give their word and keep it." And just like the rest, Morrell was a Caterpillar lifer who had grown up inside the factory, benefiting from the good days and suffering from the bad ones.

But there was a difference about him. He had a certain eagerness, a willingness to throw himself into the union's projects. He seemed to be a thinker, someone who didn't just slam his hand down on the table, cussing the company. Though he was 49 years old when the trouble with Caterpillar began, he seemed to represent a change from the old guard within the local. He was not as hard-headed and militant as Larry Solomon. He wasn't rash. He seemed to think over his plans and search for new ways of doing things. He had an infectious enthusiasm that went beyond just kicking the company in the butt. He was like the others his age: the people who felt put upon by life. But he seemed to want to do something about it. He was not a whiner. He had plans, ideas.

ONE MORE TWIST OF FATE

Life, Randy Morrell believed, often seemed to move opposite from where he wanted it to go. If he wanted to go here, somehow it took him there. If had planned on this, that is what he got. And what did he usually get? The short end of the stick. He was always catching up with the rest, the ones who didn't go to Vietnam, who went to college and earned a degree and got a good job. He was always behind those who got the good breaks, ever a victim, he was sure, of bad-luck coincidences, one after another.

In late 1991, when the strike at Caterpillar began, he had one plan in mind: He would retire in five more years. He had started at Caterpillar when he was 19 years old and never figured on staying all those years.

Morrell's hometown of Mowequa is not far from the central Illinois mines where one of his grandfathers, a French immigrant, went to work at age 13. His mother's roots were mostly Dutch and Irish, but his great-grandmother on his mother's side had been a full-blooded Cherokee. Working in Decatur was a tradition in the family. Not long after 54 miners were killed, their bodies buried in the mine on the bitterly cold Christmas Eve of 1932, a lot of workers in Mowequa got factory jobs in Decatur. Randy Morrell's relatives were among them.

An athlete of some local fame, a legacy that he cherished for years after, Morrell went to Southern Illinois University and got a summer job at the end of his first year in college. Gambling on a low draft number, he stayed on at Caterpillar, thinking he would earn some money before going back to school. But the Vietnam War's thirst for draftees grew, his draft number was no longer safely low, and he faced being called up. Rather than be drafted, he signed up for the Air Force and spent just less than four years in the service.

Allowed to leave early to return to school, Randy was at Southern

Illinois University when his father, who did not have insurance, was hurt. Serendipitously, Caterpillar called at the same time, saying that Morrell had three days to return to his job or lose his chance to work there. So he put school aside to help out at home. Then he married, and somehow he just stayed on at Caterpillar.

High interest rates and the recession in the early 1980s crushed the small flower shop and greenhouse he was running on the side at home with his wife, forcing him to sell it. Then came the union's 205-day strike, at the time the longest ever against Caterpillar. Financially, he had never been in worse shape. It took him years to catch up.

Once the strike began in 1991, he figured it would be like most of the rest, a few weeks of strike duty and a settlement. The company and the union always worked things out in the end. He thought he knew the rhythm of these things. Even though he had been devastated by the union's strike nearly a decade before, he somehow felt that this time was different. He was gambling, so to speak.

A few years earlier, Morrell had eagerly joined in the worker participation efforts at the plant. All throughout Caterpillar, workers responded to the company's pitch, supported here and there by the union, for them to pitch in and help the company come up with ways to improve the job. It seemed to be the new way of doing things not only in Decatur but around the country.

That was before the strike.

STIFFED, ONCE AGAIN

At the beginning Randy figured he would do his picket duty and that would be it. But the strike dragged on, and then Caterpillar threatened to replace workers. He was dumbstruck by the company's intent to get rid of all of the people who had spent their adult lives inside the factories. Caterpillar was a bully, and he had always hated bullies.

One step led to another, and he was soon asking to help out at the union. "Some of the ideas they were coming up with to get the company were kind of dumb," he said. Hanging company officials in effigy seemed amateurish, so he offered his own ideas and linked up with others who agreed with him. He started writing letters to the *Decatur Herald & Review*, making sure the paper ran one of his every 30 days, the paper's limit on exposure for any one reader. He went on the morning talk programs on WSOY-FM, one of Decatur's popular radio stations, to offer the union's interpretation of what was going on.

It seemed there was always much more he could do, and he threw himself into the union work. He swept through the union hall upbeat, energetic, and eager. Increasingly, he felt he could relate to the majority of workers, who shared his patriotism, sense of honor, and determination in the face of tough situations. They had gone off to Vietnam because they thought it was the right thing to do, and when they came home they were told they had done wrong. But they put that shock and defeat behind them. Working hard on the job at Caterpillar had meant winning a different American battle, the victory of the blue-collar middle class. The spoils were the ability to live a good life and the building of a world-class industrial core.

But he also felt that they had become lazy. They took much of what they had won and earned for granted, the union included.

Then came the fight with Caterpillar. One more mess-up. One more rotten deal. One more problem to squeeze out of—he hoped. It reminded Morrell of how things always went bad for him, and always just when he was catching up.

> "We were taught how everything was right in America, and then we learned that it wasn't. We were told all through the 1980s that we had to share ideas and benefits with the company. I joined in the ESP program (an employee involvement effort) the program that worked with the company. And here came 1991, and the whole thing was jerked out from under us. Oh my God, after all that, it wasn't going to come out good. We were not going to reap the benefits.
>
> "Damn it, here I was in the middle of the bullshit. Always coming up with the short end of the stick."

NO CHOICE BUT AN EXIT

The last thing UAW secretary-treasurer Bill Casstevens wanted was a strike. He didn't think it would do any good and feared that it would only backfire. But he couldn't smother the fire down below that the union had ignored. It had done the job of morale building well, convincing workers that they were fighting a moral fight, a fight for them and their families, not just a cut-and-dried contract dispute or a struggle to preserve pattern bargaining. It was the workers versus the company. The workers holding the line for blue-collar America. The new proletarian battle.

Gathered in Detroit, the union local leaders were hungry for a strike.

How about putting it off? No, they wanted a strike.

How about sending postcards to Caterpillar's board of directors, complaining about what was going on? Their members would laugh themselves silly over that idea.

They were driving Caterpillar crazy with their operations inside the plants. Why not go on? No, it was time to show Caterpillar what they stood for, to show the company that they wouldn't put up with what was going on in the factories.

So they struck again in June 1994.

C H A P T E R   2 1

Desperately
Seeking Solutions

July 1994

Amid the hubbub, one gray-haired, balding, slump-shouldered worker, 61 years old, 43 years on the job at A. E. Staley, softly whispered to another worker waiting beside him in the vast sea of metal chairs set up for the night's union meeting.

"I'm scared," said the older man, an electrician, in a low voice so others nearby could not hear. "It's hard to sleep at night with no health insurance. It's like playing Russian roulette. Can't get any 'cause of my wife's health. I feel like in a way I want to give. But I don't want to give up. And I don't want to retire."

The man beside him nodded at his neighbor's words, offered apologetically because in the heat and furor of the union's effort to win its battle with the company the theme was sticking together, outlasting the company, and here he was admitting what everyone feared: his weakness. Should he or should he not retire and walk away with his retirement benefits in hand, a decent amount, relatively speaking? Should he quit the struggle? What should he do? He wondered out loud, but softly, and almost to himself.

He was wavering, something the union had struggled with from day one.

Around the two men nearly every metal folding seat was taken for an event few seemed to want to miss. Husbands, wives, and children, mostly older children, chatted on and on as latecomers kept showing up at the Staley workers' weekly solidarity meeting to keep their ranks unified. The last-minute arrivals were crammed along the sides or in the rear of the local's cavernous meeting hall.

The meeting began with a prayer by a visiting Teamsters Union member from Local 705 in Chicago, a short, heavy-set African American man, who was also a minister and was wearing his clergyman's collar. His mention of the fact that he had brought with him a donation from Chicago workers stirred wide applause and cheers.

"America was built by the sweat of hardworking people like you and me," he said. "Lord," he asked in a deep voice, pausing and lifting his arms upward as he wound up his remarks, "what's happening in the heartland to workers?"

. . . Now on to tonight's meeting.

To begin, an update on the support drive:

A. The bucket collections are going well, but there are fewer road warriors, fewer people out collecting money around the country. (It is not clear why, but the point is lost.)

B. New donations came in from the railroad workers and the oil, chemical, and atomic workers unions.

C. Also, don't forget to take home bread, donated by the supermarket. It will be out there on the tables when you leave. Thanks to the stores in town that are helping us out with the bread and other items. And there are children's clothes to pick up. Oh yes, how many of you need school supplies? Okay, come up later.

Any questions from the floor? Quiet, please, this is important. Can everyone hear?

"We need to make the town know we are still here," a man said shyly.

"We gotta get jobs," said another, raising his voice a notch.

"We got families to support," another followed, his words sounding more like a plea than a complaint.

Life was beginning to bear down on some.

It was not easy living on the $60-a-day pay from the union. Gene Marquis, a 28-year veteran at Staley who never missed a solidarity meeting, who had been trained as a counselor at workshops run by union officials, was running into all kinds of shortages and problems faced by fellow workers. There were people without medicine. People without clothes for their children. People without money to make their car payments or mortgages. And people without hope.

That was one of the biggest problems he faced. Some wives were deeply discouraged because their husbands were not working but just sitting around drinking. Saving marriages became a full-time job. And there were some who talked to him about killing themselves. With help from the churches, hospitals, and counseling groups in town, he was able to find assistance for the ones who seemed most fragile and most in danger.

They had a lot on their minds, indeed, as they gathered weekly at the union meeting.

Up to the podium microphone stepped Ray Rogers, smiling, seeming confident. This is when he was at his best: connecting with the workers, telling them in their terms how they are going to win, how they are fighting the good fight, how they are the ones in charge. It restored their energy and uplifted them.

Solidarity meetings had been a key ingredient in Rogers's other campaigns, in his efforts with the paper workers union and International Paper and at the Hormel strike, and they quickly filled the same role in Decatur. But it was the Staley union officials who, after studying what they should do in such confrontations, had also decided that they needed weekly meetings and all the solidarity they could conjure up. Thus the weekly sermonizing.

"You have a choice, Decatur," Rogers began intently and forcefully.

"Is this the pride of the prairie or a company town? If there is any place in the country that has shown how big business cannot put down its workers, it is Decatur, the heartland of America. Just think of the spark you've created in this country."

Applause rippled, flowing from every part of the room. All of the faces were focused front.

Then on to more discussion about union strategy and then details about what to do to get by with few resources. Sister Ethel Ferguson had some updates on the help available.

Off to the side of the large room, with the meeting nearly ended, Rogers, still pumped up, talked philosophically about what lay ahead.

"When I got involved, I made it very clear that it was a David and Goliath thing. I said always, 'Look at this as a very tough fight.' And we have certainly notched the company down. We have sent a message:

You may take us on, but you will pay a heavy price if you do. These people are not being led to the slaughter. These people would've been totally crushed long before now."

Afterward, following several hours of speeches and debates, the room was still full, something that never happened before in Decatur and rarely happens at any of America's union meetings. American workers hardly ever attend union meetings in such large numbers or pay attention to what is happening with their union locals.

Nor did the room empty out when the meeting ended. Instead, people sat in small groups, spread across the room, talking, listening, or, in many cases, just being there, visiting for a few more minutes. Families and union members. Some simply sat in their seats, quietly watching a short video that the local had made about its struggle. It was about them. They felt connected. They seemed caught up in something bigger than themselves.

And they were. Indeed they were.

LATEST CASUALTY REPORTS

Swept aside, swept away, swept in circles, Decatur's labor disputes became rivers that carried people to places they had never been before, places they had never expected to be. Places of the heart where they felt overwhelmed and lost but also fully engaged. Some became radicalized and even militant. They became people they never thought they could be. They were excited and exhausted, and the exhaustion, likewise, overwhelmed them.

They were caught up for the first time in something beyond work or home, and it became a riveting experience. Some were attracted by the militancy and drawn by the emotional appeals it made to what they believed in—the long-term bonds of loyalty between workers and their company, the right of blue-collar workers to stand on their feet and to better themselves—values they felt had been violated by the companies. They found a new meaning in the events swirling around them. They were comforted by a new sense of community.

The demonstrations were growing. There was a momentum in the air.

For the Caterpillar workers, the troubles were approaching three years now. It had been two years since the Staley workers' troubles began. The rubber workers were the newcomers, and many of them seemed shocked somehow to have joined the fray.

In early June 1994, 48 people were arrested outside of Staley's facilities for blocking an exit that led to Eldorado Street. One of the protesters, a Methodist minister, toted a 10-foot-high cross. The Reverend Martin Mangan of St. James Catholic Church waved to a crowd of onlookers as he sat down with others, blocking the gate. Larry Solomon, wearing a tight-fitting T-shirt that made his paunch stand out, was one of those arrested by police. The charges were mob action and obstructing the police. A few weeks later there was another rally, and this time the Decatur police used pepper gas to push back some of the demonstrators. Only one person was arrested.

"THEY ARE THE BACKBONE OF AMERICA"

After the police used pepper gas, the Staley workers stopped talking with them, and that really worried Lieutenant Richard Ryan, a veteran with the Decatur police in his forties. All of the unions had regularly kept in touch with the police as the disputes wore on, and Ryan was convinced that that was one way the violence had been kept under control. At least, as much as possible.

Shots had been fired through the windows of the homes of union workers who had deserted their unions. Pipes had been thrown too. Rocks and sharp objects and planks of wood with nails driven through them were laid down on the driveways of company officials, strikebreakers, and the union deserters, and in front of the factories.

Several homemade bombs had been tossed onto Staley's grounds. Luckily, nothing serious happened; Ryan figured that they could have set off large explosions if they had combined with the chemicals stored there.

The police had been told by several video stores around town that they had been warned by different union members against carrying copies of *The American Dream*. This was the documentary that drew such a devastating portrait, from the workers' point of view, of the strike at Hormel and showed Ray Rogers leading them to defeat.

For Decatur's police, Ryan was the man who decided how to handle the marches and occasional scuffles at the factories' gates and the man on the scene most of the time too. It was not a new experience; he had dealt with labor disputes before around town and had lectured to other police departments throughout the state about what they should do. For years he had taught criminology and sociology classes at the community college, and the issue of dealing with labor disputes came up occasionally there.

As soon as the troubles began, the department sent a team of officers to Austin, Minnesota, where the Hormel workers had been caught up in the heated dispute with the company. Ryan, the head of the department's emergency response team, a swat team for crises, urged the officers to prepare for what they would be facing. He knew it would be a challenge.

They are us, Ryan—who grew up on the south end of Decatur and whose father had once been a blue-collar worker at Caterpillar—would say to his men to explain why they had to be extra careful when facing the union crowds.

They are the backbone of America, he would say. They are the people we grew up with, played ball with. They are our brothers and relatives and neighbors. They are the people who went to Staley and Caterpillar and Firestone after school as it always has been here in Decatur.

So when they spit in your face, don't take it personally, don't get angry, don't lose your control. It will not be easy. You can count on that.

That was his standard lecture, and he meant it.

From the start he thought he could predict what was ahead. There would be intimidation and sporadic violence, and neither took long to start. But he felt reassured somewhat that the unions were trying to keep a lid on things. That is what they told him, and he believed. Through the grapevine, he also heard that the unions were doing their best to keep outside troublemakers away so as to restrain the militants within their ranks.

What truly worried him was whether the growing desperation he saw on the streets and outside the factory would turn to rage one day. He feared that a radical faction or a handful of workers would suddenly lose control.

As he saw it, the workers' world was collapsing right in front of them, and they could barely comprehend it, let alone accept it. And their unions seemed of little help. It was not a dispute like any they had gone through before. It was as if they were on a set of railroad tracks, and they didn't see the freight train coming at them. The things that had worked for them in the past, he thought, had no hope for them in this time.

He realized that the reaction around town to the disputes was not making the situation any easier or calmer. People were mad at the unions and furious over how they were hurting Decatur's name. He could tell this by the juries that faced the workers who were charged with trespassing or other minor crimes that grew out of the disputes. In one case after another the jurors readily found the workers guilty. "Slam-dunked" was the term that came to his mind. The police, he concluded, did not have to worry much about losing these cases.

PLEASE JOIN THE BATTLE TO SAVE AMERICA'S DREAM

Indeed, some in town were truly turned off by the angry words, by the growing rift with the conservative, small-town Midwestern ways they had always known. Distraught over what they saw taking place, frustrated either by their unions or their companies, some sought to distance themselves from what was taking place. They began to think about moving their retirement dates forward from the ones they had long counted on. They pulled away from the others. They isolated themselves. They avoided the local diner, the bowling alley, the hardware store, the church parking lot, the traditional picnics. They stayed out of town. They simply withdrew.

And then there were those for whom life became only more difficult: the people who had crossed their own union picket lines, neighbors or family members who had temporarily taken the jobs of those waiting out on the streets, the workers who felt wounded but could not speak up about their wounds, the activists who felt lost or abandoned and could not explain away the wrong direction in which the disputes seemed headed.

But it was not easy to escape in the neighborhoods where workers knew each other, where their children went to the same schools, where they attended the same churches, and where they faced each other on the streets. Nor was it easy in the wide sprawl of small country towns from which many of the workers commuted.

At Caterpillar, the UAW under Bill Casstevens initially went about things as it had before: with signs and talk about what it meant to uphold pattern bargaining. At first there was little resonance among the union's rank-and-file workers for such abstract concepts as bargaining used to rope together similar companies. That changed, however, as the union translated its dispute into more personal terms, as it began calling its struggle with the giant manufacturer a battle to save the American dream.

On the edges of Decatur and the other major towns where Caterpillar's plants were located, the union put up signs saying "Welcome to a War Zone." If the union were truly at war with Caterpillar, however, it was mostly a prolonged war of words and gestures, a war of minor campaigns until June 1994, when militancy bubbled up from the bottom and overcame the plans and thinking of Casstevens and other UAW leaders. The result was another strike that again proved the union's inability to pressure Caterpillar.

For the most part, the UAW had preferred to go it alone. There was no commandment from Detroit for its local union leaders to link up with other unions, because that was not the way the UAW usually did things. In its own eyes, it was a powerful, self-directed union. A union that had once walked out of the AFL-CIO because the big labor organization was too conservative, too backward. A union that had stood up again and again to the automakers and others and did not need to ask others to come to its rescue.

A different kind of fury filled the Staley workers.

There the local's sentiment had instantly seguewayed into a sense of outrage. Almost from the start a greater willingness to condemn and demonize the company filled the union local. As he had done before, Ray Rogers became the local's proselytizer of labor activism, fervently preaching the need to raise the battle to a higher, national level. It was at his urging that teams of the so-called road warriors mentioned at the weekly solidarity meeting had been set up. The road warriors—at one point as many as 80 of them—would travel around the country, collecting money from union meetings, from like-minded groups, from anyone who would offer them support.

The local's war room coordinated reams of literature and posters churned out by Rogers. Because the local had no large benefactor like the UAW to rely on, the money that poured in from all over the country was parceled out as its aid. The money was given to 100 of the most needy Staley families, who remained anonymous. On a large map in the union's campaign office were pins and arrows showing where the money-collecting road warriors had traveled. The campaign office was separate from the union hall. You drove a few blocks north, parked in a strip mall, and there it was. You could find the road warriors there, and one of the most enthusiastic of them was Dan Lane.

"IT BECAME NOT JUST DECATUR"

Good-looking, tall, dark-haired, Dan Lane seemed to change as time passed and the lockout dragged on; his hair became longer, his clothes scruffier, more "alternative." There were others who did the same, and it worried local president Dave Watts. Long hair, beards—these were symbols that Decatur people usually didn't feel comfortable with, and Watts feared that this look would isolate the workers from the community.

But such fears were not bothering Lane. He was going through one change after another. When the showdown with the company came, Lane was a member of the union's bargaining committee. Not known for being outspoken or assertive, he had shown few signs of the kind of labor activism that he later preached. He had little sense of labor's recent history, and so he was not familiar with what had happened to the Hormel workers when Rogers acted as their shepherd. He had even voted for Ronald Reagan when he first ran for president. But Lane's voice soon became one of the loudest for taking on the company, for resorting to a stronger, more combative battle strategy.

He was one of the first road warriors, and he seemed to delight in speaking up for the union at rallies here and there. He would be gone for three to four weeks at a time, crisscrossing the country, making the pitch for the union, but also soaking up a reality that many of his fellow warriors had never before seen or anticipated.

"As I got around, what became even more real to me was that this was not an isolated situation. It became not just Decatur—not just Decatur that was being exploited. All of a sudden I'm in the middle of people in a struggle, and it was a very real part of my life," he said.

This was all a great change for Lane. He had followed the route taken by so many others at the factory. He had finished high school in Decatur, joined the U.S. Marines, and gone off to Vietnam. Afterward, he had wandered through several jobs in town and then joined Staley, where his father had worked for 25 years. With his wife and five children, Lane lived in a large, white two-story house in a quiet development on the south side of Decatur.

As the negotiations showdown between the company and union grew, Lane was thrust into the limelight because he was one of several workers fired for disciplinary reasons. He had been fired several months before the lockout began, accused by company officials of making derogatory racial remarks to an African American supervisor, charges he denied.

Traveling around the country, Dan began to frame the dispute in a different way. It was more about dignity and justice, he decided. As he talked to others, he found himself focusing on issues that had never crossed his mind. "I lived through the civil rights era, and I can't tell you a damn thing about it," he said. He hadn't realized what had happened in the South and what civil rights groups had done. "I didn't have the awareness of what the struggle was all about."

He felt himself becoming more and more passionate about what he was doing and what he was seeing. He was convinced that a larger plan was being carried out by corporate America. It was the elimination of the middle class as represented by people like him. "The only reason we woke up was because they were going to replace us," he said. He saw himself more as a leader and felt the local did not have to rely so strongly on Ray Rogers's vision. Rogers, he thought, had a plan for a long-term battle. He, Lane, wanted to see something that would bring things to a head sooner.

Within the union's leadership, some became uncomfortable with Lane's growing alignment with some of the leftist groups that identified with the Staley workers' struggle. They feared that his rhetoric was turning off other members and dividing the local. But he persistently rejected such signs, saying the situation called for more and more outspoken steps, more aggressive actions.

The words seemed to come smoothly. One cold Sunday afternoon at a meeting at a Teamsters union hall in Chicago, an old building with a creaking wooden floor, Lane's voice moved the crowded room to wild, foot-stomping applause. "We're sick of workers dying, of 12-hour shifts, of watching communities die because there aren't enough jobs when there are too many jobs that need doing. We're tired of being second-class citizens. We need to start making the laws. This fight in Illinois has to be won." Almost as compelling was the brief talk of his 16-

year-old daughter, Melissa, who faced the two-tiered audience in the old wooden-floored meeting room with an initial nervousness and ended with an absolute sense of conviction. "I'm mad at the company for depriving us of the family life we had and for what they have done to our fathers and our families," she said.

BETRAYED AND ABANDONED: "DOESN'T ANYONE CARE?"

Bob Hull, the local's vice-president, felt almost as passionate about what the Staley workers were doing, but, unlike Lane, he did not put it into a larger political scheme. He felt driven by the need to do his union job not just right, but well. Tall, thin, and blond, he wore steel-rimmed glasses and looked more like a detail-driven, small-town junior high school principal than a factory worker.

A local official on and off for 20 years, he had become the Staley workers' cautious, mindful planner, a conscience for Watts to rely on. He had gone to work at 18, straight out of school in Decatur, and stayed there for 40 years, revering the work he did, using large cranes to move heavy equipment around the sprawling facility. Over the years he had saved and invested well, so the money he was losing during the lockout was a far lighter burden for him than for others.

As time passed, he found himself growing weary and overwhelmed by the dispute. He saw how hard Dave Watts worked, spending all his time on the union's business, and he tried to keep up because he felt loyal and close to Watts. "Dave, he was the hardest worker," Hull said. "He was in the office night and day. I said, 'Dave, don't burn yourself out. You have a long way to go.'"

But it wasn't easy keeping up with Watts, who himself rarely disclosed his feelings.

One fall day in 1994, Hull went to a solidarity meeting at the UAW hall for all of those caught up in the town's labor confrontations, and only 400 persons showed up. He was stunned. He stopped, looked around, and quickly calculated that there were about 4,000 persons out on Decatur's streets because of the three disputes. And this was all that showed up on a perfectly nice day. Four hundred. It felt like a jab to his heart.

Here he was, he told himself, working so hard for this cause, and so few people cared enough to come to a meeting. Others from Staley had gone off and gotten jobs, good jobs too, and they were leaving him behind to fight their fight. Plus he was feeling tired and not himself, physically or emotionally. He felt let down by the town and by everyone around him. Despite pleas for help, union leaders in Springfield and Washington were not coming to the local's rescue, and that troubled him. It seemed to him that all they wanted to do was drive around in big, new cars and enjoy their well-paying lifestyles.

Meanwhile, he saw the chances for his tiny local to turn things around fading day by day. His family doctor, who had known him for years, had sat him down a few days earlier and warned him that the mental stress was weighing very heavily on him. He could not recall Hull looking as bad. It would take a good year of rest, his doctor said, just to recapture his old self. That was it. He wanted out.

So he announced at a union meeting that he was giving up his vice-president's position and soon left for Florida, looking for a place to get away temporarily—and possibly to retire. He had no location in mind. He just wanted to escape. His wife, Susan, still had her job as an elementary school teacher in Decatur, but Hull felt an overpowering immediate need to be somewhere else. Behind him, he felt, he had left betrayal and loss.

COMMITMENT AND MEANING: "THIS WAS ABOUT MAKING A DIFFERENCE"

For Dave Watts, a worker at Bridgestone/Firestone with the same name as the head of the Staley workers' local, the experience of the strike and his union's efforts were new and exhilarating. A tall, broad-shouldered man in his early forties with long, dark hair curling down toward his collar, Watts, a tire builder for nearly 20 years, had never cared much before about what went on with the local. This time, however, when the rubber workers went out, he found himself drawn into the squabble.

The same was true for his wife, Suzie. Their two children were grown and out of the house, so she had extra time on her hands. Indeed, Suzie took to the issue faster than her husband. She started a scrapbook the first day the URW went on strike and loyally updated it with notes, pictures, and news stories about what went on with the rubber workers' struggle. One by one the pages grew, and she filled one after another scrapbook. Then the rubber workers union asked for help in creating a group that would back local political candidates for city offices, the first such effort the unions in Decatur had made to raise their voices politically since the disputes began. The group was called Friends of Labor, and Suzie and Dave quickly joined its first workers.

What made the work even better for Suzie was the companionship of Annie Floyd, whose husband, Jerry, was also a rubber worker. Dave joked about how the two of them, Suzie and Annie, had become the female labor radicals of their day. Together they went to rallies and political meetings, and Suzie kept notes on them in her scrapbook.

Whenever the call went out, Dave and Suzie were usually eager to help. In the heat of the struggle, they and others decided it was time to learn more about organized labor, so they signed up for labor history classes taught by Bob Sampson, a local labor historian whose day job was as a public information official at the University of Illinois.

Sampson, with a deep passion for the long sweep of union history in Illinois and the United States, was teaching on Saturday mornings at Richland Community College in Decatur. Some of his students drove for miles to the classes, saying they wanted to learn about how their situation fit into a bigger picture of organized labor. As the classes progressed, Sampson was struck by how much the workers who were tied into the disputes seemed to have changed, how much more radical their words and arguments had become. They were unlike the Reagan Democrats he had met over the years in town. They were not complacent. They were angry but did not seem to know whom to be angry at. They had a feeling about class differences that he had not encountered before. They saw themselves not getting the breaks others had, and they were convinced that the government was not helping them.

It was clear that they had begun searching out whatever they could read—leftist, alternative magazines, books not easily found in Decatur, anything that explained labor history to them. One or two would drive up to the University of Illinois in Champaign–Urbana to pick up magazines they could not find elsewhere. Their hunger to learn moved him.

Slowly, however, some stopped coming to his labor history classes, and soon he understood why.

As the disputes wound on, the labor history they were learning, starting with the 19th century, became increasingly personal. The terrible defeats labor had suffered on the railroads and in the steel mills and coal mines, the saga of the Homestead workers' defeat and labor's crushing setbacks at the turn of the century, seemed too familiar, too painful, too immediate. They identified with the defeats as if they were their very own and they were reliving them.

But Richard Zerfowski, who had worked for Caterpillar since graduation from high school and whose father had put in more than 30 years in a factory that no longer existed in Decatur, stayed on for the classes. He became so caught up in the history he heard in the classes that he took one after another. Whenever possible, he would compare his reading of history to what he was seeing take place between the UAW and Caterpillar.

What attracted Zerfowski to the classes was the sense that he was living through a repeated cycle of history. It was very clear to him. Just as the coal miners had risen up and been beaten back 100 years ago, so, too, factory workers like him were suffering through the cycle of gain and defeat.

AT LEAST THE WOMEN CAN TALK: "MY HUSBAND'S DEPRESSED"

Six months after the Staley workers were locked out, a group of the wives began holding biweekly potluck dinners to help each other out. The men did not form a similar group. A few men from Staley took a stab at it, but nothing ever came of it.

One hot July night almost a year after the lockout began, the Staley wives had gathered in the basement at Diana Marquis's house in a leafy Decatur neighborhood of well-trimmed lawns and newer cars parked out front. I was lost on the meandering streets, but then found the right one. It was easy to locate the house because of the number of cars parked on the grassy lawns up and down the street.

Gene Marquis, Diana's husband, was not home that night.

The downstairs room was cool and dark, a comfort after a sunny, sweltering afternoon. The women made small talk at first, some chatting about a weekend getaway they were planning—a chance to escape, they called it—and they admired the night's spread of dishes that filled several tables. Everyone remarked on Ethel Ferguson's peach cobbler. They were not patronizing her. It really was very good.

Then they sat down and talked intensely for several hours, letting the conversation float freely. They didn't mind that I listened along.

There were points they wanted to make. They had a few rules, and one of the basic ones was that everything they said was confidential. When this group had begun meeting, they had invited wives from the Caterpillar and Bridgestone/Firestone disputes. The women came, but they eventually dropped out.

On this night the women wanted to talk about how embarrassing it was to ask for food stamps, about how some of their husbands thought only about the union and not about them, about how hard the holiday seasons had been, about how difficult it had been scrimping to buy clothes for the children. And about their anger and isolation. Especially their anger.

"There are no jobs out there, and they won't let us live the lives we are used to," grumbled one middle-aged woman. But she didn't explain who "they" were.

Another woman giggled and nervously said she constantly dreamt of breaking the windows of her neighbors, who had picket-line crossers in the family.

Another woman explained how she cried and unloaded all of her feelings on her husband one night recently and how much better that had made things. Not easy, they said, shaking their heads. Some of the men drank, and some of the men just did not talk, they agreed. Not easy at all. Ten marriages had broken up so far, they calculated.

Another woman looked around the small group and flatly said that, emotionally, she felt up and down, up and down, all the time.

Christmas was hard, very hard, Ethel Ferguson said. And the future—a future without Staley—worried her. "There are no jobs that will let us live the lives we are used to."

"I don't like the way I've gotten lately," one woman said shyly. "Because I'm not like that."

They nodded, but their minds were on their husbands, whom they saw as afraid—afraid of the future, afraid of what would happen to their jobs, and afraid of the fact that they didn't know what to do about it. If they seemed protective and troubled about the men, they said that was because the men behaved as if something truly had been taken from them.

"My husband is ashamed. He hasn't done any sabotage, and he can't go back to work," one wife said. Another picked up just as she stopped. "My husband hasn't lost his job; he just can't go in to do it.

That's the frustration. They feel baffled by what's happening and the loss of their security. They feel like something was taken from them. They feel reduced to what they came from."

"A lot of the men came from nothing," said Diana Marquis. "A lot of them are Vietnam vets. And so here they are again. How many times are they going to get beat down?"

As time passed, Judy Dulaney found the meetings helpful because they were the only place where she could share feelings that the others would easily understand. Her neighbors, and even relatives, as supportive as they were, did not seem to understand what she was going through. One night as the husbands were sitting at the union hall in a meeting—one of the meetings where votes taken were restricted to union members—the women's group gathered in a small back room and went over the latest shipment of food and clothes that had been donated or for which money had been raised. As they went through the bags, the women suddenly realized that there were candy bars. Someone yelled out that she had found a Hershey bar, and another woman cried out that she had found a Snickers. "We were all so excited," said Judy Dulaney. "We had all cut out candy because we could not afford it, and here we were, like little kids sharing what we had gotten. After that night I got to thinking that is something you couldn't share with anybody else," she said.

The women of the group, most of whom did not have young children, had thrown themselves into the drive to find Christmas gifts for the local's children. That was a bond that they shared too.

As the first Christmas was coming up, they feared there would be hardly anything for the children. Dave Watts had asked the women to help coordinate a little bake sale to raise some money. They raised $1,000, far more than any of them had imagined possible. And then word came that people around the country were going to be sending gifts for the children. Eager to help unload the gifts, Judy Dulaney, Ethel Ferguson, and Diana Marquis went down to the union hall a few days before Christmas.

Just as they arrived, a caravan of large trucks, filled to the brim with gifts that had been sent by supporters in Chicago, pulled into the union's parking lot. The women hadn't expected such kindness and support. "We looked at that, and we just stood there and cried like little kids," Judy Dulaney said.

This was a hard time for Sandy Gosnell, because the whole experience did not fit into anything she had ever expected. She had been raised in a family where the father worked and the mother stayed home, and if you had a job at Staley or any of the big factories in Decatur you were set for life. That was it. But it wasn't. Even though she still held a job at Staley as a clerical worker, it wasn't the same. "All of a sudden," she said, "you felt like the rug had been jerked from under you. We didn't know what was going on."

Mary Brummet couldn't believe how many friends were no longer friends. She had to explain everything about the union and its struggle to them, and they still didn't understand. Worse, some of them didn't want to understand. "They thought union people make a lot and they deserve what they get." That didn't go over well with Brummet, who had to go to work soon after the dispute began. Previously, she had stayed at home.

Mary Brummet's way of dealing with things as the dispute dragged on was to make sure her voice was heard in town So she started attending city council meetings. It made her feel good to be "boisterous" and outspoken. "The city council and the courts were going against the union," she said. "And I took it personally. I felt it was time for me to stand up in the city council and say this is how I felt. It made me feel so much better."

Almost everything about the women's group made Diana Marquis feel better and lift her spirits. It was a way of healing. It made her feel that she was not alone. She grew increasingly angry and distrustful about the way the top leaders of her husband's union, first in Milwaukee and then in Nashville, were dealing with the situation in Decatur. She was furious about what she read in the newspaper about the dispute, and she grew outraged over politicians who seemed to lie to people like her.

Amid all this fury, the women's group was a way to laugh, to spend the night without spending any money. Although Diana Marquis was hurt that so many people did not care about what was happening, she was also moved by the fact that some people were so charitable, sending $1 or $2 for the children's Christmas gifts. The women's group basically took over the Christmas gift operations. With money raised by the union, the women shopped together, buying the gifts. They did most of their shopping at one large retailer in town, which gave them a special discount, something to let each other know.

But more often what mattered to Diana Marquis was the insight she got from the meetings. "Some of us didn't realize what our husbands were going through. I watched mine get up in the morning, sit in the chair, go out, walk around the garden, and then he would go back to his chair. I didn't really understand what was going on. And the group helped me with that because their husbands were going through the same things. I remember one day somebody said, 'Isn't that a form of depression?' and I said, 'Oh, yeah.'"

ANSWERING LABOR'S CALL: "I WILL NOT STAY SILENT"

All of this seemed so foreign, so removed from the world of small Midwestern towns where he had served. Union squabbles and labor issues had never been high-priority issues for the Reverend Martin Mangan. When he arrived in Decatur in 1991, he was 61 years old, a Roman Catholic priest who had grown up on the southwest side of nearby Springfield, a slow-going Midwest state capital like any other.

He had gone to St. Louis University and Mundelein Seminary in suburban Chicago, studied canon law in Rome, and spent most of his life and career in small central Illinois towns. His deep passion for years had been civil rights. Unfortunately, the higher-ups in his diocese had not shared the level of his passion and had never given him the approval to go ahead with the kind of policies he thought mattered. But he never relented.

He had come to Decatur to take over St. James Church, a set of timeworn red brick buildings, a church and a school in an old lower-income neighborhood on the edge of Decatur's shrunken downtown. It was feared that the 100-year-old parish, which had once served German immigrants—there was another one for Irish immigrants not far away—was going to be closed down.

Saving the parish had a special meaning for Father Mangan, because the school had a sizable African American enrollment. As for the church, most of the 550 families that belonged to the parish were retirees and blue-collar families, among them Staley workers, people with whom Father Mangan thought he could find a kindred spirit.

As the disputes grew, news about them filled the *Decatur Herald & Review* and his parishioners told him about the problems the dispute was causing them, Father Mangan became increasingly intrigued. The more he learned about the situation, the more convinced he was that the veritable destruction of the factory workers' way of life was taking place right in front of him, right there in Decatur. Instantly he saw parallels with the Holocaust and the failure of religious leaders to stand up. It touched his deep sensibility about speaking out. By no means was there any comparison between the labor troubles in Decatur and the loss of lives in the Holocaust. But the image of a silent clergy hung over Father Mangan, and he decided that would not be his way now. So the silver-haired priest, short and slightly hefty, an easy-going man with a warm cherubic smile and soft voice, began attending the unions' public rallies and solidarity meetings. He always wore his collar, because he wanted to show the people that his church cared about their concerns.

The first time we met at his parish, I was surprised when he came into the room. I knew little about him, but from what I had heard I thought he would be young and full of himself, a champion for the working stiff. I was surprised by the small, gentle man before me.

So were the union people.

At first they didn't know what to do about him. The first time Judy Dulaney of the Staley women's group saw him, she was stunned. "This little leprechaun of a man came to us and asked if he could hold one of our signs," she said. "He was always there for us, with a laugh or a shoulder to cry on." In a nighttime English class she was taking, she got an A+ for a paper she wrote about the person who had touched her most, Father Mangan.

At one meeting the local's leaders asked the elderly priest to offer a prayer, and Father Mangan found himself unsure of what to do. He didn't want to choose sides, but he quickly decided he had to. Things seemed headed that way. There were a number of other clergy in town who similarly had spoken up or shown an interest in the unions' cause. A young activist couple from Chicago had come to town for several months and were trying to rally the clergy on behalf of the unions. He had felt himself pulled along. Then the company had locked out the workers.

"The whole issue was, why lock out all 760 workers? Why, if only a few did the sabotage? It was the classic way to downsize. That was where the real moral issue was for me. A lockout simply takes away the rights that unions have," he said.

Without much experience in union issues, he decided his role would be to offer moral support and swore he would quit the day the disputes turned violent. Yet he found himself more and more willing to stand out front and take chances. The sisters at the Eighth Day Center for Justice in Chicago, a religious community devoted to social justice, put on a demonstration for him and others on how to carry out civil disobedience. The sisters were upholding a traditional alliance between activists within the Catholic Church and organized labor in the United States. When labor was on the rise, it had easily found allies in some Catholic clergy. But the two groups had drifted apart over the years.

Invited to a meeting of community religious leaders by Staley's officials, Father Mangan decided, after listening to Pat Mohan talk on behalf of the company, that Staley really wanted fewer workers. That was the significance of the lockout. He also decided that he would speak up, raising the analogy that had been on his mind for some time. "In Germany there was a systematic destruction of the people called the Holocaust, and I really believe that there is also a systematic process going on now to destroy the economic lives of people. In Germany, the ministers were silent; I'm not planning to be this time," he said.

On Labor Day, along with others, he chained himself to a fence outside the Staley facilities to show the workers' opposition to being chained to 12-hour shifts.

Despite his growing identification in the community with the labor disputes, his church superiors had never uttered a word of criticism, nor of praise. He took this as a sign of acceptance. He did, however, receive two anonymous letters and an anonymous telephone call. Their message was the same: Stay where you are supposed to be; keep out of the union disputes. He was not deterred.

On the night after a Saturday rally on behalf of the unions, when he and several others took part in an act of civil disobedience resulting in his arrest for mob action and disobeying a police order, charges that were later dismissed, Father Mangan had troubling dreams that haunted him all night long.

What would have happened if he had been held by police? He had already arranged for another priest to say the 5:30 P.M. mass. But what might happen to the parish and school? He dreamt that he went to Sunday mass and nobody was there.

Why was he risking this at all?

Was everyone going to turn on him now?

Would he lose the parish?

He had come to Decatur to save the church, and now what was he doing?

Still, he told himself, "I could not not take part and be honest with myself."

Nothing came of his fears. And so he stayed involved, accepting the Staley workers' invitation to travel to London to describe the plight of the workers at a stockholders' meeting.

In a letter to the chairman of Tate & Lyle, to whom he publicly presented a petition signed by more than 400 religious groups ranging from the Little Sisters of the Assumption in New York to the Reconstructionist Rabbinical College in Philadelphia, the Catholic priest called for an end to the company's lockout. "From an ethical and moral perspective," he wrote, "we believe that ending the lock-out would be a gesture of your commitment to the common good of the wider community, not a sign of weakness."

His presence at the meeting was noted by a number of British newspapers. But they also noted that British shareholders, upset by the time taken up with the talk about the labor dispute in America, pressed for the annual meeting to get on with its business. Company officials promptly heeded their complaints.

As Father Mangan stood at the microphone, one thought kept returning to him. "I had no doubt that what I was doing was right," he recalled.

> "I know people who say they don't want to drive by that part of town. They don't want to see that conflict."
> —JAMES FRASER, mental health therapist,
> *Decatur Herald & Review*, July 17, 1994

CHAPTER 2 2

The Ballot Box Rebellion

April 1995

Journalist Gary Minich thought he understood what was motivating Father Mangan. After first meeting him on the picket line, Minich was moved by the man and deeply respected him. In fact, it was because of Father Mangan that he converted to Catholicism two years later. Minich was not surprised by the priest's motivation to get involved in the disputes. Staley's handling of its workers seemed brutal to the priest, and this had compelled him to speak out. That made sense to Minich.

What Minich didn't understand was the overwhelming lack of concern he saw everywhere else in Decatur.

We met for lunch at a small, timeworn restaurant on a side street not far from the newspaper's office just off the downtown. The restaurant had the feel of a family gathering. It didn't seem that any strangers ever wandered in.

As a business writer and columnist for the *Decatur Herald & Review*, Minich naturally covered the festering labor disputes in town. Thin, soft-spoken, with the air of a small-town college professor, he knew Decatur's economics and business communities backward and forward, knew who spoke out at what business meetings, who thought what about whom, and why it mattered.

He had been a wire editor for the Decatur-based chain's five Illinois newspapers and an editorial writer. But there had been changes and staff cutbacks at the paper in the late 1980s, and so he found himself, in his late fifties, a business writer, sitting among reporters with far fewer years on the job than he had. There seemed to be few reporters his own age. And even the young ones, who often came from out of town, stayed on only a while before finding work elsewhere. It wasn't an unusual reaction. Others in the newsroom felt they too were witnessing the disappearance of older reporters.

He had come to Decatur from Terre Haute, Indiana, in 1973, a time when the town's factories were booming. And he was dumbfounded by the lack of emphasis on college education among Decatur's youth. He soon understood why. It was widely assumed that there would be a factory job waiting for those who wanted one after high school, and it would be a job paying as well as some of the jobs a young person can get after college.

But the good fortune vanished, and he witnessed close up the spiraling unemployment in the early 1980s, when nearly one out of five persons in town was jobless, one of the highest jobless rates in the nation at the time. And he had seen the slow evaporation of good-paying blue-collar jobs; jobs that paid $10 an hour were being replaced by jobs that paid no more than $6 in town.

That was the real story behind the factory disputes, he thought, the loss of good-paying jobs and companies that no longer made providing work for the community a high priority. There were no more patrician owners like A. E. Staley. On Labor Day, 1992, Minich wrote a gloomy and openly critical column that said profits no longer guaranteed job security:

> American workers are being asked to accept less. No lifetime careers. More dependence on temporary and part-time jobs.
>
> Without Staley, or Caterpillar, Bridgestone/Firestone, or Mueller Co. or Wagner Castings—and the jobs they provide—there will be fewer reasons for others to locate businesses, and jobs, here.
>
> Even if our children and our grandchildren won't be working in Decatur's factories, there is little hope they will return to Decatur as lawyers, accountants, marketing specialists, retail clerks—unless someone's children and grandchildren work in the factories.
>
> It is one thing for labor and management to agree on purpose. It is another to ask workers to trust their futures solely to the bosses.

STRANGERS IN THEIR OWN TOWN

Even more baffling to Minich was the anger and apathy toward the workers. For a town with a blue-collar heritage, Decatur didn't seem to show much warmth toward the unions when the disputes began. Many of the letters sent to the newspaper were full of gripes about the unions: The union workers were overpaid whiners. They were spoiled, well-paid bumblers, people making $18 an hour when others were lucky to get half those wages.

Minich wasn't the only one who was struck by the way people had turned on the unions. Joe McGlaughlin, chairman of the Macon County Board and a leading Democrat, heard people saying on the street, "Good. They're getting what they deserve." There was real resentment toward the unions for the fix they had got themselves into.

After Staley officials complained about his pro-union bias in several stories, Minich found it even more difficult to report on what was happening. If Staley officials did not like what he had written, they would complain loudly to him and his bosses. The routine became tiring, frustrating. Behind his back, some of the union leaders grumbled that he did not seem to be giving them a fair chance.

Increasingly, his stories were cut-and-dried efforts. He thought much more ought to have been done: stories, for example, about how the union families were surviving. But nobody was asking him to write those stories, and neither was anyone else on the newspaper doing them. He saw no pressure to go out and dig up the news.

Just before going on vacation in the midst of the unending labor crisis, he finished one long story wrapping up the situation, a story that his editors thought was too favorable to the unions. When it did not appear even after changes were made, he decided not to put out as much effort again.

The problem for the newspaper, as George Althoff, the editor of the *Decatur Herald & Review*, saw it, was not that the story had been told. Rather, it was a painful story, a story that regularly promoted angry calls regularly from readers, who complained that the reporting was either too negative or too pro-union or too pro-management.

Union leaders were furious with the coverage, and equally so was the Chamber of Commerce, but for different reasons. It seemed to be a no-win situation for the town and the newspaper. Feelings toward the paper were so strong that Althoff checked his driveway for nails for a month or so.

Althoff had arrived in Decatur from another small Midwestern newspaper in 1992, just when the situation was heating up. Tall, blond, outgoing, he would not look out of place or feel lost at a table of small-town businessmen. His quick assessment of the labor situation was that it would get worse before anything good took place. He thought Staley held all the cards, and he didn't understand why Staley felt the 12-hour shifts were so necessary. How, he wondered, were older workers going to adjust?

ALL EYES AND EARS ON DECATUR: "I REALLY FELT SORRY FOR THEM"

With one in every fourteen workers walking the picket lines in Decatur, National Public Radio came to town in July 1994.

> KATHY LLOHR (reporter): At a city council study session last week, more than 200 workers showed up to protest a proposal which would have required workers to get a permit before holding a rally or demonstration.

> MAYOR EERIK BRECHNITZ: Well, it's charged. It's emotionally charged at the moment.

> KATHY LOHR: Mayor Erik Brechnitz has often been a target of protests.

> MAYOR BRECHNITZ: We have demonstrations continually. We have pickets, who are at the plant gates and sometimes get emotional when people try to cross the picket line. You have people in the community that are starting now to write letters to the editor. So, it's a very tough situation, and the atmosphere is becoming more and more electric.

Tensions were high—higher than ever since the troubles began.

At one of Decatur's Celebration Days, a major annual summertime bash held downtown, someone had slipped up behind Mayor Brechnitz and poured beer all over him. Threatening phone calls awaited him at home. One night, as he was driving home late, in the darkness Brechnitz's car hit a chain someone had placed across his driveway. It shattered a headlight.

Brechnitz was taunted and ridiculed by the union activists because they thought he should have shown more support for them. They were convinced that his only allegiance was to the business community, that he always sided with business. He wasn't scared or angry. He felt bad for them. They didn't understand, he was sure, what was happening.

"They needed somebody to blame and I was a fairly easy mark for them," he recalled. "I felt sorry for them. I really felt sorry for them."

At a meeting with union leaders, he reached over from his desk at his brokerage firm and handed them photocopies of a motivational guidebook for workers put out by a business consulting firm: *New Work Habits for a Radically Changing World*. Filled with snappy quotations, it talked about altering expectations, about adjusting to the global economy and becoming a fixer, not a finger pointer.

With the help of U.S. Representative Glenn Poshard (D-Ill.), a former schoolteacher from nearby who related well with the workers, he set up several meetings between union and Staley officials. They were held without any public mention. Nothing came of these meetings, and Brechnitz was convinced it was because the union didn't realize that something different was taking place: the company had its eye on something different from ever before, a reworking of its scheme for its workers and their union.

BATTLING APATHY

So what to do next?

The answer came by chance when Suzie Watts was asked to help out with Friends of Labor, the group organized to help union-backed candidates get elected to the City Council. Suzie and Annie Floyd got involved, and so did Dave Watts.

In the spring of 1995, one area in which there seemed to be some momentum in Decatur was politics. A new passion, with almost a revolutionary feel to it, had heated up. Typically, union involvement in politics involves the Democrats calling on the union leaders, who call on their reliable workers to hand out pamphlets or man telephone banks. What was developing in Decatur went way beyond that routine and had the feel of rank-and-file fervor, probably because the rationale seemed to make so much sense.

The thinking was that labor needed a visible stake in the town's politics. Randy Morrell firmly believed in pushing the union's political agenda. Others agreed and signed onto the effort. Dave Watts, the head of the Staley workers, thought it might be one more last-minute way of giving a boost to a fading struggle. With a voice on the city council, or with a mayor friendly to labor, maybe the unions would see better days. Maybe the police would be less pesky about enforcing the rules on the shacks or picket stations the unions had set up outside the factories or on where they could demonstrate.

Dave Watts agreed to run for City Council. Mike Carrigan, an official with the International Brotherhood of Electrical Workers, was also put up as a city council candidate. And the unions decided that their man for mayor would be Terry Howley.

Affable and easy-going, Howley made a good impression: a middle-aged businessman in a dark suit with a warm smile, a good laugh, and a strong handshake. His current job as a stockbroker gave him good credentials and earned him points with small businesses. But he earned more points with the unions because he was very much in their corner. He fretted openly about the loss of good-paying factory jobs and said the town had not done enough to save its jobs base.

He said the old forces that held Decatur together, the wealthy families and leading businesses, had long since been erased, leaving a vacuum. He commiserated with the unions but privately felt that strikes no longer worked. The town needed to connect with the companies that made decisions, even if that meant going to their home offices. Much had to be done to put things back together.

If his message sounded evenhanded and his pitch appealed to frustrated union members, something else made him unique in terms of Decatur's politics. He was a registered Democrat. Although the town elections were nonpartisan, the veil between reality and party politics was very thin. Decatur had not had a Democrat mayor in well over half a century. It had never at all had a mayor who was Catholic.

Howley was a Democrat and a Catholic, with deep blue-collar roots and not-so-deep business roots. He had been a social studies teacher at St. Theresa High School in Decatur and had coached football and basketball there before stepping into a dark suit and financial dealings.

With the help of the unions, who made up about one-fourth of his campaign funds, he campaigned heavily against some significant opposition. The word went around town that organized labor was going to take over and that voters had to do something. He was told about a fax that had circulated at the Caterpillar plant urging the company's managers to vote against him. Asked about that, Caterpillar officials said the company had no interest in local politics.

In the first round of elections, Dave Watts finished fifth among 16, though he didn't make the cut in the final elections.

With the largest turnout in years, both Howley and Carrigan were elected in May 1995. Most could not remember the last time a union member, clearly linked to organized labor, had been on the city council.

Suzie Watts enshrined the victories in her growing pile of scrapbooks about Decatur's labor disputes.

The Road Warriors Meet the Labor Mandarins

February 1995

Absolutely brilliant sunshine, powdery blue skies, delicious surf. A picture-perfect south Florida day, a postcard worthy of sending home in the midst of the depressing backstretch of a gray Midwestern winter.

It is two months before Decatur's ballot box rebellion. The Decatur workers gather by the palm-tree-covered sidewalk outside the regal-looking Bal Harbour Sheraton. Breakfast is just over, and they are in their favorite red T-shirts, jeans, and union logo baseball caps, ready to make their case for defending the American dream with the people who are supposed to defend them.

They are wearing buttons and lugging boxes full of leaflets about the labor struggles back in Decatur. Larry Solomon, who has driven down from Decatur in his full-sized 1990 van, bringing his wife and daughter and son-in-law along for the ride—their first trip ever to Miami—thinks he sees some union presidents pull up to the hotel's long, sweeping entranceway in stretch limousines and hustle inside. He is amazed and infuriated.

So that's where our dues money is going, he quips to the others, who have driven down in their own cars or come with the bus rented by the three union locals in Decatur.

Most are staying in a $49-a-night dive farther up the road, camping out there, several beds to a room, and some are sleeping on the floors in one of the timeworn Miami Beach motels where fresh sheets do not seem to be standard. Nothing like the plush pastel-colored hotel in the middle of one of the most exclusive areas in all of Miami. At the luxurious resort, which has a fair sprinkling of upscale European tourists, rooms are going for up to $325 a night. Some union heads prefer the hotel's airy cabanas, with refreshing views of the ocean down by the pool, to the large executive suites in the main buildings.

The union presidents are in the midst of their annual winter schmooze in the sunshine, a tradition that organized labor established more than 50 years ago and has relentlessly clung to despite the image of fat cat union leaders lounging luxuriously in the sun.

At the moment, however, the leaders of the nation's working stiffs are unavailable to their surprise visitors. Off in closed meetings. Very important meetings. Can't be interrupted. Visitors cannot just barge in and demand a hearing. Hmmph. The AFL-CIO bureaucrats roll out as many excuses as they can.

Labor's mandarins cannot see the union members even if they are down-and-out workers mired in disputes that seem to be going nowhere. The mandarins are debating labor's future before their lunch breaks. Forget about trying to catch them at night. They fly off to fancy restaurants. Dave Watts insists that he has never seen so many limousines in one place, and he is amazed at the union leaders getting in and out of them.

So the 70 or so visitors from Decatur, workers from the conflict-ridden Caterpillar, Bridgestone/Firestone, and Staley plants, scatter and spread out in search of union leaders to talk to at the hotel.

They wander by the hotel's large pool on the way to its private beach and meander through its exclusive shops. They pass a few silent, suntanned middle-aged labor union minions sprawled at poolside.

They stop and tell their stories of labor distress to everyone in sight, to middle-aged guests in bathing suits slowly heading toward the beach, to puzzled hotel workers, some of whose English is rather limited.

The road warriors from the Central Illinois War Zone, as they call themselves, are middle-aged folks with slightly sagging waistlines that leak over the thick belts they are wearing. They are husbands and wives marked with smatterings of graying hair. They look more like guests at a small-town Midwestern church picnic or American Legion gathering than a delegation of wild-eyed, fire-breathing labor militants.

They also stop occasionally to take photographs of each other to take home and put in their photo albums.

Here are the road warriors from Decatur standing by a fancy hotel fountain. Here are the road warriors posing on one of the hotel's sunny terraces. In this photograph the road warriors are out under some lush trees. And in this one the road warriors are waving their hands in victory signs and smiling. They don't look miserable in the photos.

Edith Marques, a veteran tire worker, who ran a wire-winding machine in Decatur before her union struck, has stopped some guests wandering toward one of the sunny restaurants and is politely telling them her story.

"What about the small guy?" she is saying as other guests in beach outfits drift by and throw her a curious glance.

When they finally get a chance to meet with the union presidents, only the presidents of the three union locals and their union presidents are permitted by the AFL-CIO's leaders to make a presentation. The rest of them have to wait outside.

Larry Solomon feels awkward facing the large group. They stare at him, he thinks, as if he were an apparition, a ghost of the radical labor days of the 1920s and 1930s. Once stares of that kind would have thrilled him. They would have given him a feeling of strength, a recognition that the Decatur unions had created something that had rarely existed in organized labor in the United States in recent years: an ability to come together, to stand up for the right cause and make some honest-to-goodness headway. It was everything he had dreamt about.

But that feeling had dried up long ago. The thrill of speaking out, of being the maverick, is gone. Now Solomon and most of the Decatur workers are tired and turning desperate, convinced that their battles are going nowhere. They want their union leaders and the AFL-CIO to use the mythical resources of big labor to come to their rescue.

Dave Watts is especially glum about the future for his local's effort, but typically he does not talk about it with the others. He hopes that by going to Miami they will wake up organized labor and get the kind of support that would make a real difference. But by Watts's calendar this is their last chance, their very last hope, because everything is coming apart. Everything they counted on is collapsing, and they are growing weary of the burden of keeping the struggle going.

Bob Hull, who stood close beside Watts as the local's second in command at the start but then gave up, exhausted and depressed by the experiences, is here too. He came down to Florida a while ago, having made the painful decision to forget Decatur, to abandon the battle that was making him seriously ill, physically and emotionally. Alongside Watts, he wanders the elegant hotel in search of help.

PART VI

Surrender and Retreat

Slumbering into Oblivion

February 1995

What the road warriors got from the union leaders at Bal Harbour was a handshake, not a lifesaving embrace.

They got promises of solidarity and visits from a few union leaders. They got a handful of donations and promises to spread the word. But they didn't get the call for an all-out war, the kind of effort they thought was critical to their cause. They wanted the unions whose members were crossing the pickets lines at Caterpillar and Bridgestone/Firestone, workers from the Teamsters and several trade unions, to stop that right away. But the workers kept on crossing the picket lines.

Organized labor was not about to launch a jihad in their name. Not only that, it also stirred some of the Decatur union leaders to wonder whether they had not become too radical, an out-of-control gang waging a fight that wasn't worth such sweat. At best the workers crossing the lines were a distraction for the union leaders, drawing their attention from the furious internal battle beginning to take place, a showdown unprecedented in big labor's recent history and provoked somewhat by what was happening miles away in Decatur.

Press conference, AFL-CIO conference, Bal Harbour Sheraton:

REPORTER: Are you going to run for re-election?

LANE KIRKLAND (AFL-CIO president): I'll deal with that question in good season—as I normally do. In the meanwhile, we have fish to fry.

201

REPORTER: Have you been reading the reports?

KIRKLAND: I read the papers, yes. Some of it I even believe.

REPORTER: Assuming that someone is elected in October, what do you think should be the strategy of the AFL-CIO in the future?

KIRKLAND: Our strategy and our goals haven't changed since Gompers spelled them out as "What Does Labor Want?"

We want more schoolhouses and less jails. We want more learning and less vice. We want more leisure and less greed. We want more of the opportunities to improve our lives. We want the earth and the fullness thereof and we pursue that as best we can through collective bargaining and through trade union solidarity.

And that hasn't changed.

REPORTER: Has anyone come to you and said they thought you should retire?

KIRKLAND: No.

BIG LABOR IS A MIRAGE

Crusty, aloof, a shy intellect who often chose to ignore most of Middle America by clothing his most important messages in difficult-to-understand Proustian syntax, Lane Kirkland, at a few days short of 73 years old, was only the fourth president ever for the AFL-CIO, and he was not surrendering easily.

He was a symbol of American labor's great dilemma: It had withdrawn into its own cocoon. Just as basic American industries had withdrawn into their shells, as the auto and steel industries had retreated after being been whipped mercilessly by foreign competitors, organized labor seemed stuck, with its head twisted backward and left with no blueprint for the future. Time had passed Kirkland and organized labor by.

As labor's woes mounted from the 1970s onward with the growing loss of blue-collar jobs and increased resistance by the business community to sharing power with it, and as its percentage of the American workforce steadily dropped, organized labor drifted off, headed, it clearly seemed, for insignificance.

Gatherings of its leaders often resembled meetings of the Kuomintang, the exiled Nationalist Chinese leaders who sought refuge in Taiwan and once dreamed of going home. They were out of touch. They were mostly old. They were men. They were mostly white. A few of them would doze on the dais as their long public meetings droned on.

In the early 1990s the crisis for unions worsened as their numbers continued to slip. American unions were desperately in need of new blood and new thinking. They were drowning in people who blithely operated by timetables that were badly out of date.

They had too many hangers on, too many friends of friends of friends who slipped into top jobs with a nod and no credentials. There were too many people who had tasted what seemed like a better life and did not want to lose the material perks of union leadership. Too many union leaders who could only remember the good old days. Too many unions were run by people who had few ties to the changing face of their unions. Although these unions were organizing women and newly arrived immigrants, although their membership was brown and black and yellow, the leadership was white and old and male and stuck mentally in their best of times, the past.

And then there were still some unions pinned under the thumb of mobsters and others who did not mind stealing from those who worked very hard for their living.

The image of labor leaders gathered in Miami—sitting around a pool during a break, smoking cigars, anxiously waiting at the end of the day's business to get into taxis to go to expensive restaurants—was everything that union haters could ask for to further deride them.

At a time when hopes for replenishing organized labor's roots rested heavily on finding new recruits among women and workers of color, the unions' elite offered at best a nostalgic portrait of another time. Only a few unions put forth any serious organizing efforts. Worse yet, organized labor's political victories were few, so few that big business no longer seemed to show any real concern about labor's political clout.

Corporate America still went through the routine of wringing its hands publicly about labor bosses' undue influence, but it was a charade. Companies privately realized that the labor bosses rarely got what they wanted. They were being generous in even calling them "labor bosses."

If there was any hope for organized labor, if the Decatur workers had made any impact, then the gathering in Bal Harbour seemed a true test of where American unions were headed. It was highly unlikely that the AFL-CIO was going to have a sudden change of heart and throw itself open to the workers. But the Decatur organizers had crossed a barrier by presenting themselves to the union leaders. Rarely had such a group of workers—heretofore similar to offstage actors in a Shakespearean play—ever shown up at the labor chiefs' meetings. Their arrival in Bal Harbour was fortuitous. The first real showdown in labor's ranks in years and the beginning of an unprecedented palace coup was about to take place.

As the Decatur workers milled about, the union chiefs met for five hours in a closed-door session. At one point during the meeting, Wayne Glenn, the president of the paper workers union, who himself was in his late 60s, point blank told Kirkland that if he wasn't going to change his ways, he should retire. Ever since his union had been beaten by replacement workers in the strike with International Paper, Glenn had held the AFL-CIO accountable for not seriously taking up the cause on behalf of his union.

Later, at a press conference, it was clear that Kirkland felt badly bruised by this attack from his rivals, who had kept their plot largely in the dark until then. It made him sentimental, defensive, angry, a bit unhinged. He seemed old, older than usual. His jowls shook. He peered solemnly through his thick glasses. The large, fancy hotel meeting room was full of reporters and union people drawn to hear him describe what was happening within the AFL-CIO's inner circle. He was King Lear, furious, surrounded, weakened, lashing back.

Asked about the impact of the hard-core Republicans' Contract with America on the AFL-CIO, Kirkland's mind wandered. It leapt backward through decades and settled on his childhood in the South during the Great Depression. It was a time, he said in his slow, somewhat mumbled South Carolina drawl, when the rivers ran red from the runoff of every farm, when people suffered from rickets, pellagra, and hookworm, when farmhouses were lit with kerosene, and when the country depended on the tender mercies of corporate enterprise. It was as elegiac as ever, a classic Kirkland offering that later read as well as it had sounded. Clearly there was a reason why he had twice been a ghost writer for Adlai Stevenson's presidential campaigns. But his oration while under attack was not what his supporters wanted to hear, not what they thought would revive the fate of the long-suffering organization.

WHO RULES THE HOUSE OF LABOR?

Never before since the federation of unions took root in 1886 had one of its leaders been forced out of office. Samuel Gompers, William Green, George Meany—they had all died in office or retired. Kirkland probably would have followed the same route, headed toward retirement at about the same age as his predecessor. Meany had stepped down in 1979 at age 85 after a quarter century at the helm of the AFL-CIO. He had personally anointed Kirkland, then the organization's number-two person, its secretary-treasurer, one of a new breed of well-educated labor technicians.

As in a Third World political party, there was no opposition, and barracks rebellions were unthinkable within the AFL-CIO. The decision on who was to rule the house of labor was not up to the workers who belonged to it, nor to middle-level union politicians. It rested with the union leaders, who made their decisions among themselves and then voted as if they had polled their membership individually. The larger unions had the real clout. That was the way things were done within organized labor in the United States. And it still is.

That was why the campaign to unseat Kirkland had begun as a whispering campaign only a few months earlier among a handful of union presidents. They were running against the traditions. Because of the clandestine nature of their effort and their somewhat guerilla-like tactics, they were dubbed the "gang of seven": This group was going against the grain, against all AFL-CIO traditions. And because such action was out of the normal, others, who rallied to Kirkland's side, were furious. How unkind. How divisive. Above all else, they did not like the break in tradition.

At the AFL-CIO's dark, musty offices not far from the White House, Lane Kirkland witnessed the union's development for years, first as a labor bureaucrat and then from 1969 on as Meany's top aide. Even though he was the chosen heir and showed more acumen for dealing with the latest issues than Meany, who led by a "committee of one," a term coined by Kirkland, some wondered whether he was the right man.

As A. H. "Abe" Raskin, the *New York Times*'s veteran labor writer, had pointed out, labor's ark was leaking and Kirkland faced many challenges. He was a different kind of leader from Meany, who, as Raskin wrote, had seemed cut from Bronx concrete. Where Kirkland seemed ill at ease with the press and avoided public appearances, Meany had been "Mister Labor," a gruff, outspoken, cigar-chomping plumber who had gone to work at age 16 and worked his way to the top. He became a well-known icon of organized labor, disdaining the leftist, populist urges of union leaders like Walter Reuther and framing himself in the image of the popular tough guy. His legacy to organized labor was the stamp of practicality and his inclination to keep labor unions at least united under the AFL-CIO.

He oversaw the merger of the AFL and CIO in 1955, but the new organization never lived up to expectations. All of the critical issues for labor—reversing crippling labor laws, invigorating its organizing efforts, wielding its political clout for gains in Washington, D.C.—were heartbreaking dreams. Year by year organized labor accounted for a smaller share of the American workforce. By the end of his rule, Meany was seen as dogmatic and distant from rank-and-file workers and their concerns. He had once been praised for his progressivism, but he seemed to have forgotten his liberal instincts as the years wore on. Ironically, the arc of his career at the end very much resembled that of Kirkland's: downward and quite diminished.

As much as the two men were dissimilar individually, they shared an almost seamlessly similar view about the AFL-CIO. When Kirkland was about to step into his new job, he showed no indications that labor was in distress or should expect a departure from the past. "There will be a different face in charge if I'm elected," he said at the time. "But as far as changes go, I don't feel any need for drastic departures from the policies that George Meany and I have developed over the last couple of decades. I hope to have some good ideas in the future, too. I recognize that we are in a changing society. I expect that we will keep pace with it and try to anticipate it."

LABOR'S VALEDICTORIAN

Son of a small-town cotton buyer in South Carolina, Kirkland was soft-spoken, erudite, a college graduate who had considered a career as a diplomat. He rarely exhibited a passion that the average worker could easily fix on. Unlike most Americans who rarely consider overseas issues, he had never lost his fascination with foreign policy matters and organized labor abroad. He made sure, for example, when he headed the AFL-CIO that the Polish Solidarity Movement had support from its American brethren when others did not rally to its side. And his speeches were gems.

"We are blessed," he said in one of his most memorable addresses in October 1969, "and strengthened by one piece of sure and certain knowledge: that there are no lost causes for us; that the fight is never over, that as long as we stand together and the blood is in us there can be no final defeat on any battleground."

During World War II, he was a mate on ships carrying weapons and supplies to U.S. forces in the Atlantic and the Pacific. That was the bulk of his rank-and-file experience. He was a superhawk, a fervent anticommunist who opposed Senator George McGovern as the Democratic presidential candidate because of his anti-Vietnam war stance. And on his watch, as he referred to his time in office, organized labor took some of its worst beatings.

In the 1980s concession bargaining raced from one union to another, wages were frozen, benefits were slashed, and patterns of contracts built up over decades disappeared. Crossing a picket line to take a union member's job no longer seemed a moral failure. Amid their defeats and losses, handfuls of American workers were outraged and fought back. In the steel making communities around Pittsburgh, laid-off steelworkers rose up with a fury not heard for years.

But most American workers swallowed their defeat. If there was anyone to blame, they seemed to blame themselves. They did not take to the streets to vent their rage; they moved on, looking for jobs, latter-day Okies. They slid downward, going from middle-class jobs to lower-paying jobs held by the working poor. The older they were, the more likely they were to drop out of the job market, to disappear into subsistence living. Their lives were lost in frayed ethnic communities, big-city ghettoes, one-time bustling factory towns like Decatur.

How far organized labor had fallen in the public's view was obvious in a March 1994 survey of public opinion done for the AFL-CIO by outside consultants. Its findings were devastating. Did people care about unions? They largely didn't, the survey found. And if they did, they considered them dinosaurs, protectors of the past, bureaucracies caring for their own and no one else. Hostility was especially rife among those who were envious of the good pay and benefits union members receive. As envious as they were, however, they didn't see themselves signing up for unions. Even union members raised a troubling issue. A number felt disaffected, complaining about the lack of democracy and being told what to do by their leaders.

By 1995 a group of union leaders felt they had scores to settle with Kirkland for all of these losses—much of them beyond the control of the weakened arms of the AFL-CIO.

At the end of the U.S. Senate battle to ban replacement workers the year before, Kirkland had been traveling outside of the United States. Then there was the labor movement's failure to knock down or at least modify the administration's North American Free Trade Agreement (NAFTA).

The organization had done all it could to elect Bill Clinton president, and how had Clinton shown his appreciation for its time and efforts? He had turned around and battled fiercely with it to pass NAFTA. However, he was unable to show the same energy to help find votes in the Senate to make the ban on striker replacements come true.

Plus there were the Democrats' disastrous political results in 1994, and a marked drop in the turnout among union voters. Big Labor was really little labor. And its leader was a phantom. A 1991 nationwide survey had pointed out that only 3 percent of the U.S. public could identify the AFL-CIO's leader.

Wayne Glenn, still angry about organized labor's failure to ban striker replacements, was one of those who thought Kirkland's time had come. Gerald McEntee, sharp-tongued, ambitious, a politically savvy leader who was head of the American Federation of State, County, and Municipal Employees, was one of the dissident strategists. He was too sharp-tongued, too out-front, too abrasive to be the man who would unseat Kirkland and meld together the two wings of organized labor. Ron Carey, the reform president of the Teamsters Union, who was fighting his own wars within his giant union, became one of the most outspoken critics of Kirkland. That was the style of Carey, a feisty New York local leader, who had astounded his union's old guard by winning the Teamsters' first rank-and-file election ever in 1991. But Carey's own battle within his union was clearly taking its toll on him. He seemed tired, less ambitious, less outspoken about the blindness and foibles of organized labor.

For a while he had been the hope and the dream of progressive union members and their supporters. His aggressive, table-thumping attack on union corruption and the old ways of doing things was a break with a union that had become a kleptocracy—it could not stop itself from stealing from its members and others. Carey had brought new blood and new faces into the Teamsters. Yet he became a victim of their adoration. He seemed to lose control of the union's daily business as he became engulfed in all-out war with the union's old guard, who furiously fought him. The war against evil in the Teamsters engulfed him years later, when he was barred by government-appointed monitors for campaign wrongdoing, carried out largely by supporters who thought they had to break the law to keep Carey in office.

Months later, when the efforts of the AFL-CIO's rebels' needed an extra push to rally votes from unions fighting the dissidents—the margin of victory was never very strong—one of those carrying out the last-minute lobbying and arm bending was George Becker, president of the United Steel Workers union.

OVERCOMING THE PALACE GUARDS

But Kirkland did not step aside easily. He was undaunted by his opponents' boasting and stubbornly clung to the hope of staying on until it was clear that his time had run out. His delayed departure set up a bitter, almost fratricidal feud between his right-hand man, Thomas Donahue, the organization's secretary-treasurer, who had served him loyally for 16 years, and John Sweeney, president of the 1.1 million-member Service Employees International Union. Longtime friends, the two had climbed the ranks of the same union and upward within labor from similar New York, Irish American roots.

In a drama played out for a very select audience, the union presidents, who were truly the ones who cast the votes of their members, the two old friends turned increasingly hostile. They agreed on the basic issue: The labor federation had to change.

Donahue and Sweeney, the longtime drinking partners, attempted to project competing images of how to get there, but in reality the differences seemed to be a matter of degree. Donahue, who clearly saw where change was needed, became the candidate of the established order. And Sweeney, who had ascended to the top by learning how to live with the old order, became the supposed radical. The images did not really fit, but the view of Sweeney as a believer in reckless street confrontations was more out of focus. Soft-spoken, reserved, Sweeney was a less-than-inspiring public speaker who relied heavily on speeches written for him. A silver-haired, slightly paunchy man, he resembled an elderly uptown Manhattan doorman. In terms of America's labor unions, however, he was to become an evolutionary leader who straddled both the old and the new.

He had never been a militant within union politics, but his union had become one of the most progressive despite pockets of old-time cronyism and good-old-boy politics. He was skilled at promoting new voices and stoking new ideas within the union. He was not, however, a fire-breathing reformer; that kind of forcefulness, the other dissident union leaders had feared, would doom their effort. They wanted a change, but not an abrupt one that would weaken and split their ranks. So, Sweeney became their man, and he, in turn, supplied a vision that appeared, with help from the news media, much more ambitious than Donahue's.

But that vision was strong enough to scare the supporters of Donahue and Kirkland, who feared it and thought it would bring a wrenching break with their old ways. They thought it would alienate the American public. They imagined street demonstrations and union officials in Washington telling unions how to get out the vote. They wanted to press ahead, but not at a pace much different from that of yesteryear. They seemed to think the older ways had been working.

But those ways no longer worked, and the situation was becoming even more dire.

WHERE IS LABOR GOING?

Union membership was sinking toward 11 percent of the private workforce in the mid-1990s. Only a tiny handful of unions were actually organizing workers. The U.S. economy was booming, but wages were frozen for millions on the middle and bottom rungs of the pay ladder. The gap between the top and the bottom was growing, because the top was doing so much better financially. Wall Street analysts continued to fret about the day when workers would wake up and realize how the market's boom had been constructed partially on starved wage increases.

A whole new army of temporary workers—workers largely without rights or voices or benefits—was rising up across the economic landscape without a single link to organized labor. Foreign manufacturers like Mercedes-Benz were eager to build their products in the United States because American factory workers' wages were so much lower. Like a Third World nation, the United States was luring bargain hunters. It had been a long time since organized labor had so significantly failed to perform.

Yet the idea of wholesale change struck some union leaders as absolutely unneeded and, worse yet, dangerous.

On Dave Watts's mind, when he got home from Miami, was keeping it all together now, keeping the Staley workers from splitting apart. That was going to be his biggest challenge, he thought. The longer this lasted, the more people became divided. Beards, long hair, radical words. And others worrying about losing their pensions and all they had. And the mess with the AFL-CIO. He sensed a real divide in the ranks, and it was growing steadily, but he was not sure how bad it was. He knew for sure that fewer people were coming to rallies or passing out handbills or going around the country as road warriors. And he was getting more and more flak at the local's meetings.

This was not what he had thought he would be best at. He had never been a great speaker. But he found himself changing in the way he talked and thought. He felt betrayed by his union and the AFL-CIO. Dave's wife, Pat, noticed that he was quieter. He seemed to be burrowing more into himself and the local's quandary. He was so caught up in the challenge that there was little time for himself or his family.

Unions Add New Members

Union membership grew by 150,000 persons in 1994, the second consecutive year of growth after 14 years of decline, the Bureau of Labor Statistics reported.

"Where the jobs are growing, unions are growing," said AFL-CIO Organizing Director Joseph Schantz. "The most significant gains occurred in the services sector, which has been growing as the other sectors have declined in recent decades."

—*AFL-CIO News*, February 1995

CHAPTER 25

Still Waiting for Victory— Or Something

January 1995

Jerry Floyd faced an awful choice. He had built tractors and made shoes, but he considered himself a tire builder because of the 28 years he had put in at the factory in Decatur, and that is the way he wanted people to know him. So when the company called to say it was willing to offer pensions to strikers over 55 years old with 10 years of service, Floyd could not accept the offer; he didn't want to retire. He was working part-time at a grain elevator, earning less than half of what he had made at the tire factory, but he told himself he was a tough old guy. He could hold out. He made tires.

Then the union called to say that the company's bid was still being offered. Didn't he want to reconsider?

Sitting one night at the kitchen table of the old farmhouse where he lived with his wife, Annie, he decided he might as well get it over with. For 28 years, 7 months with the company, he walked away with a monthly pension of $750 plus health care. With his salary from the granary, he and his wife figured they would be able to get by. Annie was working at a small fireworks factory, earning just about minimum wage. Later, whenever any of his friends brought up the issue of the strike and his retirement, he would feel suddenly caught in the throat, as if there was nothing he could say.

It didn't seem right to workers like Floyd that they should be stuck in such dire situations. They couldn't understand how their unions had let such things happen. The truth was the unions were virtually helpless. They had called on their members to give everything, but the unions themselves did not have much to give. Their game plans did not work any more. Moreover, they either didn't have the financial clout to put up terrific battles or they weren't prepared to go all out.

It was a lesson for the old guard leaders of the AFL-CIO on how far the movement had fallen. But they had their own battles to focus on, battles far from Decatur and average union members like tire builder Dave Watts, a close friend of Jerry Floyd.

Watts had just come back to work after being laid off at the Bridgestone/Firestone factory for nearly two years when the union went on strike in July 1994. Financially, he was not in great shape, but he didn't think he was in any great trouble.

He figured it would be the same as always.

He figured the union could handle it.

But when the union's 4,200 workers struck Bridgestone/Firestone, the rubber workers' leaders merely threw up picket lines and waited for Bridgestone/Firestone to begin hurting as its production was halted. Union leaders in Akron figured time would be on their side.

So the rubber workers waited. And waited.

At the start of the strike, the union had considered launching a corporate campaign against the tire maker, but it did not have much money and anything ambitious was quickly considered unlikely. It leaned on outside consultants and the AFL-CIO's Industrial Union Department, which had been building a repertoire of experience in running corporate campaigns.

The combined advice was to go after unions around the world and have them help run a consumer boycott of the world's largest rubber maker. Bridgestone also made golf equipment, hence the idea of sending striking rubber workers to golf tournaments. Targeting Japanese government officials in the United States was another suggestion.

Getting the Clinton administration to back the campaign was a key point of the advice given to the union. And there was more. The campaign had to be without racism or anti-Japanese fervor. The union had to take the high road, but it had to go after the company aggressively, said the memos from the consultants to the union leaders in Akron.

The union waited some more, but it was not making much of an impact on the company. Bridgestone/Firestone continued to make money, its profits going up to $29 million in 1994. It had a hefty supply of tires shipped from overseas. It had been prepared for a strike. Because of its strikes against three other tire makers, the union had begun to drain its strike fund. By November 1994, the URW was still waiting, and its $12 million strike fund was gone. The company had canceled the insurance coverage for the workers months before.

When the giant tire maker sent letters to its strikers saying, "You did not report to work because you were on strike, and you were permanently replaced. Please address any questions you may have to the Labor Relations office," the number of line crossers' names on the "Wall of Shame" in the union hall's major meeting room grew from 73 to 325. One of those who crossed was a worker who had shifted from Decatur to the Oklahoma City plant and had crossed the lines there. He later committed suicide.

Dave Watts had a cousin who crossed the lines, and Watts quickly swore he would not speak to him again. Most workers had friends or relatives who took the jobs at the factory, and this also made their strike futile.

NO WAY OUT

On the mind of Roger Gates, the local's low-key, soft-spoken president, was the feeling that he had to hang onto his hopes. The most moderate of all the local leaders of the rubber workers, he was spending seven days a week at the union hall doing a job that had seemed a comparative breeze several years ago. That was when few showed for union meetings and the union simply rolled ahead. A tall, hefty man who did not need the extra pounds, Gates continued to put on weight as his days at the union hall stretched around the clock.

Other local leaders within the rubber workers union itched for a showdown. They were far more radical, far more willing to engage the giant Japanese company, taking a real stand on behalf of American workers. Gates had no such visions. And despite his deepest hopes, it seemed to him that the strike would go on and on.

A Sad Armistice

The Staley Workers Lose Out

Fall 1995

A crashing end was ahead, dead ahead, and Ray Rogers, undecorated veteran of many such battles, knew it. He saw it in the critical letters sent to Decatur from the paper workers union headquarters in Nashville: Where was the local headed, exactly?

He sensed it in the growing frustration within the local: When was it all going to end? And then Dave Watts finally flat out told him that the union's top leadership in Nashville wanted him and Jerry Tucker out. The two had too many enemies within the AFL-CIO, and the giant labor organization would not budge on the local's behalf or help the union as long as they were in Decatur, Watts told him.

BATTLE PLANS AWRY

At one time their overall strategy—Watts's and Tucker's—had seemed so clear and workable. It was to link up the disputes, to put pressure on the companies, and to enlist the big unions to help draw attention to Decatur and how the workers were taking on the corporations: Decatur was the battlefront for American labor in the 1990s.

And at times it seemed to go so smoothly.

One warm day in June 1993, more than 3,000 people had come out

215

to link arms in a human chain that stretched from the Caterpillar plant all the way to the Staley facilities. It was Jerry Tucker's idea, and it drew people from miles around to stand in the bright, warm sunshine, waving to the cars that passed them as they stood arm in arm. The message: Workers were fighting back in Decatur.

But more often the strategy for the Staley workers was not accomplishing what they had hoped for: It was not forcing the company to end the lockout or to back down on its bargaining strategy. As time went on, the union's two high-exposure gurus increasingly disagreed on the way to go. Ray Rogers felt that Jerry Tucker didn't appreciate the corporate campaign strategy Rogers was pursuing, and Tucker didn't think that Rogers saw the bigger picture of rank-and-file organizing. Considering the money Rogers was getting monthly from the union to run his New York office, Tucker considered Rogers as much an entrepreneur as a labor strategist. Rogers had warned that the union would suffer mightily if its workers were put out on the street because of Tucker's work-to-rule campaign—as they were when the company locked them out.

Convinced he would find a way to apply pressure to Staley, Ray Rogers went after the corporate links to the company. He called for a boycott of the First of America Bank—Decatur, and as a result Robert M. Powers, Staley's chairman of the board, had resigned from the board of the bank, which was based in Kalamazoo, Michigan The same tactic worked with Magna Bank of St. Louis. Miller Brewing Company canceled its purchases from Staley too, and the union celebrated the event. But Staley officials insisted that that had been strictly a business decision by Miller, not a result of the union pressure.

Rogers also went after Archer Daniels Midland (ADM), the giant agrichemical firm in Decatur and the biggest company in town, as well as State Farm Insurance Company in nearby Bloomington, saying that they were both investors in Staley. But nothing came of those efforts. Then the local went after Coca-Cola and Pepsi Cola, trying to get them to give up buying sweeteners from Staley, but the choice of these two targets was not Rogers's. He thought at that point the local was taking on too much.

Rogers felt he was operating a national campaign, somewhat like the one he had waged at Hormel. He had made the Staley dispute visible, given it a national image. He had shown the workers how to raise money, as much as $3 million before the whole battle was over. He was sending out as many as 65,000 pieces of mail at a time. But there were not as many warriors traveling on highways across the United States as there had been during the Hormel dispute. And he was not there on the spot, directing things, as he had done at that time.

The Staley workers had held demonstrations that drew support from across the Midwest. At one rally in mid-1994, 48 persons were arrested, among them several clergy members. A few weeks later they faced off with police and security guards, and several demonstrators were sprayed with pepper gas as police pushed the crowd back from Staley's gates. Primed to look for ways to pressure Staley, the local finally hit a small well.

One of the workers, Art Dhermy, researched the tax breaks that Staley had received and realized that the company was no longer eligible for some state funds since its employment levels had dropped below a certain point. The local pressed the case with the state, and it, in turn, ruled that Staley was no longer qualified for two tax breaks. The local estimated the cost to Staley at $3 million. (Staley reapplied three years later, based on its investment in equipment and machinery, and received another tax break in 1999.)

Just when Rogers was convinced his corporate campaigns were going to pay off, the doors to the union closed on him. Paper workers union head Wayne Glenn had called off Rogers's corporate campaign against International Paper seven years earlier, just when it had built up steam, and now he was doing it again.

The union leaders in Nashville felt the Staley campaign was going nowhere and that it was becoming a drain on the union's strike fund. But they also believed Rogers's strategy did not make much sense. They felt the local needed to pressure the company to put the workers back to work and that it did not have the leisure of long-term challenges. They also felt that the local had been stubborn and unbending. A number of paper worker locals had already gone over to 12-hour shifts, the issue that seemed to get the Staley workers really worked up.

And it was known around the union headquarters that there was pressure from the AFL-CIO to get Rogers out of the picture. Other unions opposed to Rogers would not help out as long as he was taking part at Decatur.

Faced with the union's case against Rogers, the local put the issue up to a vote and recommended that Rogers bow out. Dave Watts felt that the local had no choice. When the local's leaders went to Nashville after scuttling Rogers, he went along, still eager to make his case personally with Glenn. He told Watts about what had happened before with the paper workers union in the showdown with International Paper, and how the union had backed down then. They are going to bury this fight, he predicted to Watts.

When Rogers met with Glenn and several other union officials, Glenn told him that the campaign was being put aside so the company and the union could return to negotiations. And there was a problem in Washington, Glenn explained, because of Rogers. Rogers followed Glenn into his office and confronted him.

"All I'm doing is the job I am supposed to do," Rogers said. "And how can you live with yourself? All you are doing is burying the workers, again. Put down on paper what you are doing to do for these workers."

Rogers was livid. Once again, he felt, he had been used by a union official as an excuse to call off a fight the union couldn't stomach. He was sure the union would not carry on the fight. His old partner, Ed Allen, called soon afterwards, saying he had heard that the local in Decatur had let Rogers go and he suspected that Rogers was depressed. He was let down, he replied, but he was also relieved. He was broke, having spent nearly everything he had on the effort, and he was exhausted. Whenever he went to Decatur, people would stop him and tell him to slow down or he was going to drop dead. Now he could slow down.

AN UPRISING OF THE DISCONTENTED

Within the Staley workers' local, the edges of support were already badly frayed, and the center was no longer holding.

At the factory, a group of locked-out workers were chaining themselves daily to a nearby metal fence, where they sat for 12-hour shifts to symbolize their protest against the 12-hour workdays. They called themselves the "the chain gang."

Dismayed by the lack of progress and increasingly urging the local to take more militant steps, Dan Lane went on a fast in a small room in the rectory of Father Mangan's church, St. James. Others came by the church and fasted briefly to show their solidarity with him, but the tall, dark-haired former Marine infantryman and Vietnam veteran made the fast his statement.

As he saw it, he was taking part in a battle for lower-middle-income people like him, people who had left high school and thought their career plans were set for life once they got a permanent job. He thought if only something dramatic would happen to make people pay attention to Decatur, then maybe the AFL-CIO or others would suddenly rally to the cause. At least within the local, it might get people excited again. "We need something to make people stop and think this is pretty serious stuff," he said. "There is almost a front line out there advancing against middle-class America. People ought to be able to make a decent wage and go home and be with their family. People get on the bandwagon about family values. How about me being home with my kids?"

Lane and his wife still had three children at home to take care of. Toward that end he was bringing home $60 a week from the union and delivering newspapers in the mornings. His wife was working 25 hours a week, earning minimum wage at a local jewelry store.

As he fasted at the church, going from 215 pounds down to 165, Lane was encouraged that he was doing the right thing, making some headway, when National Public Radio called one day and asked how he was doing and another day he talked with a woman from Portland, who told him that people had to take a stand. He must be drawing attention to himself and, therefore, to the issue at hand. One day Staughton Lynd, a longtime peace and civil rights activist, who had become a lawyer in a small Ohio town, stopped by to visit Lane and give him a copy of a book about nonviolence in America. At Lane's bedside in the small room were the writings of Martin Luther King, Jr. and Henry David Thoreau.

Many in the local, however, were not enthusiastic at all. They thought Lane's action gave an appearance of militancy to the dispute that they didn't feel comfortable with. They worried about his family. They didn't see his hunger strike moving the union any closer to going back to work. They felt that Lane was consumed with himself.

But Lane stayed on the fast for 64 days and then went to New York, where the AFL-CIO convention was about to elect John Sweeney, by a small margin, as its new president. On the podium before hundreds of delegates, Lane was the angry, militant worker, who fit in with Sweeney's image of the newly revived organized labor. It was good timing. Tall, gaunt, but as furious in his words as ever, Lane waved his arms in the air as he spoke and then strode through the vast hotel meeting room to wild cheers of support.

TIME TO SURRENDER

Nothing was happening in Decatur. But that would end soon.

Worn out by a dispute that seemed to go on forever, a small group of workers began privately discussing ways of changing the direction of things. One way was to get their own man elected to head the local. But they were reluctant. It took guts to stand up at a meeting and say that all the efforts of the past had failed and it was time to cut a deal with the company.

Then along came Jim Schinall.

Every time he met another worker, he heard stories about people losing houses or cars or control over their lives. He was convinced the local's leaders thought they could walk on water. It had to stop. And so he became one of those pushing to put the battle to an end.

Schinall started putting in calls to see how deep were the roots for rebellion, and those who liked what they heard made more calls. The dissidents figured they had at least half of the local on their side. And they counted four, maybe five, votes out of the nine-member executive board.

Schinall had been the chairman of the bargaining committee when the dispute began and then left the local's leadership, saying he needed to earn a living. But he was disgusted, too. He didn't think the local needed Ray Rogers anymore. Rogers had brought in money for the local from across the country, but his strategies were no longer working. And he was convinced that Jerry Tucker had only made things worse. "He, Tucker, was the reason we got locked out, 'cause we did what he told us," Schinall said.

Schinall had taken a job as a truck driver, but had kept an eye on what was happening with the dispute. With so little money coming from the union, only $60 a week, many of the workers took full-time jobs to get by.

By late 1995, Schinall was 57 years old and had 29 years in the factory, almost all of his adult life. He was a blunt, straight-talking man, and he and Dave Watts were dead opposites on thoughts about what the local should do. No doubt about that.

Soon came the showdown moment. At a local meeting, Schinall

and his backers put up a proposal requiring the executive board to bring any contract offers from the company to membership for a vote. They no longer trusted the local's leaders to decide for them. It was an open declaration of war between his group and those backing Watts. And Schinall's group won. The motion passed. Watts was furious and told them so at the next local meeting.

Schinall was on a roll, and he decided to take the next step, to run for local president, not because he wanted the job but simply because he thought the others would endlessly drag the fight on. Time to cut and go, he explained. The time had come to make a deal and move on. He vowed that he would make a deal and retire soon after. It was an unusual campaign promise from an unusual candidate.

Then came the local's election, and Schinall won, taking 60 percent of the vote. Watts was disheartened. He knew the local had been divided, but he had never guessed that the split had been so deep. He had kept asking people to tell him about the mood among the membership, but deep down he sensed it. He felt that he had started the dispute with 98 percent of the membership's support. By the end, however, he counted no more than maybe a dozen who were still committed, who were still pulling their weight.

He was disgusted, disheartened, and yet he was relieved. The pressure was off him. He was no longer the one trying to be upbeat, trying to keep people together, trying to come up with a solution that seemed tougher and tougher to find.

Once again the company and the union were bargaining, and the company pushed an offer that it insisted was the best it could do. Watts was still the local's head, and he, along with the local's lame-duck leadership, decided not to present the offer to the members for a vote. They didn't consider it a good deal.

But union officials from Nashville interceded, saying the members had to vote or they could face charges by the union for violating union rules.

With Schinall now the local's new president, the members voted on the contract and accepted it by a vote of 285 to 226. It was virtually the same contract they had turned down four years before. Twelve-hour shifts rotating monthly.

Four years for nothing.

It was not a good contract, Schinall thought. But it was an end to the fight.

Of the 740 workers that had been locked out, the company expected 350 to be called back. But far fewer took the company's offer. Only 146 returned to their old jobs. The rest turned their backs on the company. They were worn down and wanted to take their pension or severance pay and leave. Or their fury toward the company would not let them return even if they had no other plans.

So, they too, took their pensions, if they had qualified for them, and moved on.

After 29 years on the job, Watts got a severance payment of $30,000, which, after taxes, was $18,000 in his pocket. Under the company's pension plan, he could begin drawing $650 a month when he was 65 years old. Sixty-five years old seemed a long way off to him. And $650 monthly after so many years working at Staley's seemed so little. He was furious, absolutely furious.

The company expected that in a few years it would need no more than 200 to do the work once done by more than three times as many. Technology, round-the-clock shifts, and less restrictive job categories had wiped out hundreds of jobs.

The day the contract deal was reached, Dave Watts, who was now just a union member, was cool and somber. "We virtually lost everything we had [gained] through 50 years of agreements with the company. This contract just barely bargained back some improvements," he said.

The union had slightly improved the language for the way it would work out grievances with the company. But there were hardly any real improvements. It was more as though they had ever so slightly worn off the edges of the changes that the company wanted to carry out. For example, the company won the right to use outside suppliers and contractors and to lay off permanent workers when it meant an improvement in cost, quality, technology, or operating efficiency at the plant. But now it had to discuss the layoffs with the local. That was it. The local had no power to stop the slow bleeding away of its jobs.

Nor was Watts particularly pleased by organized labor's show of support.

"We gave some opportunity to put some soul back into a sleeping giant. I hope somewhere in the future it happens, but it hasn't happened yet. The people in Decatur, in the three disputes, particularly my union—we accomplished goals that many tremendously wealthy and large unions couldn't. But it wasn't enough in light of the corporate challenges to workers. They've got far too much money and far too much clout."

Schinall wasn't any happier. He was simply relieved that the fight was over.

"We were divided by a war of attrition," he said that day, as the contract's meaning first sank in. "The company kept chipping away at our solidarity and ability to hang on to what we had. We had 350 people without health care for three years. The family disruptions were my biggest heartaches. The divorce record was terrible. Dying without health care was equally bad. There were a lot of people who stood up for the values of what this fight was all about. The real heroes who surfaced, unfortunately, were in the minority. They were the . . . road warriors who raised the money, the people who ran the food pantries, who rallied the clergy. This is the biggest faction of quality people, and Staley has lost them forever."

His mind more than ever on larger battles, Dan Lane was philosophical about what labor unions would have to do to win such battles. "The fatal flaw was trying to outlast the companies. You are not going to outlast them. Some of the people went to the edge but never as far as they could have as far as civil disobedience goes. There has never been a sense of urgency about what was going on in Decatur. We got help, but we never got any real serious help."

Bob Hull, who had worked his entire life at only one place, A. E. Staley, stubbornly refused to walk on company property once more to sign up for his retirement. He did all of his dealing over the telephone or by fax.

Sitting late one afternoon at the union's campaign office soon after the upheaval in the local, Mike Griffin, a 50-year-old who had put in 28 years in the plant and who had been one of the die-hard activists during the dispute, was despondent.

The new local president had just ordered the office shut down. It was a separate office that the union had set up to run its charity drive, to sell its T-shirts and other paraphernalia promoting its cause, and to coordinate its road warrior operations. A large U.S. map dotted with pins showed where the warriors had traveled. At the peak of activity, there were about 35 warriors traveling at the same time and 6 people working in the office. It had the ambience of an election campaign office for an underdog, antiestablishment candidate.

With all that had happened, Griffin could not believe the effort was coming to an end. He had been fired by the company a month before the lockout and had become one of the most outspoken workers. The Staley workers had made so many far-reaching contacts with unions in the United States and overseas, he said. They had worked with 87 support groups and backers in 11 nations. They had learned so much about unions and companies. They had raised over $2 million.

What they had done was not just for workers in Decatur, he said, but for workers across the United States. He grew bitter, angry amid the piles of recently packed boxes.

"There is such a big need, I hate to see it go," he said.

"HE WAS NOT THE MAN I KNEW"

Mike Dulaney was one of the few who decided to go back to Staley. During the lockout, he and his wife, Judy, considered themselves survivors and prided themselves on having learned how to live without the factory paycheck.

Mike and Judy had known each other from grade school, had begun dating when they were 15 years old, and had gotten married right out of high school. During the lockout, Mike had found odd jobs here and there and Judy had cleaned the homes of elderly people who needed the help. Not a lot of money was coming in, but they were getting by. Mike finally found a job at St. Mary's Hospital in town as a security guard, earning about half of what he had before. But he liked the work at the hospital; more than anything, he liked the way the hospital treated him. Then the union signed the contract, and he was called back to work. He decided he would go.

But his return to his old job was short-lived.

"The week he was back at Staley, he was not the man I had always known," Judy said. "The man I married was always easygoing. He played Santa Claus all the time. But [once he was] back at work, he was withdrawn and an entirely different man. I came home one day, and I found him in tears at the thought of going back the next day. So we talked, and the next day we went back to the hospital and he got his job there."

In his large office at Staley, just off of the old main entranceway, Executive Vice-President Pat Mohan was as polite and philosophical as ever. Out in the hallway beyond the door to his office was where the farmers used to sell their grains decades before.

Now, after the company had won the battle, there was no gloating, no public display of bitterness. No need to trounce the people who had haunted him and his family. In terms of profit for the company, 1995 had been a very good year. Mohan saw the big picture. The one the company had focused on. The workers didn't. Four years down the drain.

"We realize change may be difficult. These changes are causing a lot of anxiety for us in the workplace," he said.

CHAPTER 27

All Things Fall Apart

The Caterpillar Workers
Suffer Defeat Too

December 1995

The strike begun in June 1994 went on and on and on. A wealthy union with a nearly $1 billion strike fund before the strike, it was digging deep to keep its picket lines up. It boosted the monthly strike pay from $100 to $300 and was paying about $600 a month per member for health benefits. The tab: at least $12.3 million a month. Clearly, the union was willing to foot the bill for the effort and to ensure solidarity.

Much to the amazement of the union—and to company officials as well—the factories kept going. First they were operated by white-collar workers whisked away from their desks, and then the company brought in temporary workers to help out. At $13 an hour and with heaps of overtime, the temporaries, mostly out-of-work Southerners recruited by agencies that regularly fill factories during strikes, swallowed up the work. But there were also workers from nearby. Farmers who wanted the extra money. Young workers stuck in dead-end, low-paying jobs. Also, there were UAW workers who had deserted the picket lines.

By the company's count, about 5,200 workers had quit the union. But the union put the figure closer to 1,000, and officials who saw the union's books suggested that the company had inflated the number of deserters as part of its psychological warfare. Still, the point had been made. The union's ranks were miserably torn.

CATERPILLAR HOLDS THE WINNING CARDS

Their ability to run the factories without any glitches left Caterpillar officials elated. They had never realized what changes they had wrought with new technology. They now saw which tasks they didn't need workers for. And, ultimately, they saw no reason to surrender to the union now that they too had suffered so much. The union kept looking for confirmation that the company had stumbled badly. It never came.

AN UNWANTED DEPARTURE

A year later, as the union's convention neared, and he was likely to give his job up because he would be over 65 years old, the limit for union officials, Bill Casstevens wistfully hoped that the union would make an exception. Over a cup of coffee in a suburban Detroit restaurant, he offered a rare glimpse at his dismay over what had taken place at Caterpillar and within labor's ranks.

The division in the Caterpillar workers' ranks, lack of solidarity with the union's goals, the workers who gave their votes to Republican politicians who then opposed labor unions: These were troubling shifts to him.

"It is discouraging. There is no question that the labor movement developed a middle class. So we are victims of our own success," he said. "In the 1980s you had Reagan and Bush, and unfortunately we had a lot of members who chose them. They voted with their emotions and I am sure it will come back to haunt them."

He met the local leaders and promised them he would find a way to stay on. He told them he would not walk away. He told them he was with them for the duration. Meanwhile, he had exchanged a series of letters with the company, each side accusing the other of not bending. Nothing had changed.

And the union leadership was not on his side, either. At a lunch in Detroit, Casstevens told Larry Solomon that the union's leadership seemed determined to drive him out. If the union would bend the rule, all he wanted was to stay on and finish the Caterpillar dispute. He put the offer to Owen Bieber, the UAW's tall, silent president, who himself was retiring. But the response from the union's leadership was a resounding no.

So he packed and left Solidarity House, the UAW's headquarters in Detroit. He never had a last good-bye discussion with Stephen Yokich, the UAW's new president. Nor did he go over his Caterpillar files with Richard Shoemaker, who replaced him as the person in change of dealing with the giant manufacturer.

It was widely known that Yokich did not think much of Casstevens's way of dealing with Caterpillar and wanted the unhappy affair ended. He had made it clear that putting the Caterpillar debacle to bed was a high priority for him and would be one of the ways in which he would be measured as the new leader of the UAW.

Whereas Bieber looked like a Hollywood image of a union leader— tall and rugged—Yokich acted like one that Hollywood would like. He was sharp-tongued, aggressive, feared by the union bureaucrats and local union politicians because of his reputation for casting aside foes and publicly ripping apart those who got in his way. Where Bieber always seemed to be slowly summoning his thoughts and strength, Yokich gave the impression of being wired and ready to spring.

He was. Within days of taking office, Yokich talked with Don Fites and Caterpillar officials. The relationship formed would continue in private between him and Fites. Almost as soon as he took over, Yokich also ordered an end to the public hostility toward the company. The union wanted a contract; it didn't want a 100-year war.

Shoemaker, quiet, reserved, fearfully shy of the news media, was a one-time factory worker from Iowa with John Deere who had worked his way up the union ladder. He also operated very differently from Casstevens. He didn't berate the company. He didn't stage tirades. He was direct, precise, focused. He was not the kind of bargainer Larry Solomon admired. But Solomon was not much admired at Solidarity House.

On a clear, cold day in December 1995, Yokich's drive to end the losing battle was put to a vote by the rank and file. Those UAW members who had not crossed their union picket lines were asked to vote on a contract that the central bargaining committee had rejected and the union had not recommended.

As the union members gathered to hear the details of the contract before voting, the union handed them another surprise. It told them that whatever happened, their strike was over. They were going back to work. The feeling in Detroit was that the union could not put up with the great expense while gaining little. The fact that so many workers had crossed the picket lines was a serious threat to the union's existence at Caterpillar.

Larry Solomon ridiculed the offer with his usual rebellious humor. As his members gathered to vote in Decatur, he handed out small brown paper bags with the words "Barf Bag" printed on them. In Peoria, a union official stood up at a closed meeting and called the proposal a rape. But, he said, it was the best the union could get. The 17-month strike, the longest the union had ever attempted against the company, had cost most of its members at least $30,000 each in lost wages.

AN UNWELCOME DEAL

The contract they were voting on was largely the one the company had offered before. What made it more frustrating was that the agreement made no provisions for the more than 100 workers whom the company had fired during its confrontations with the union. After furiously battling the company over the firings, portraying the workers as hapless victims of a cruel company, in the end the UAW could not protect them. Those it had held up as heroes it now seemed to abandon. It would keep up its legal battle on their behalf. Everyone that the company had fired was still on the outside. They would not go back to their jobs as their union brothers and sisters would. A sense of betrayal hung in the air.

The union members overwhelmingly voted the contract offer down. Nine out of ten workers in Decatur voted against the contract. The company immediately informed the union that the workers could not simply show up tomorrow at their old jobs. Changes had taken place inside the factories. Moreover, the company was going to lay down some rules about how the returning workers could behave. No more anti-company shirts or hats or other items that talked about the strike. No more disruptive acts. Hands down, the company was the winner. The strikers were going back under the company's terms and its watchful eye.

Was the union ultimately defeated?

At the union hall in Decatur, sitting in his darkened corner office one lonely afternoon, Larry Solomon said, "There is no question that the union will win. But I can't tell you when. I can only tell you we will win. We went through all kinds of tribulations in Decatur, and now

Caterpillar's really the one in the bind. Let's say we go out again; this could be played out again. The union was in a tough struggle, and we drew a line in the sand. We said we are really prepared to take on a full battle. The AFL-CIO was totally shocked when they saw this happen. There was no plan. They saw what was happening, but they had no solution. I think Decatur could have been a laboratory. If the fire had caught on, this thing should have led to a national shutdown. We ought to have had people who were willing to go to jail. Someday, somebody in labor is going to say enough is enough."

"IT IS NOT YOUR FAULT"

Soon afterward the local UAW leaders gathered in Detroit for two days to think over what lay ahead for them.

At the meetings in Detroit, Joe Vasquez, the president of Local 1415, an organization in Denver with only 150 workers, was openly upset. How would he face those union members whom he had called scabs and who would now be on the job beside him? How would he face the company foremen whom he had challenged?

Unlike those of most other union leaders, his was a part-time job that he did on his own time and at home. He had been the local's president for only a few years when the union's squabbles began with Caterpillar. He had shown his mettle, nonetheless.

At one point the company had suspended him for wearing a button it considered provocative. It read, "Happiness is waking up in the morning and finding a Don Fites picture on a milk carton." He had taken the button off, but then put it back on, saying he had a right to do so. The company promptly suspended him. When a group of workers staged a walkout on his behalf, they were suspended indefinitely by the company. Finally, they were allowed back when they agreed to file a grievance over their suspensions and to leave the matter up to a third party. An administrative law judge later ruled that the company had wrongly suspended Vasquez. The National Labor Relations Board not only upheld the judge's ruling but slapped Caterpillar's hand, saying it could not continue to violate workers' legal protections.

It had not been an easy time in other ways for Vasquez.

Some of his members had also crossed the union's picket line, and some had stopped paying dues since the company was no longer collecting them. Worse yet, his small local, which made parts for Caterpillar, had voted for the contract, and Vasquez spent most of the time at the leaders' meetings in Detroit apologizing for the vote, which he had of course disagreed with.

He talked about these things with Solomon, with whom he had developed a kinship. He reveled in Solomon's stories about his simple country upbringing. He could not imagine someone growing up without electricity or a bathroom in the house. And Solomon listened as Vasquez told about his own childhood, his feelings about unions, and the marvelous night that the famed farmworkers union leader Cesar Chavez had slept at his house. Vasquez was an outgoing middle-aged man, a joker over the years at union gatherings, who usually tried to calm things down when the meetings had turned tense and combative among the local leaders. Solomon took him out to lunch and told him not to take the situation so much to heart. It was not his fault how his members had voted or how the dispute had played out. Solomon put his arm around Vasquez and urged him to put the troubles out of his mind.

"Joe," he said, "don't worry about it. It is not your fault."

"I just don't feel right," Vasquez replied. "Larry, I don't feel good about this."

"Joe," Solomon repeated, "don't worry about it."

But his worrying had been building for some time. Before the Detroit meetings, he had told Stan Royale, a UAW organizer in Denver, that he would rather kill himself than go back and face the Caterpillar officials after what had happened. Royale urged him not to take it all so seriously, while he wondered what really was on Vasquez's mind.

Yet Vasquez would not let go of those feelings. He would not bury his fears. He continually asked Royale whether he had done the right thing, whether he had been a good leader.

Back home in Denver the day after the Detroit meeting, Vasquez lay down in his garage, turned on his truck, and took his life.

An Unexpected Good-Bye

The Bridgestone/Firestone Workers Lose Some of Their History

March 1996

Nothing was working out. Their strike pay had run out. They had no benefits. The union had no money for a high-pressure campaign against the company. It could not afford a large-scale confrontation. The strike against Bridgestone/Firestone and the other tire companies had drained it financially. The only real outside help came with a hefty loan from the autoworkers union.

As a last-ditch effort to create a strike fund, URW president Ken Coss called a special convention in Las Vegas. He wanted to raise dues to replenish the strike fund. But he could not win approval for anything more than $3 a month. Roger Gates, president of the Decatur local, stood up on the convention floor to declare his dismay at such short-sighted stinginess. Back home in Decatur and elsewhere there were people losing homes, marriages collapsing, and people in need of help, he said. The union had asked them to strike, and now the union was not helping them. He was downhearted but felt somehow things would go on. Coss felt terrible. Never before had he had been so embarrassed by the union's failure to do something. The money would only be enough to pay loans the union had taken out to keep its strike fund afloat. There would be nothing to really help the strikers.

A DESPERATE MARRIAGE

Salvation was nearby. At the Bal Harbour meeting of the union chiefs, steelworkers union president George Becker, talking casually with Coss, had raised the possibility of a merger of the two unions. Coss immediately warmed to the idea, and the two kept up a string of private meetings in Youngstown, Ohio, over the next few weeks.

The steelworkers were rich and well staffed. They had over $150 million in their strike fund. The rubber workers were gasping for air, though they had received plenty of advice about what to do. The Industrial Union Department of the AFL-CIO, which had set up a corporate campaign office years before, had been sending a stream of memos pointing out ways the union could take on the company. The union had also hired Washington consultants Fingerhut, Powers, Smith and had them plot out a campaign. But the union could barely stay alive.

In Japan, meanwhile, Bridgestone's officials were saying that the company's profits worldwide and in the United States were up. The company publicly showed no sign of quitting the fight it had begun to rewrite its contract with the union. It had decided it needed to wrestle control back from the union to boost its finances, and it could not relent.

A small local of about 150 workers in Akron had broken ranks and gone back to work. Pressure to give in was building in Decatur too, out of fear that the replacement workers were going to vote the union out in a decertification ballot. A meeting was hurriedly called on a Sunday, and a vote was taken in a loud, chaotic meeting.

Gates truly believed the replacement workers and others in the plant would vote out the union. He didn't think there was time to kill. He also knew that by quitting the strike the local would be abandoning some workers who would not be able to go back to their jobs. He could not recall making a decision as difficult before. The local said it was giving up and going back to work. It would be the first of the four large locals to surrender.

And its surrender stirred bitterness among the others. Within weeks, however, the rest of the locals capitulated and told the company they would go back to work under its terms. The longest and last strike in the rubber workers' history had ended. But it was not the ending the union had expected. Rather than welcoming back the strikers, the company said it had enough manpower on hand and would take back the workers when they were needed. The union was dumbfounded and furious.

DETERMINING THE FATE OF THE URW

Awaiting the rubber workers union was another question: Did it have a future?

At first, it had seemed plain to Coss and others in top union positions that the tired and beaten 98,000-member union would join with the steelworkers. The union's executive board had voted for it unanimously. Yet resistance within the ranks began building against the union's merger. A new drive was launched to prevent the URW from being swallowed up by the much larger steelworkers union.

For three days in July the union met in Pittsburgh amid furious debate. Was Coss doing this for his own advantage? someone asked. He emphatically denied any personal gain and offered to step down. He felt as though he were in a dogfight.

Finally the vote was taken, and when the totals came up, the ballots were counted once again. For the merger to pass, two-thirds of the delegates had to vote yes. By a vote of 617 to 304, the 60-year-old union faded from history. Three votes had made the difference. The union that had stood up to the tire makers in the 1930s and won a 36-hour week, but had also witnessed the rubber industry's flight from Akron to lower-wage Southern communities and to nonunion facilities, was history.

Although Coss was given a high-ranking position with the steelworkers, he left by the end of the year, retiring from union work. He was 60 years old and had prostate cancer. Some of the promises the steelworkers had made to him did not pan out. But he had liked being a union president, and when he quit he felt he was not walking away in bitterness. He looked on it as a business: Sometimes it was good; sometimes it was tough. It was like any business.

Whatever happened, he said, he had never lost a night's sleep.

A FIGHTER'S INSTINCTS AND STILL IN GOOD SHAPE, TOO

A loner, a tough boss who didn't forget and who would not accept defeat, George Becker had earned the reputation of having fire in his belly.

He clearly was not an intellectual like his Canadian predecessor, Lynn Williams. An economist and labor bureaucrat, Williams had brought a new sense of priorities to the steelworkers, a willingness to fight companies when necessary, but also an understanding of the need to sit down and compromise. Williams's argument had been that the steelworkers could no longer let the steel companies commit suicide. So they had to work with them.

Of the nation's major unions, few had been humbled as much by the death of blue-collar jobs and the collapse of North American companies as the steelworkers. From more than 1.4 million members in the late 1970s, it was down to just over a half million by the time Becker took over in 1994. This was a union that had made history, and now it was fighting not to become history.

The son of the son of a steel mill worker from southern Illinois, a former U.S. Marine, Becker looked far younger than in his middle sixties. A devotee of physical fitness, he had the strong arms and flat stomach of someone whose only hobby was riding an exercise bike in the mornings and lifting weights. He had gone to work at age 14 at a mill just across the street from his family's home.

Whereas Williams had been supreme at creating big plans for the union, but miserable at following up on the details, Becker's strength was in marshaling the union's forces: plotting and carrying out campaigns that would beat the odds.

That, too, would be the game plan for the AFL-CIO dissidents who, like the Decatur workers, saw in Lane Kirkland an outdated way of handling things. And they saw their chances only growing dimmer down the road.

Once the merger was complete, and he learned all of the details about the rubber workers' problems with Bridgestone/Firestone, George Becker was struck by what a mess the rubber workers had gotten themselves into. The union was flat on its back. It was busted, and he was convinced he had to rebuild it. He knew it was useless to wage a fight on a picket line against the company.

Besides that, he was convinced that unions rarely win fights that way nowadays. They have to wage corporate campaigns, like those the steelworkers had staged against Ravenswood Aluminum Company. The company had locked out its 1,700 members at a West Virginia mill and hired 1,000 replacement workers. The steelworkers took on the company as if it were waging a holy crusade. It went after the man it considered the investment force behind the company: Marc Rich, a one-time commodities investor who had fled the country amid charges and was living in Europe.

It took the union 22 months for an effort estimated at $20 million to beat the company and claim one of the very few victories for unions in recent years. It was like a drenching downpour in Las Vegas in August. Only a handful of workers had broken ranks with the union. The union had sketched out a worldwide campaign that showed far more imagination than usual. Rarely before had a union waged such an international campaign. And rarely before had an American union plotted such a complex strategy aimed at a company's pressure points. And best of all, the company's shareholders had revolted, leading to the downfall of the company's hard-line president.

The winning campaign was Becker's springboard to fame beyond his reputation with the steelworkers, and it guaranteed that he would go from number two in the union to the top when Lynn Williams stepped down.

Within the union, Becker was known for having street smarts, for being a fighter who liked to be out front in a dispute. And once a decision to do something was made, his style was not to back down even if legal problems came up. Let the union's lawyers work things out, he would say. The steelworkers have a tradition of carrying a number of lawyers on their staff and relying heavily on them.

Late in 1994, before the merger with the rubber workers was even a likelihood, Becker had called a meeting of more than a dozen steelworker officials in Pittsburgh and voiced his dismay at the beating suffered by the rubber workers. It was a black eye for all of organized labor, he said. It couldn't be allowed to go on.

He asked Jerry Fernandez, who had worked his way up with the union bureaucracy to become its international affairs director and his guru on corporate battles—his most famous was the Ravenswood campaign—to take a look at the situation. After several months, Fernandez concluded that the union was overwhelmed and had no real resources to hurt the company.

It needed to whack the company 20 different ways, and it couldn't. Becker instructed Fernandez to help the rubber workers whether or not a merger deal came off. Afterward, when the merger had become a fact, Becker told him that Bridgestone/Firestone was the union's number-one fight and to put everything into it.

Tall, soft-spoken, with a hangdog moustache and a slight middle-aged spread, Fernandez was a third-generation steelworker of Spanish and Polish origins from Homestead, a gritty steel mill town up the river from Pittsburgh. He was an unusual mixture of sorts within the union's white-collar ranks.

The son of a former union local president, he chewed smoking tobacco and had an honest-to-goodness feel for what went on in the mills. He also had an MBA and spoke Spanish.

He knew the ropes of the union's bureaucracy very well, emerging after years of paper shuffling into a high-profile job. And he was creative in tough situations. He was the perfect person to pick up the pieces after the collapse of the rubber workers. He had first felt the passion for what he was doing as a teenager, working as a runner for the union during a strike in the late 1950s.

His theory was that you need to think creatively in disputes. More often, he had no plan as he went about putting together a strategy for the Bridgestone/Firestone effort. Rather, he relied on a bunch of hunches, assuming that something would work out. He believed in putting a human face on the campaign, so he enlisted several rubber workers and their families. He used their pictures in news media campaigns and sent the workers and their families overseas to campaign at Bridgestone facilities worldwide.

In Argentina, Brazil, and Turkey, the union was able to stir brief plant stoppages. It brought on rallies at Bridgestone plants in Spain and France. He sent demonstrators to Bridgestone/Firestone meetings and to industry conventions in the United States, hoping to embarrass or disrupt them. On the theory that a consumer boycott might hurt the giant tire maker, about 60 workers were put on the payroll full-time to demonstrate at malls. It's not clear whether the boycott ever made a significant impact on the company's finances.

That was not the point, however. Fernandez was searching for more pressure points and more ways to apply pressure. Because the union had the finances to back him, he was able to keep trying.

The union peppered Japanese officials in the United States with complaints about the company's treatment of its workers and orchestrated demonstrations outside consulates across the nation. Late at night he would regularly fax the union's doings directly to Yoichiro Kaizaki, Bridgestone's president, making sure he would not be sheltered from what was happening. He had Kaizaki's private fax number.

Then he decided to take the battle to a higher level, to Japan. For months, the rubber workers had asked for help from the Japanese unions and gotten nowhere. He first asked Rengo, the large Japanese national labor federation that also represented Bridgestone's workers. But this labor group, which had cooperated with Japanese firms' belief in company unionism, would not go along. So he took a chance. He approached the much smaller Zenrokyo, a left-wing union group. With its help, the union was able to carry out street demonstrations in Japan.

To add to the flair of the street theater, he sent over a 15-foot-high puppet of Mother Jones, the legendary labor organizer. Five families of striking rubber workers—husbands, wives, and children—joined in the demonstrations in Japan. Rengo complained to the AFL-CIO that the steelworkers were cooperating with radicals. But Rengo was nudged into speaking up on behalf of the American workers with Bridgestone officials.

ON THE HOMEFRONT: CAMP JUSTICE

Then another inspiration struck Fernandez. He would take the battle to Bridgestone/Firestone's front door, as he had once before with Ravenswood.

Near Bridgestone/Firestone headquarters on the edge of the Nashville airport, Fernandez secretly rented an empty grassy lot. Then the union announced the creation of Camp Justice right at the doors of the company. Tire workers from all of the struck plants were invited for a mass demonstration and the initiation of Camp Justice. Thinking they were seizing the land, the workers were greatly inspired by the union's show of bravery.

As they marched by the company's headquarters, several workers up front decided to dash toward the shining glass and concrete building, and the crowd took off behind them, racing headlong toward the building and then its lobby. It was controlled anarchy. Nothing came of it except a quick, breathless panic by Bridgestone officials. The union had shown its grit and scared the company. Fernandez was pleased. The union had to show that the dispute was gaining tension, that it was approaching a dangerous level of anger.

Camp Justice had two large tents that became home to strikers who had not yet been called back and to others who were supporting the union. It was staffed around the clock, seven days a week. Every Wednesday there was a march from Camp Justice to the front doors of the company's headquarters. Workers planted tomatoes, cabbages, peppers, and onions, figuring that the garden would be needed in a few months.

Suzie Watts and Annie Floyd drove down from Decatur at the start of one weekend in March 1996, eager volunteers for whatever the union wanted. That day they gathered at the Nashville airport and stood at the gate where Chuck Ramsey, the head negotiator for Bridgestone/Firestone, was arriving. Then they trailed him through the airport. The commotion at the airport, the feeling of being involved in a movement of such energy, the sense of being in the middle of something so important—all of it was exciting to Suzie, who told Annie how much she had enjoyed the day.

Suzie's husband, Dave, was back home in Decatur. He had been called back to the tire plant in the fall and was building tires again. He hated the new 12-hour shifts and the constant rotation from days to nights. He was falling asleep at the machine, falling asleep going home. Suzie told him he did not have to stay on the job. The strike had taught them they could live without the company. They would get by. But he felt he had to go back to the plant after all they had gone through.

Rather than spend the night in the tent at Camp Justice near the Bridgestone/Firestone headquarters, Suzie and Annie stayed at a nearby motel, planning to move to the steelworkers' site the next day. They had a nighttime cookout at the camp and sat talking with others. Excited but tired, they headed for the motel. Annie woke up early the next morning, stirred by the first light pouring into the motel room, and casually took a look over at her friend. Apparently Suzie was still asleep. Some time went by, and Annie was eager to get to the camp, where breakfast was cooking.

"Come on, Suzie, let's get going," she said, in a hurry.

No response. She walked over to Suzie's bedside, stared down, and put her hand on her friend. Suzie was cold. She had died during the night.

It was her heart. A few years earlier it was discovered that she had high blood pressure. But Dave didn't realize that there were other problems with her heart. There had been little he didn't know about her. They had a small circle of friends, their children, and themselves, and that had been their greater world. To Dave, Suzie was friend and partner. He had been 17 years old when they married. He was a grandfather in his early forties. She was 41 years old when she died.

The Wattses' friends, the new ones they had made in town from the beginning of the disputes and even some from the union headquarters from Akron, as well as the old friends who knew them growing up around Decatur, came to the services at the Alter–Wikoff Funeral Home in nearby Macon. Suzie was buried in Mt. Gilead Cemetery, Decatur.

Dave dutifully copied and saved the *Decatur Herald & Review* article "Steelworkers Mourn Death" for Suzie's clippings, which he updated. *SteelLabor*, the union's magazine, ran a small article about her too, along with her photo.

> March 30, Susan Kay Watts died in battle in Nashville, Tenn. So, where was this war that Susan lost her life in? Right here in America. Not on some foreign soil as so many of our proud soldiers have before. It was a battle nonetheless—the same battle that corporate America has waged on middle-class laborers for several years now.
>
> She had devoted her time to defend the rights of all of the laborers at Bridgestone/Firestone. She was serving her time at the camp set up at the Bridgestone/Firestone headquarters in Nashville, called Camp Justice.
>
> No, she is not the first casualty of this war. Due to the extreme tension we are working under and forced 12-hour rotating shifts, we have had a lot of losses due to heart failure, nervous breakdowns and other stress-related illnesses. Most of our casualties have been the older fellows . . . you know, the ones that went to work every day, never caused any trouble, just did their job, and, as a reward for being . . . good employee[s], are now forced to work 12-hour rotating shifts, holidays and weekends.
>
> I hope that Suzie's children realize that in the eyes of all labor, she is our hero. Susan, thank you for serving.
> —ERIC W. LITTRELL, Oreana
> Letter to the editor,
> *Decatur Herald & Review*, May 5, 1996

Decatur and the labor strife that catapulted the city to national attention are featured prominently in a CBS news documentary on the decline of America's middle class, scheduled to air tonight.

The hour-long special, which will be carried at 8 P.M. on WCIA (CBS, Champaign), is titled "Who's Getting Rich and Why Aren't You?" It attempts to explain why, in 1995, more than 400,000 Americans saw their hopes of achieving the American dream collapse.
> —*Decatur Herald & Review*, August 8, 1996

PART VII

Heartfelt Losses

C H A P T E R 2 9

Unhealing Wounds

1996

Large, thickly wrapped bales of natural rubber from Southeast Asia sit piled in a high-ceilinged warehouse room at the Bridgestone/Firestone factory. Across the smoky, timeworn, red-brick tire factory, newly finished tires weighing 15 to 50 pounds are rolling off a conveyor belt. From start to stop, if all goes well—if there are no breakdowns, no machinery snafus—it should take about 40 minutes to build each tire.

In the heart of the mechanized rush and cacophony are the factory's tire builders, each working alone, working almost like an individual artist, a medieval craftsman at a single machine. The tire builder works at keeping up with the pace as strands of rubber and steel, melded together, hurtle along a warren of conveyor belts and through massive machines that bake and mold and press the rubber amalgam, throwing out smoke and heat and noise and a product that has to be shaped into a tire. The tire builder sculpts an industrial gem.

Most tire builders work against the clock, hurrying to beat the factory-set line speed, because that is how they are paid: by how fast they cut the rubber with their knives and then knit and shape together the rubber parts. The faster they go, the more tires they build and heave onto the pile beside them, the more they get paid. Some tire builders are paid by the hour. But the risk and the gamble, when they are winning, go to those working against the clock.

For all of the years Dave Watts had built tires at the Bridgestone/ Firestone plant, and for all of his massive size and strength, he was not

243

doing the job the way he once did. He could not adjust to the changing shifts after he returned to work from the strike: 12-hour days, 12-hour nights. Going from nights to days and back to nights. He could not adjust to life without his wife.

Alone, uneasy, unattached to almost everything around him, he drifted.

Seven months after his wife, Suzie, had passed away at Camp Justice, a foreman called him in one day at the factory and handed him a reprimand: He was not building tires fast enough. He was stunned.

Didn't they understand that his wife had died a few months ago, that the last few years had changed so much for him, and that he was still recovering from all these traumas?

How cold.

How insensitive.

He returned to his tire-building machine, stood there, and then started to cry. A feeling of being out of control welled up in him. A rage to smash the foreman and all of the people who had crushed his spirit. A union official who had sat with him through the meeting with the foreman by chance saw him crying on the factory floor and rushed to his side. He was going to smash them, Dave said again and again. He was going to get back at them. The union representative, thinking quickly, whisked him off the factory floor.

Union and factory officials agreed that they knew what to do with him from then on. They listed him in the temporary employment category loosely described around the union hall as "mental," otherwise known as being on psychological leave. That way he would get his pay while recovering.

After the strike ended in defeat for the rubber workers, there were a handful of other so-called mentals at the factory. But in another sense there were many mentals. Indeed, there were far many more who were still suffering emotional bruises from the labor disputes. The difficulty was telling how serious the wounds were.

In some cases the bruises seemed to heal with help from friends and relatives; in other cases, with the passage of time or with space put between the hurt and the person's life. Retirement was a common solution. Many of the workers were in their late middle years already, so retirement was not out of the question. They found work, like Jerry Floyd, in town, usually at lower-paying jobs. Some went to work for the farmers, who could always use farm hands.

But, so, too, many could not be healed—neither right away nor anytime soon. They could not retire or find another job and forget so easily.

This is the cost of labor disputes that endure, that turn into contests of blind will and grit, that is almost impossible to calculate. There are loosely based mathematical formulas for the number of deaths associated with plant closings. A labor dispute is sometimes the emotional equivalent of a plant closing and a job loss and more. It is disorder for people who live their lives by order. It is the uprooting of traditions for people who set their lives by tradition. It is chaos and confusion for people who get through their lives by what they do day-to-day on the job.

FACING THE BEYOND

Dan Lane delivered newspapers and worked as a church janitor, all the while itching to do something with the passion about labor that had been stirred within him. He felt that his life had been changed, but he was unsure what came next. He was filled with ideas, uncertain as to what he would do about them.

Dave Watts, the former president of the Staley workers' union, quit the plant and vowed never to have anything to do with unions again. He was going to do outdoor work, home repairs. He needed time to forget.

The problem was that the situation could not be forgotten readily because it refused to fade away so easily—not just for the workers but also for the town, the companies, and many of those caught up in the confrontations. There was no quick cure for an economy that had devalued blue-collar jobs. As Caterpillar's workers slowly began returning to work, called back by the company in groups, not en masse as some workers had expected, worries continued. What would happen to those who, with so little to do for a year and a half, had developed a drinking problem? How would those whose marriages had broken up, whose lives were disordered, whose family squabbles had grown more intense, whose old furies had awakened from the dark, do now?

In Peoria, where the largest number of Caterpillar workers were located, social work agencies had seen a rise in family problems as the strike had lingered on. Union officials talked loosely about a dozen suicides but backed away from mentioning any names. One social work agency offered to help the union with advice for workers, and the union quickly accepted the offer.

The time he spent with a number of Vietnam veterans among the Caterpillar workers caused Richard Shepherd, a psychologist with the Veterans Administration in Peoria, to have a frightening premonition. He feared an explosion of anger as they returned to the factories, an explosion not unlike those that had surged for a while at U.S. post offices. A few Caterpillar workers had, in fact, set up a dirty tricks division during the strike. They had staged nighttime forays onto the plant's grounds, decked out in camouflage garb and wearing night vision glasses. They were just looking around. Nobody was hurt. But it was very real to them. It was as if they were in combat again. Fear and excitement filled them. They felt they were really alive again.

For others the feelings were far more mixed and confusing. There were nightmares not unlike those they had had after Vietnam. They had feelings of mixed loyalties: Whom did they serve, the company or the union? Workers who had rushed to fill in for the strikers had pangs of uncertainty about what they had done to neighbors. Factory floor bosses who found themselves at great odds with workers were caught up in the confusion, because these were the same men they had fought with in Vietnam.

Some veterans, who identified closely with the union's cause, had trained themselves, as in Vietnam, to see things as black or white: the union versus the company, themselves versus the enemy, themselves fighting the right fight, sacrificing themselves to protect their buddies. The pressure of the moment had forced them to narrow their understanding. A number of those who came to Shepherd for help felt that way.

There were some who recalled the grim downside of their return home from the war in Vietnam, how they felt rejected and reviled for what they had done and for what they initially thought had been right. The strike's collapse and their neighbors' coolness or, worse, the rejection of what they had thought was so important all of a sudden brought the bad old feelings rushing back. And there were others who were simply swept up, or felt as though they were, by circumstances beyond their control.

A month after the UAW had voted down Caterpillar's contract but collapsed its strike and agreed to go back to work under the company's terms, 50-year-old Bob Griffin returned to the factory in Decatur. Every day when he came home from work, he would sit by himself, breathing deeply and trying to calm his thoughts. His wife would urge him to relax and to accept the fact that the union's fight was over. He had a family to live for. He had a life ahead. He had already suffered a heart attack in 1992 after the UAW first struck in Decatur.

It was not easy for him, however, to put his mind at rest. The factory seemed more like a prison than ever before. He was so sure that the foremen were watching for any wrong steps or signs of continued rebellion by the union. He was convinced they were watching him. A veteran machine operator, he had been assigned to new equipment that he did not know how to use. The company had reassigned the strikers to new equipment and new tasks on a wholesale basis.

So two younger, recently hired workers had to teach Griffin how to do his job. What a slap in the face, he thought. Here he was, a veteran worker, and he had to be trained by two young outsiders.

He had not been back at work a week before he hit the button for his machine to start, stepped back, and just blacked out. His heart had failed him again. He spent the next few days in the hospital, wondering what was ahead.

"As we pause to reflect on this past year, many of us wonder what we have accomplished. For the working stiff, there probably has not been much change, but let me at least point out some positives."
—RANDY MORRELL, quoted in *Decatur Herald & Review*, December 31, 1996

Leave No Bodies Behind

The Autoworkers Live Up
to Their Word

1996–1998

Being back at work changed nothing. The Caterpillar workers were still miserable, still angry. They didn't like being losers, didn't like facing continued uncertainty, didn't like the feeling of always being watched by their bosses, didn't like working next to scabs. Didn't like, at all, the way things had turned out.

They had only one outlet left for expressing their dissatisfaction, and Randy Morrell was ready to give it to them.

Morrell believed the local could have made its decisions differently over the years. He believed the local needed a new, young leadership and sensed that the members agreed. He was right. When he ran for local president against Larry Solomon, he won by a two-to-one margin.

Larry was stunned at first. He had heard talk before the election that Randy would be a better person to get along with the company now that the strike was over. But he couldn't believe the members would turn their backs on all his years of experience. Larry was convinced that Detroit had set up Randy as his opposition to punish him for siding with the union's dissidents over the years. There was no question that he was not popular at Solidarity House. Detroit saw Larry as a loose cannon, a troublemaker, a maverick like the handful of others that gave it a hard time. Larry saw Detroit as putting its own interests before whatever else mattered for the local.

Larry quietly went back to work in the factory in June 1996, where he had not been for nine years. It took a long time for him to return to the union hall, and when he did, he stopped by only briefly.

Back inside the plant he showed his grit, he said with a crusty smile, by telling his bosses flatly that he wouldn't take any garbage from them. And they didn't give him a hard time, he bragged. Not Larry Solomon. They had assigned him to inspection, and he found the work that he would be doing until his retirement fascinating. He had just less than two years to retirement. He could have retired in May 1993 if the company had counted the time when the union had been on strike. But that wasn't the situation when he went back to work.

Every day there was something different for him to review on the job. He worked in salvage, going over rejected industrial parts and materials.

GRIEVANCE BY GRIEVANCE, RULE BY RULE: HOW CATERPILLAR AND THE UAW MEMORIALIZED LEGAL TRENCH WARFARE

After all the turmoil that had taken place, after the parades and marches within the plants, after the union's harassment of scabs and line crossers, Caterpillar officials felt they had to enforce rules that would control the returning strikers. They were terrified that the factories would be cauldrons of seething UAW fury. So for eight weeks the returning workers would have to abide by strict new rules: The returning workers could not discuss the strike or wear anything that smacked of the strike. The company had discussed its planning for this with the National Labor Relations Board, through its office in Peoria, and was positive it had the NLRB's approval. But it didn't. The NLRB balked, saying the rules amounted to a gag rule, and, furthermore, they were unprecedented.

As soon as the company enforced the rules, the union had the NLRB on its side. Once again a battle began between the UAW and the company, and as had become the case over time as the confrontation developed, the government in the form of the NLRB was on the union's side.

From the start of the situation that led to the strike the union had had skirmishes with the company in the courts, but as other tactics used against the company proved ineffective, the union stepped up its fight through the NLRB. After a short while, Stan Eisenstein, an attorney with a veteran labor law firm who represented the UAW, concluded it was going to be a long-term fight and decided he would not even look for short-term victories.

Whatever the costs—for the high-priced Chicago law firm that had represented it for years, as well as for the local attorneys it used in all of its NLRB cases—Caterpillar was prepared to go the distance, figuring it would be far cheaper than losing to the union. Its officials repeatedly pointed out to their attorneys that what had happened to one-time manufacturing giants like International Harvester, the industrial dinosaurs that had shrunk or disappeared, would not befall Caterpillar. Caterpillar, its officials said, would not follow that route.

HAND-TO-HAND LEGAL COMBAT

So Caterpillar and the UAW turned their dispute into legal trench warfare. Stuck in the middle was the NLRB, overworked, understaffed, and underfunded, a victim of long-term government indifference and political squabbling between the Clinton White House and congressional Republicans cheered on by the business community.

By the time the battle had ended between the union and the company, the UAW had filed several hundred complaints and the NLRB had issued more than 400 charges against Caterpillar, the largest single amount ever filed by the agency against one company. The legal bills were staggering for both, but even greater for the company. There were days in court when the company had more attorneys on hand than the union and the government combined.

But did Caterpillar back down? Never.

BROTHER, CAN YOU SPARE A LEGAL PAD?

They battled over what was written on the buttons that some of the union members covered themselves with. They battled over what was written on the shirts some UAW members wore. They battled over who said what to whom and when on the job, how the company disciplined workers for what they did on the outside, as well as inside its factories. Caterpillar was determined to stay in charge, determined not to let chaos take over again inside the plants. And the union was determined to assert its rights and make trouble for Caterpillar as it persisted. The bickering went on and on.

Furious that some union representatives had taken part in a demonstration against the company at a business convention in Las Vegas, the company stopped paying them to do the union's work—dealing with grievances and other workplace issues—on company time. Over the length of their dispute, more than 400 workers were disciplined in one way or another by the company, according to the NLRB's count.

Slowly these cases worked their way up through the NLRB's paperwork chain of command and reached the board itself. After the board's fourth ruling against Caterpillar, it slapped the company's hands and declared that two years of negative decisions did not appear to have had an impact on the company. The only way to stop the company from continuing its unlawful behavior, the board announced, was to issue a wide-ranging cease and desist order.

Caterpillar fumed, appealed every ruling against it, and publicly castigated the NLRB. When the NLRB ruled that Caterpillar had to treat strikers the same as replacement workers, and thereby compensate the strikers for the free meals and other goodies that the replacement workers had received, the company was livid. It was only further proof, the company said, that the NLRB was willing to "go to ridiculous lengths to support the UAW's harassment tactics against Caterpillar."

Ever the righteous warrior, Caterpillar went further with its attack on the board's "anti-business bias."

Undeterred by the possible lack of propriety in attacking a federal agency, Caterpillar flatly said it could not expect a fair ruling from the board because its chairman, William B. Gould, had once been a UAW attorney and board member Margaret Browning had been a union attorney and, on top of that, her husband had had clients who had sued Caterpillar. It didn't matter that Gould had only briefly been a UAW attorney more than 30 years ago, some time before he became a respected law professor. Caterpillar asked for Gould and Browning to step down.

They refused. The NLRB cases, the company declared, were not bringing the two sides any closer to a bargain.

BUSINESS ON THE ATTACK

For 12 years the nation's unions had grumbled about the Reagan–Bush NLRB, but now business was having its turn. However, there was no equality between the two battles. The Republican control over Congress meant that the business community's gripes were easily translated into anemic budget increases for the NLRB. Starved financially by Congress, the NLRB began to function even more slowly. Its backlog mounting, its ability to move fast on urgent issues dulled, it was increasingly ineffective at getting its job done.

While the business community was fuming about an NLRB out of control, board chairman Gould saw the agency suffering from "political intimidation" and himself facing a political inquisition. He never really had a chance on the job. The business community had tried its best to stall the appointment of Gould, the board's first African American chairman, and he had waited on and on for his appointment to come through. Erudite, outspoken, unwilling to temper his words, Gould had drawn more criticism for what he said than what he did.

Ironically, organized labor did not make much of a fuss over Gould's appointment problems. It pointed its fingers at the Republicans and said not much could be done in Congress, its typical excuse. But if the White House and the unions had really cared about Gould's appointment, they would have put up a stronger fight to overcome the Republican opposition to the Stanford University law professor, who finally took office in 1994.

Under Gould, the NLRB issued an unprecedented number of injunctions, showing an unusual willingness by the agency to step in immediately. The goal, Gould often explained, was to stop companies from using delaying tactics. Though he was certainly a believer in unions, his attacks were not one-sided, and he considered himself independent. Gould, who often proudly pointed out that he was the great-grandson of a slave who had fought in the Civil War, had written about racial discrimination within the nation's unions years before, and during his tenure the NLRB came down strongly on unions that violated labor laws.

"They [unions] must rid themselves of the lethargy and radically restructure their organizations along the lines of early industrial unions. This, of course, is unlikely to happen unless some external force, economic or otherwise, prods them to do so," he wrote in 1993.

CATERPILLAR TURNS ON THE NLRB

Privately, NLRB officials in Washington and Peoria were at a loss over what to do about Caterpillar's attack on the agency's impartiality. They expected more and more cases down the road and saw little chance that either side would settle them. If any deals were to be struck, the union insisted, they had to be formal; Caterpillar would accept only informal arrangements. The UAW would not bend. This was not a formula for industrial peace.

For those somewhat removed from the legal battle, it all seemed tiring and endless. After the NLRB overruled a decision by one of its administrative judges, Caterpillar was furious again and the UAW was beating its chest, boasting that it was clearly standing up for justice. The *Peoria Journal Star*, whose reporting had infuriated the company at times, pondered Caterpillar's outrage in a December 1996 editorial:

> Come now, the entire world can't be against Caterpillar, can it? Actually this is what we get when both sides believe they are right—not just mostly right, but absolutely, 100 percent, willing-to-bet-the-mortgage-on-it right. Problem is that is not where most of us live.
>
> Isn't it possible, even likely, that some UAW member really did deserve to be fired? Isn't it possible, even likely, that Caterpillar went too far with others? Isn't it possible that both sides are right? And wrong?
>
> Unfortunately in the black-and-white world occupied by both Caterpillar and the UAW, there's no room for second guessing, no room to open that door a crack. If you're not with them, you're against them. It's why we still don't have a contract settlement.

MEANDERING TOWARD A DEAL

Months passed, and nothing seem to be happening. Then, in January 1998, the company and the union were locked again in talks, but little news leaked from the bargaining table. Finally, in February, the union announced that it had a deal, and Richard Shoemaker parroted what was beginning to sound like a laborwide union motto: It was the best the union could get. The company, as cautious as ever but insistent on asserting its will, said a great bargain had been brokered.

The union's members were not convinced.

Although he himself could not vote because he had retired some months before, Larry urged the workers to vote down the contract. The union should not drop the NLRB charges against the company, he said. Nor, he said, should they be dropped from the record so that they would no longer hang over Caterpillar. These conditions were part of the contract deal.

In a move that stunned Detroit, the workers voted down the contract offer. Decatur was the most resistant of the locals. Nine out of ten of its votes went against the contract. Shoemaker had expected the rejection, knowing it was a measure of the deep distrust and resentment that had overtaken many members. And he had warned the company to expect it.

It was nearly the same contract that Caterpillar had offered six and a half years earlier. It contained all of the concessions and had unraveled years of bargaining. It would mean the end of the union's NLRB battles, freeing the company from paying out millions to the strikers. But it also had no amnesty for the more than 150 workers who had been let go by the company during the strike, and on that the company would not bend. Refusing to grant amnesty was a fatal move for the union and the company. After making these workers martyrs, the union had failed to bring them back into the fold.

The day after the vote Richard Zerfowski was outside the plant's gates at the start of the shift change, holding up a large green bucket for donations for those like him who had been fired by Caterpillar.

The deal making seemed dead. But within weeks the company had returned with a new willingness to deal. It would take back the workers.

In Decatur and Peoria and all of the Midwestern towns where the Caterpillar workers live, in the diners and at the post offices and gas stations where people bump into each other, this was what they talked about. The company had backed down. And the community was abuzz with speculation. What had caused the turnaround? Had the decision to bargain come from the top? Was this a signal that Fites had relented?

Some close to the negotiations claimed this was the real scenario, but Shoemaker doubted it. The company was simply determined to get a contract, and it was making a compromise.

The Decatur workers still didn't like what they saw. The contract represented almost everything the union had resisted. It marked the end of an annual raise. There would be only one true pay boost in six years; the rest would be lump sum payments or cost-of-living increases. New hires would come in at 70 percent of the top wages and work their way up. The company could hire temporary workers at low wages and not offer any benefits. The company did not have to keep a fixed number of workers on the job, which meant it could whittle away at the workforce in Decatur and elsewhere. That would ultimately weaken the union. And there were changes in the company's health plan. To top it off, the contract would lock the union in for six years, far longer than previous contracts it had signed with the company.

Again, Decatur was the most resistant, voting by more than 70 percent against the contract.

This time, however, the contract passed, winning the approval of the Caterpillar workers. In the following days there was a spin among the workers that made the contract more acceptable. It was said that the contract wasn't a complete defeat. The difference this time was that the union didn't leave anyone outside the gates.

It was not like Vietnam, as one veteran told Randy Morrell. They didn't leave anyone on the battlefield.

Small victory. The company had set out to break loose of pattern bargaining, and it had done so. It had set out to trim wages, to end years of annual increases, and it had done that. "The union's concessions underscore the degree to which employers have the upper hand, despite jobless levels that are the lowest in a generation," wrote labor writer Aaron Bernstein in *Business Week*.

What Caterpillar proved most of all is that it no longer had to share its good fortune with its blue-collar workers. And the company had reason to feel good about itself in 1998. From 1993 to 1997, its sales and revenues had grown 63 percent, its profits had jumped 155 percent, and profits per share had soared 176 percent. *Fortune* magazine had put it once again on its list of the "World's Most Admired Companies." Caterpillar chairman Don Fites, in a statement issued by the company, said that the honor "clearly reflects on our highly motivated employees who are committed to meeting the needs of customers around the world."

WE ARE STILL STANDING
ON OUR FEET

A few months later and almost 2,000 miles away in Las Vegas, an exuberance radiated from Stephen Yokich, a man of many moods. He smiled. He embraced people. He joked. It was June 1998, and he was the master of ceremonies for a celebration, his reelection as head of the UAW.

Halfway through his speech Yokich came to the sensitive issue of Caterpillar. It was a victory for the union, he said. A victory, he explained, considering the fact that the union had almost lost the strike inasmuch as "there were just as many workers that crossed the picket line as the good ones that stayed out there."

How had it won, considering all of the concessions and so-called give-backs, the loss of protections won years ago?

"We still have union recognition," he said. "We still have pension plans. We still have paid holidays. We still have representation on the plant floor. None of that was on the table before."

Up from the convention floor came a wave of applause, and Yokich urged the Caterpillar workers to stand up and acknowledge the hand they deserved.

"Where are you, brothers?" he asked. "Come on," he implored them.

But there were hardly any Caterpillar workers present. Only two of the locals could have afforded to keep up their dues and send voting delegates halfway across the country. Not Peoria or Decatur. That didn't mean they wanted to stay away. Randy Morrell had asked officials in Detroit whether there was money for some people in Decatur to come out to Las Vegas.

No, there wasn't any, he was told.

At a reception later, where free food and booze drew hundreds to a massive, darkened hall in the convention center and a country and western band was going through its loud routines, Yokich explained again why the Caterpillar workers were winners.

Go anywhere in the country, he said cheerfully, and you will not find many factory workers earning $20 an hour as well as being the recipients of such good benefits. That's why they are winners, he said, and moved on, shaking hands.

Bob Edwards, host: Members of the United Auto Workers have approved a contract with heavy machinery maker Caterpillar. The agreement ends a six-and-a-half-year dispute that began when the last contract ended in the fall of 1991. . . .

Edwards to Harley Shaiken, labor specialist, University of California at Berkeley: What do you know about the agreement?

Shaiken: Well, given all the alternatives for the union, it survived, and that in itself is a victory.

—NATIONAL PUBLIC RADIO, April 23, 1998

Strategic Instincts

The Steelworkers Think Globally

December 1996

Jerry Fernandez had a real dilemma on his hands. Where was the one big shot, the big blow that, along with others, would knock Bridgestone/Firestone down? George Becker wanted the strike over. And Becker was an impatient man who wanted results and not philosophy. He had made clear his feeling that you follow your instincts in a fight and you do what you have to do. Becker had told him point blank, this is the fight. Fernandez liked his job and did not want to disappoint Becker.

But after a sophisticated series of tactics carried out throughout the global network of factories run by the company, Bridgestone/Firestone still was not backing down. From $142 million in losses in 1992, the company's profits had reached $130 million in 1995. The strike and consumer boycott didn't seem to be hurting the tire maker. Bridgestone/Firestone was talking with the union in late 1995, but the talks were not going in the direction the union wanted.

After days of intense talks in Chicago in early 1996, the momentum toward a deal suddenly dissipated. The company was offering to let the union make what it thought was a graceful surrender, but the union wouldn't accept it. The company seemed to be calling the union's bluff, but to the union it didn't make sense to surrender after putting forth so much effort and lifting the hopes of so many.

Meanwhile, organized labor had raised a collective eyebrow at the recent hiring of Ron Bloom as Becker's assistant for special projects. What did Becker have in mind in hiring a 40-year-old investment banker with very upper-crust credentials? Hailing from Philadelphia's Main Line, Bloom had graduated from the very respectable Wesleyan University and earned his master's degree from Harvard's School of Business. He had been an investment banker and then had formed a small firm with another investment banker. Among unions he was known for his intelligence and his sharp mouth.

For all of his dogged, blue-collar ways, Becker was clearly interested in diversifying the thinking at the top of the union.

PLAYING BY EAR AND GUT AND CHECKBOOK

The union kept reaching overseas, after forming an association of Bridgestone unions, hoping that would put pressure on the company. It set up demonstrations at the company's tire and service outlets, targeting more than 800 of them. The thinking was to convince the Japanese leadership that the union would not give up. It had lost the legal battle in the federal appeals courts to block federal contracts for firms that use striker replacements, and the Clinton administration did not push the case any further.

One by one, however, the union added up boycott victories in an era when boycotts rarely worked. More than 30 city governments, including that of Atlanta, agreed not to buy Bridgestone/Firestone products. In an even more stunning win for the union, the Saturn Division of General Motors Corporation said its customers could swap their standard-equipment Bridgestone/Firestone tires for others.

Although company officials continually downplayed the impact of the boycotts and the corporate campaign, saying sales were not down and they were not troubled by the noise the union was making, a path toward settlement was opening up.

The NLRB had filed charges against the company, and company officials were convinced that the NLRB was merely acting as part of a troika, the White House and the unions being the other two. Bridgestone/Firestone expected a ruling from the NLRB any day, calling for an immediate injunction so that the order against the company could be carried out. The company didn't give much credence to the charges, but it expected an expensive court battle over them.

Months before Becker had gone to Tokyo to meet with Bridgestone executive Kaizaki, a meeting that the union considered critical to showing the union's unbending spirit. Kaizaki was not deterred from his campaign to change the way the company did business in America. But the message that came back from Tokyo was that he understood the union's determination not to sign a deal unless its workers were back on the job.

The union's goal soon became a reality. The company had vowed it would not let go any of the 2,000 replacements it had hired during the disputes. Gradually, however, it brought back most of the strikers, so the real obstacle between the union and the company was no longer there.

WAS THIS WORTH IT ALL?

When company negotiators went to a meeting in Chicago, they assumed they would be talking about the NLRB charges and that would be it. But it was quickly clear to them that the union was willing to move ahead: The issue of the replacement workers was no longer a problem because most workers were back on the job.

Over the 27 months of the dispute, the company had established the changes it wanted. It had lowered top wages for new hires from $17 to $12 an hour, set the 12-hour shifts in place, and tied any pay increases to productivity. An annual raise did not exist in the union's absence from the bargaining process, and the contract the company had laid down.

The union deal brought back an annual raise, the first in the tire industry in 14 years. The company waived any charges against workers it disciplined and welcomed back 40 workers it had discharged for strike-related actions. The company also agreed to pay $15 million to the strikers, in amounts that varied according to when they went back to their jobs. The union kept the company's paid health care program, the biggest concession by the company. "Essentially, we wore the company down," Becker told reporters in Pittsburgh when the deal was announced. The union, he said, had waged its battle in 26 countries and faced "the greatest challenge that our union or any union" had ever encountered.

While the union trumpeted its victory, so did the company, but quietly. It had won some controls for overtime and job assignments. It had pushed ahead on incentive programs, arguing that the hourly rate was so close to incentive pay that workers did not have to strive hard to be rewarded. The result: the gap increased between hourly pay and incentive pay for those who worked against the clock. The company had also shifted its plants to 12-hour, seven-day-a-week operations. Moreover, it had killed the NLRB suit, which might have cost it millions.

It was not the pattern agreement the rubber workers had had in mind in 1994. It was a setback for the union in many ways, but the might and lasting power of the steelworkers had beaten back the predictions that the company was going to prevail. Realizing the changes that had been brought and the fury that had been stirred, company officials figured the contract would be defeated and might pass only on the third try. Peter Schofield, one of the company's negotiators, saw it as a real victory inasmuch as the company had redone chunks of the contract that had not been revised in 50 years. Still, he realized it would become difficult to put it all together again. Strikers now worked beside line crossers and replacement workers. That was a fact some in Decatur would not accept, and so they retired.

Much to the company's surprise, the contract passed overwhelmingly. It was the best the union could do, and many grudgingly realized it.

Lost on Eldorado

Late 1999
Decatur, Illinois

Decatur is not the place it was during the strikes. Long gone are the large signs that stamped it as a strike city and a war zone. Traffic on Eldorado, the street that slices through the heart of town, passing the Staley facilities and the downtown, has been increasing. Merchant Street downtown has more stores. A new office building has gone up. A handful of sandwich shops and boutiques are struggling to get by. Most downtown buildings are being turned into professional offices. The hope is that the offices will attract clients who will become customers for the handful of restaurants and shops. Millikin University has been expanding, too. Unemployment has been edging downward, reaching low levels not seen for years

A widespread contentment seems to float on the surface in Decatur, as elsewhere in the United States. In much of the Midwest, it is as if the 1980s and the brief bad days of the 1990s never happened. The old job-producing engines are running again. Auto factories are working overtime, with the auto industry, American and foreign firms, and all of the parts makers employing almost as many workers as a few decades ago. Hiring at some Midwestern companies has even slowed in some places because there are not enough workers.

A SUPERFICIAL HEALING

A cocky sense of well-being flourishes in Decatur. But underneath the faith in the future that has returned to most people lingers a fear of losing out, of falling behind, of coming up short in the end. It is a fear fed by the recent labor disputes: a fear that the good times are over for some, a fear that not everyone clearly shares the same vision, a fear that not everyone benefits from the same payoff.

Some workers are uneasy, unsure, and unnerved about the scenarios they see. They sense that long-term job stability may no longer be an asset. It has turned into a burden, a mark of a lack of flexibility. They see how pensions have been curtailed and how benefits have been trimmed back. They watch as layoffs are no longer synchronous with the bad times, but come and go as their companies change direction or need to bleed themselves to keep profits up. They watch as older workers are pared from the payrolls through massive cutback schemes. They watch as their children earn less than they did when they were starting out. They watch and wonder. Nothing much happens. Meanwhile, they seem to be working harder.

In Decatur, the new jobs pay nothing like those at the still operating large factories with union contracts. In Flint, Michigan, where the remaining middle-aged autoworkers earn $45.06 an hour in wages and benefits, nonunion factory jobs start at $7, the benefits are slim, and the plasma center seems to be one of the big businesses in the heart of downtown. And although wages at the bottom of the pay ladder began growing once again late in the 1990s, cost cutting pares away the quality of those jobs. Low-income workers are losing more of their benefits, their vacations, their company-paid health care, their pension plans.

The way race is discussed in Decatur and who runs Decatur became much louder in debates after the Reverend Jesse Jackson came to town in 1999 in defense of several African American high school students, who had been expelled after a football game brawl. Jackson felt the school board had punished them excessively. The board disagreed. The feud segued into a howl from African Americans and some whites that when it comes to schooling and almost everything else in town they matter very little. Decatur's decision makers did not agree.

Downtown Decatur seems somewhat abandoned. Most of the time an incredible hush fills Central Park, a small grassy green spot downtown where the old Transfer House sits facing the old Civil War monu-

ment. All three of the locally owned department stores closed down
long ago or moved out of the downtown area. Applebaum's, a clothing
store founded in 1910, shut down in 1995.

But don't get the wrong impression.

A Wal-Mart Supercenter recently went up on the east side of
Decatur. Now there are two to shop at. And as soon as the new giant
store opened, other stores, smaller ones, joined it. Someday all of small-
town America will look the same, and they will hand out brochures to
show the strange old days, when from coast to coast across the United
States the scenery actually changed.

THE UNIONS: STILL SINGING THE SAME OLD SONG

Meanwhile, in a great irony, 60 years after the United Automobile
Workers union spilled its own blood in Flint to stand up to General
Motors (GM), the two were fighting the same battle over jobs and the
production line. In 1998 the union was engaged in all-out combat with
GM. Toppled from its perch as the Goliath of U.S. automakers, GM had
been trying to close plants and shed workers. It had far too many workers for its much diminished share of the nation's auto market. But it
could not bring itself to face the union in a showdown, as Caterpillar
had. Nor could it relent if it wanted to thrive.

By calling strikes at two parts plants in Flint, the UAW forced
nearly the entire GM system to come to a halt. The union seemed con-
tent to take the risks that hobbling GM would bring on—retaliation by
the company or such damaging competition from its rivals that it would
have to shed even more workers. After all, the strategy had worked
again and again.

It worked this time too, although there was not much rejoicing
within labor's ranks, and not much of the nation paid attention to the
workplace issues raised by the union. By the time the company and the
union faced each other in negotiations for a new contract in the fall of
1999, the company had learned its lesson. It went out of its way to
avoid angering the union, and the union, realizing that GM had undergone such an intense personality conversion, was quite willing to let
GM share its profits. The same was so for the two other major
automakers. Fighting the union was far less important than reaping the
fruits of a very good year.

For the steelworkers, too, there were still battles to fight. Bridgestone/ Firestone built a new tire plant in South Carolina, an area where unions are not exactly strong, and experts said the steelworkers would have a hard time organizing the new plant. *May 2001 that had proved to be true; the facility was still nonunion.*

The steelworkers faced another gritty battle with a tire maker, German-owned Continental Tire Company, at a plant in Charlotte, North Carolina. Not unlike Bridgestone/Firestone, the company said it faced global competition and pointed to the new nonunion plant owned by Bridgestone/Firestone in South Carolina as a reason for its tough bargaining stance. Not long after the plant's 1,450 workers struck, the company brought in replacement workers. Claiming that the U.S. government had failed to protect workers and failed to live up to international labor standards, the steelworkers and a global alliance of related unions, known as the International Federation of Chemical, Energy, Mine and General Workers' Unions, filed a complaint against the U.S. government with the International Labour Organization in Switzerland.

At the outset, the business–labor relations experts didn't give the union much of a chance. But the steelworkers put pressure on the company at home, in Germany, and in the United States. They spoke up at the firm's shareholders meeting. They demonstrated outside tire dealer's facilities. They targeted the Ford Motor Company with a campaign that said the automaker used tires made by inexperienced workers and strike breakers.

And the union won. In September 1999, a year after the strike began, after only 15 of the striking workers had crossed the union's picket lines, the company and the union signed a six-year agreement. It was the first wage increase for the workers in a decade, and the union had held the line on a number of benefits that the company wanted to shrink. The steelworkers had learned their lesson well in Decatur.

More and more it seemed the only battles the steelworkers faced were do-or-die efforts. Steelworkers president George Becker was convinced the union had no alternative.

At a small meeting of steelworkers during the AFL-CIO's biennial convention in Los Angeles in October 1999, Becker celebrated the union's victory at Ravenswood and all of the others that followed, including Bridgestone/Firestone. Becker lingered long, giving detail after detail and pointing out what a great victory it had been for the union. "We all grow with these things," he said. "We always come out learning something different."

Despite the steelworkers' victories, including one in which Wheeling-Pittsburgh Steel Corporation bowed to a relentless 10-month campaign, unions staged fewer strikes each year. United Parcel Service was beaten by the Teamsters union because the union had its foot on the company's hand: It could not do business without workers. But such union victories were the exception. If anyone had doubted it before, it was now clearer than ever that only fools or brilliant strategists led unions into strikes.

For security provider Chuck Vance, this reality has meant a number of last-minute cancellations of contracts and continuously dropping business after his company had grown to claim nearly two-thirds of the business of guarding companies in labor disputes. It seemed to Vance that corporate management was willing to give up more as the economy was so good, and that the unions were less likely to put up a battle, realizing they could not win. "There is just not the militancy of the unions anymore," he said.

Likewise, the AFL-CIO's John Sweeney proved to be more moderate than the bomb thrower his foes had feared. Rather than turning loose howling union crowds to tie up America's streets, he met with Chamber of Commerce types and traveled to Switzerland to tell the world's richest executives what was on labor's mind.

Organized labor did awake from its near fatal slumber, but it remained haunted by the question of what comes next. Under Sweeney, it poured more money than ever into the 1996 presidential election and then geared up to beat back a drive in California to tie its hands by forcing unions to let workers opt out of funding their unions' political efforts. Fearful at first about the challenge, it won.

Where it had been a hapless victim of the Clinton administration's rush to embrace the North American Free Trade Agreement, it found new strength and helped block Clinton from gaining "fast track" powers to push the new trade agreement with Latin America through Congress. But organized labor couldn't withhold its embrace of Clinton and the Democrats. Al Gore got its endorsement early in his presidential campaign, and it threw more muscle than before into the election. That seemed to make a difference among voters from union households. They made up 26 percent of the nation's voters in 2000, up from 23 percent in 1996 and 1998.

CATERPILLAR'S GLOBAL IMPERATIVE

A few months before he stepped down as Caterpillar's CEO in early 1999, Don Fites sat behind a table in a small auditorium within the solemn confines of the Federal Reserve Bank's Chicago regional office. It was a conference on global trade, and Fites, a grand champion for corporate America on the need for free trade, had come to recite the dictum that he had been delivering for several years.

He seemed older, heavier than more than half a dozen years ago. He sat slumped shouldered. His face was covered with a frown from the start, and he seemed ill at ease, impatient with some of the points raised by others as the conference wore on.

"Caterpillar is particularly committed to free trade. We are today globally competitive from a U.S. manufacturing base," he said. And in a few years, he said, the company's commitment to the world market would grow significantly. It would sell, he predicted, nearly three-fourths of what it makes outside the United States, a sizable jump from its current rate of about 50 percent. Foreign trade was especially important, he said, for factories like Decatur, which exports more than 60 percent of what it makes. He railed on about the threat to the United States from "isolationist, protectionist lobbies." He complained about those in Congress who have "no real understanding about trade."

Then he drew a grim portrait of what would happen if his vision of the future of free trade failed to come true and his opponents prevailed. It was a strange but telling insight, a stolid Midwestern CEO foreseeing the day when the only way to compete would be outside the United States.

"If they prevail, leading companies will be forced to move overseas," Fites began, speaking almost in a huff. "You can bet we are going to move manufacturing outside the United States. That is not our strategy. That is not our thinking. But we have our shareholders and our employees to think of."

And the company had done well for its shareholders. Its stocks and its profits headed upward for most of the decade. For several years there was one record harvest of profits after another. But the Asian economic slowdown and the troubles facing American farmers began to eat away at sales for the world's largest construction equipment maker. That didn't faze the company, however. It had plenty of faith, its executives said, in the U.S. economy in the new century. And there were places still to be conquered.

THE SKY COLLAPSES FOR
BRIDGESTONE/FIRESTONE AND WORKERS IN DECATUR

Its cool darkness broken only by the harsh glow of beer companies' neon signs, the Sundown Lounge is normally a gloomy place. But late one fall afternoon, an unusually grim foreboding echoed through the tavern, which is just up the road from the tire plant. "It just breaks my heart," softly confided a tall, thin middle-aged worker at the tire plant, who had known no other job since he was 18 years old and who had once nearly lost an arm to a tire-making machine at the plant. Despite that near tragedy, he had kept working at the factory.

Hunched by the bar, clutching a can of beer, he barely looked up as he spoke. "I got 28 years in there. What happens if it folds? What happens to my family? Gee, I'd like to see the offspring work there."

The dreamlike sense of normalcy that had finally settled back over the factory after the labor disputes had collapsed, once again.

Following its struggle with the union, Bridgestone/Firestone seemed to have put aside its problems in the United States for a time. As the Japanese company's largest arm, Bridgestone/Firestone also became a financial crutch the tire maker learned to lean on as Japan's economy slumped.

The global rivalry among tire makers had grown more intense than ever, but the company had appeared up to the challenge. The $70 billion world tire market looked like it was headed toward being ruled by fewer and fewer players. First, the Goodyear Tire & Rubber Company said it had set up a global alliance with Sumitomo Rubber Industries. That alliance displaced Bridgestone as the world's largest tire manufacturer. Then Cooper Tire & Rubber Company and Pirelli Tires, a division of Italian-owned Pirelli S.p.A., set up their own global deal.

With 12-hour shifts firmly in place, there were many more complaints at the union hall in Decatur about sore feet and repetitive stress problems: pain in hands and shoulders. At least, though, the shifting between daytime and nighttime hours at the factory had stopped. Since incentive pay rates had been cut back slightly, there were more complaints about how much harder it was to make money. To union officials it seemed that a number of the front-line managers who had gotten along well with workers had also been replaced after the strike ended. But hiring was markedly up; more people were needed to work the around-the-clock hours, and the local's leaders were trying to calm the bad blood between the scabs and those who had remained loyal to the union.

Then came reports of Bridgestone/Firestone's unraveling tires.

In much the same way they had been stunned by the problems that arose with the strike, the plant's workers were caught off guard by the cloud that began to hover over them and their plant in the summer of 2000. Once again they talked about losing out, and how the company had treated them during the labor dispute. They talked about their fury toward those who had crossed the union's picket lines, but there was danger in such talk, as union officials quickly realized. It confirmed the swiftly growing image that the plant was a hotbed of troubles, the result of which may have been that the plant had made bad tires. The union saw that such an impression was certain to backfire on them.

They were right about one thing: they said they felt helpless to change their fate. Indeed, they were caught up in a problem of massive proportions: a widening consumer safety crisis with seemingly no clear culprit for the loss of lives, and the number of injuries suffered from Bridgestone/Firestone tires that were coming apart on U.S. highways. They were just blue-collar workers in a Midwestern town trapped between feuding global giants, a slow-moving federal bureaucracy, and a rapidly expanding army of lawyers.

The tires were the company's ATX and Wilderness AT tires, tires built for sport utility vehicles (SUVs), pickup trucks, and light trucks. They were built for a number of vehicles, but most of the tires were headed for the Ford Motor Company's highly popular Explorer-model SUV. Some of the tires were built at other Bridgestone/Firestone plants, but the Decatur plant accounted for a large number of one of the tire models, and nearly all the other's line of production. Ford and Bridgestone/Firestone clearly blamed the Decatur plant.

The initial response from workers to the crisis came from a residual anger. They had predicted, they said, such problems when the company had replaced them with new workers right off the streets during the strike. They had warned the company that their jobs could not be done by newcomers. Sought out by plaintiff attorneys searching for the blame for the tire failures, some former Decatur workers provided the gist of

an argument that the company's management style and later the upheaval at the factory were likely causes for the defective tires.

These workers testified that quality had been sacrificed at the plant
for the sake of quantity, that loose manufacturing procedures had been
followed, and that the inspection system had been compromised. As
these claims became public, company officials strongly repudiated
them, and pointed out that the criticism came from former workers
who most likely were deeply disgruntled by the labor dispute.

But neither could the blame be pinned exclusively on Decatur's
workers, according to some of the attorneys and tire safety experts involved. If it was true that Decatur's workers had been careless, whether
intentionally or not, why weren't there problems with other tire models
manufactured in the Decatur plant?, they asked. And why were so many
of the tires defective? It would have taken widespread violations of factory rules by many workers to mess up so badly. That didn't seem possible. There were also bad tires from other plants, though not as many as
from Decatur, and some experts suspected that the company was using
its labor-related difficulties in Decatur as a smokescreen to hide the real
problem.

The speculation went on and on. Maybe it was because the tires were
manufactured in short runs, and so the company incurred start-up problems, the experts said. Or maybe it was because the Decatur factory was so
old that unwanted elements, such as plaster dust, had been added to the
tires or the rubber at some point in the manufacturing process. Or maybe
it simply had to do with the way the tires were designed, not how they
were made. That was a line of questioning Bridgestone/Firestone officials
began to follow. As they updated the results from a much publicized investigation of the problem by the company, the officials said they were
looking at both how the tires were designed, but also what it was in the
manufacturing at Decatur that might have gone wrong.

Whatever went wrong, if the alarms set up by the government and
the companies involved to catch such problems had gone off, they were
ignored until the fatalities began to pile up.

In July 1998, a curious researcher for State Farm Insurance had notified the National Highway Traffic Safety Administration (NHTSA), the
government agency that oversees the nation's auto and tire manufacturers, of 21 cases of failed Bridgestone/Firestone tires that the Illinois-
based insurer had encountered. But the researcher's e-mail message
failed to prompt swift action from the long overworked and understaffed federal agency.

Then in February 2000, a news report on Houston television station KHOU-TV, Channel 11, said that Bridgestone/Firestone tires on Ford Explorers might have been the cause of a number of fatal crashes around the United States. A major source of the report were lawsuits alleging that Bridgestone/Firestone tires were defective. A handful of cases had been filed and settled in the 1990s. But the cases were sealed, as tire safety experts pointed out, by gag orders. Company officials insisted, however, that the gag orders only barred the lawyers and families from discussing the amounts of the settlements and trade secrets. Spurred on by similar news reports and its own research, the NHTSA soon opened an investigation of the tires.

In August, Ford and Bridgestone/Firestone jointly announced the second biggest tire recall in the history of the United States. It amounted to 14.4 million tires—6.5 million of them still on the road. The tires were dangerous because the tire treads could suddenly peel apart and cause accidents. A month later the government warned that another 1.4 million tires, most of them built in Decatur, might also be dangerous. But the company would not agree to recall them as well.

Caught up in a windstorm of criticism, the company flailed about, switching its explanations. At first, it defended its product and suggested that drivers had not taken good care of the tires. But at U.S. Congressional hearings in September, CEO Masatoshi Ono, who soon after stepped down from his job, issued a public apology. The company also pointed the finger at Ford, suggesting that the tire failures might be related to Ford's suggested air inflation levels for the tires, which differed from Bridgestone/Firestone's prescribed amount. A company official also pointed out that there were an alarming number of rollovers of SUVs, including Ford's Explorer. Ford officials were livid. The problem was not Ford's vehicles, but the Bridgestone/Firestone tires, said Jacques Nasser, Ford's CEO. Furthermore, the tire maker had not let Ford know soon enough that it had information about problems with the tires. But several senators were dubious about whether Ford had really been left in the dark. Hadn't the company recalled similarly labeled Bridgestone/Firestone tires in at least two countries?, they asked. Yes, Nasser replied, but he explained that Ford had been reassured by Bridgestone/Firestone that the overseas problems had nothing to do with the tires being distributed in the United States.

In Japan, Bridgestone President Yoichiro Kaizaki didn't blame the U.S. workers and managers openly. But he lamented at a Tokyo press conference that the company had failed to exert the kind of quality control in the United States that was carried out in Japan and that Firestone officials didn't deal with problems in the way Bridgestone managers do.

By the fall of 2000, the government said it had received reports linking over 119 deaths, 500 injuries, and more than 3,700 complaints to the troubled tires. The tire company said it was looking at why so many of the tire failures involved tires mounted on the rear axle of vehicles. The publicity and the financial burden of the crisis had taken a toll on the company. Its sales were down and the company said it expected to run at a loss for the year. In November it said it was also closing three tire plants for short periods. One of them was the Decatur plant, where it laid off 450 of the plant's 1,950 workers, a small number of white-collar workers included. It was uncertain when, if ever, they would come back to their jobs. The plant's shut-down took place during the end-of-the-year holidays. With unemployment low in the Decatur area, community leaders took an optimistic view, hoping that the laid-off workers would quickly find other jobs. But it didn't seem likely that with their skills they would be able to step into jobs paying the $18 an hour that most had earned.

At union local 713's meeting hall, vice-president Randy Gordon was surprised at the number of calls he was getting from laid-off workers who were wondering when they would be back on the payroll. It seemed to him that they were just standing around the telephone, waiting for the call to come back. He couldn't understand that people were so eager to get back to 12-hour shifts, let alone all of the other problems with the plant.

"That shocks the hell out of me," he said in his typically crusty, outspoken way at the meeting hall one cold wintry day. "I don't think there is much of a future here in Decatur. It's an old plant and an old building. If I were a young man I wouldn't want to be working 12s here the rest of my life. I would go to school. I would move on. If nothing changed, I would be definitely be looking."

A FAR DIFFERENT FACTORY

Since the lockout began and ended, the company began changing the way work got done in the vast, rambling A. E. Staley facility.

Not a single human sound, not a laugh, grumble, smoker's cough, or ripple of footsteps on the flights of metal steps or amid the vast rows of tanks. Building 7 felt like a giant industrial mausoleum, its pipes and tanks shifting the starch according to computerized programs tracked by numbers flashing on monitors. No one was opening or closing valves on the pipes to check on things as once was done at the Staley factory. In the building's brightly colored control room, several flights up, sat five computers but only one person, staring at the multicolored screens that blinked with rows of numbers showing how the mammoth tanks and other machines were doing. They were working just fine.

Halfway through his 12-hour shift, the attendant occasionally looked up at a large glass window that showed a colorful, spaghetti-like sprawl of pipes. But the window was an anachronism, a vestigial reminder of precomputerized days, a leftover in the very modernized building. Humans need windows; computers do not. The computer-driven automated equipment had everything under its sightless control. Before, there might have been 10 workers per shift in the building. Now there was just one. Before, the middle-aged, slightly balding worker sitting at the desk might have worked with a wrench or spent long hours walking the factory, checking the equipment, manually opening the valves. Now he worked with a computer's spreadsheet, and he was keeping watch on the machines humming in four buildings at the same time.

Only 146 of the locked-out employees went back to work for the company in 1996; the company had now pared its entire workforce down to 270, and it saw an even smaller payroll ahead.

Staley was Tate & Lyle's major American beachhead, and from there, as it had done before, it pressed on. To Australia. To Slovakia. To Saudi Arabia. To China and Vietnam and India and Morocco and Canada and Botswana and Namibia and India and Hungary and the Czech Republic. Investments here, additions there, new acquisitions left and right. A global giant, it was determined to grow in the 1990s. But the profits were not what the company had hoped for during most of the 1990s.

Declining profits in the sugar industry stiffened Staley's spine, which showed in a labor dispute in New York City that was eerily reminiscent of the one in Decatur. Faced with contract changes that eliminated jobs and most job-security guarantees, nearly 300 workers at the Domino Sugar refinery on the Brooklyn waterfront struck in June 1999. The workers, members of the International Longshoremen's Association, complained of being abandoned by organized labor as their strike dragged on. After 20 months, the union members gave in, calling their strike a failure.

In his wood-paneled office, just beyond the high-ceilinged, dark marble entranceway resembling an elegant old-time bank lobby, Pat Mohan, Staley's public face for most of the labor dispute, was philosophical about its outcome. The union had made a number of bad guesses. It had underestimated the impact of technology, he said. Even more critical, the union, first as the Allied Industrial Workers and then as the United Paperworkers International Union, had not counted on the company's showing such resolve.

These three companies, that fought their workers at the end of the 20th century, won their battles and went on to more profitable days. The unions that survived have slowly begun to regain their footing. Though they have lost ground, they have not disappeared, and that alone is a victory. The UAW threw more money and manpower into organizing and began to win more organizing victories than ever before.

All the parties moved on. But in Decatur and places like it, there's an emptiness, a hollow feeling, a sense that something has been lost.

It is hard to put your finger on it, this something that was lost. It is like the sweet-sour smell that still pours from Staley's tall smokestacks, is carried across town by strong winds, and is spread out toward the flat, endless, open-top prairie.

Though the feeling is there, a lot of people just don't seem to notice it.

A MAP FOR THE ROAD AHEAD

Maybe people don't notice the feeling of emptiness because Decatur's travail ended with hardly a whimper. No marches. Only exhaustion and disappointment that rushed in where frail dreams and stubbornness had lingered. But if you bothered to look, you could read the message the struggle left behind for America's labor unions, for the nation's Decaturs, for workers, for companies, for the rest of us.

In Decatur, American companies learned that they could step over the line and not get slammed for their indiscretion. When the Detroit newspapers, the *Detroit Free Press* and the *Detroit News*, which operate under a joint agreement, moved to replace their workers, they had the Caterpillar precedent to lean on. In Decatur, companies learned that they could divide the community from the workers locked in dispute with them and that they would not be rejected. They learned that to the

$8-an-hour worker with no benefits and little notion of financial security, crossing a picket line is no big deal. Perhaps most radical of all, they learned it was easier to win publicity campaigns when they blamed the dispute not on the local workers, but on union bosses in Detroit or Pittsburgh or Akron. By putting the blame on the union and its politics, they could send out the message that they truly side with their workers; it was the union leaders who were the troublemakers. In Decatur, the companies showed that they did not have to hide, that they could use public relations to go around union leaders and the unions themselves to make their argument. And they were heard.

The three strikes in Decatur during the 1990s told us that the balance of power has certainly shifted. That it's much easier now for global companies to rewrite the rules with unions and to win in showdowns where once they might have faltered. Thanks to logistics plus technology plus worldwide resources, it is possible for a giant competitor to take a tough stand and to emerge the victor in a labor dispute. Despite what their lawyers may say about how dangerous unions have become, giant businesses are not at a loss to reshape the deal between them and their workers. The larger the company, the more likely it is to play for all the cards on the table.

As American companies have become larger and less tied down by matters of loyalty and convenience, they have grown thinner. So when workers throw down the gauntlet today, American companies meet the challenge by shipping their work out—to another plant in the company's network, to the nonunion repair shop down the block, to a temporary staffing firm, to the lower-wage nonunion South, to Mexico or Burma—or by teaching high-priced white-collar workers to do the jobs of the union members picketing outside their factory gates.

This corporate anorexia is fearsome and very real to the workers who stand to be passed up like dessert. They know that they can be sacrificed to the swapping of workforces as well as to the shipping out of work. Rather than retrain veteran employees familiar with old ways and skills, corporations striving to become the lean machines of the new millennium are hiring new workers who come ready trained. They are blind to the reality that by shifting jobs and shaking up the system, they are throwing their workforces into a state of institutional shock. It is easy to move wires around. Not so easy to shift people

But swapping workforces is the product of short-term thinking, one of the two guiding principles of corporate America that propels companies that were once high-road travelers along the low road.

High-road traveling companies nurture their workers toward greater productivity. In return for the high wages they pay, they get back much more in higher production and higher quality. These companies know that better training, collaboration, accountability, and generous benefits up and down the pay ladder make better-producing workers. That opening their books to their workers, opening decision making to those on the line or in the computer room, and generally treating their workers like stakeholders rather than widgets, fosters a greater sense of commitment and loyalty.

Despite the fact that the high-road traveling companies insist they have the bottom-line numbers to show that their philosophy works, only a relatively small number of these companies appear again and again in the paeans to corporate brilliance written by management gurus. When a firm's health is measured solely by its stock growth, it's easy to see that in the 1990s long-term investments and long-term training plans had to yield to short-term fixes that served the guiding principle of maximizing profits. The fixation with stock growth that ties the salaries of managers and executives to the way their stock performs has put them on a detour to the low road, where they slash wages and benefits under the guise of meeting competition, keep their workers in the dark about their plans for the future, and lay off thousands but reward the CEO with endless stock options that do not relate to the way the company has performed.

As they wipe out retiree health care benefits and scuttle long-term pension plans in favor of less costly retirement options that benefit the company's bottom line, American companies tell their workers they can pay only so much and dare them to find a better deal out in the tough job marketplace. But they also say they can do better for their workers than any union can. And they do, when faced with an honest-to-goodness organization drive that threatens to bring a union in the front door. But then they forget their vows when the union threat has died and find their heart elsewhere than in the best interests of their workers.

Both Caterpillar and Bridgestone/Firestone were once prime exhibits of companies that traveled along the high road. Cooperate with me, they urged and cajoled their workers, and we will share the rewards. Their oaths did not last long. They quickly shifted routes and headed down the low road. Today, global giants like Caterpillar and Bridgestone/Firestone have given the world an updated, high-tech version of the old amorality: the belief that business comes first, and soft-headed politicians should not be able to tell money-making operations that they cannot relocate to places where human rights can be ignored.

Caterpillar deserves credit for clearing the way for this route.

Determined to reap the rewards of the world market and to keep the doors to trade open, Caterpillar led the fight against the way the U.S. government imposes country-by-country sanctions on nations that violate human rights, heading the coalition of firms called USAEngage. When a handful of religious groups, who held stock, challenged the company's dealing in Myanmar, where the U.S. government had barred American firms from partaking in new investments, the company disagreed. It was hardly a new complaint, echoing the protests made when Caterpillar kept its few ties with South Africa during apartheid. Caterpillar told its shareholders that the United States was losing thousands of high-wage jobs because of the government's sanctions. No, the company could not be held down by such policies. To be a world leader it needed to have a free hand.

Caterpillar and Bridgestone/Firestone are not alone on the low road. Trust me.

Let me offer another prediction that seems as sure as the sunrise: Some American workers will continue to lose what they once had. For middle Americans it is their way of life. For others it is their on-the-job rights, their identity, their health, their control over a profession they vowed to protect. For some it may be as basic as the loss of time in a frenetic race to perform. But these losses will not have to be permanent. They can be turned around, although maybe not entirely. That, however, calls for concerted action, and nobody is stepping forward to take on the job—especially when a robust economy and low unemployment shroud such losses and dull our senses.

Don't count on Washington to ride to the rescue. In an era of small government and small ambitions, the devolution of the welfare state means that the helping hand is withdrawn for those who cannot take care of themselves. Imagine a federal tough love program for the nation's slums and decayed factory towns. If you can't help yourself, drop dead.

Communities cannot solve their problems by themselves. Not towns like Decatur. Financially troubled communities that cannot hide their blemishes as well as the newly popular edge communities and chic suburbs, which are perched just beyond the big cities' borders, can barely muster the energy to plot their revival.

Nor can you count on businesses that fly their own flags and say they have to answer to so many others than the communities where their workers spend their workday lives.

CAN LABOR RISE AGAIN?

Labor is the logical choice for the heroic task.

As much as it has shrunk, it is still larger and better organized than anyone else likely to come to the rescue. And if the rest of us want to prevent the disaster from spreading, we will also have to back the unions—with all of their flaws.

What this means is that labor's boasts have to become real deeds. Its vow to organize once again must be replaced by dollars and manpower. Unions have to pool their resources. They have to learn how to fight legal battles and how to win elections. They have to learn how to set aside their photo albums, shrug off old rivalries, divide the workplace into whole industries assigned to single unions to organize and merge into stronger, more viable organizations. In short, they have to remake and renew themselves.

First, they need to invite new workers in, to truly open their own doors to women and minorities, something they have barely done. To reach the millions of immigrants who fill up the bottom rungs of the economy, unions need to speak their languages and feel their pulse. They have to learn again what it is that drives people to risk careers and to stand up against the boss. Not all workers want the same thing. Highly paid pilots have little in common, in terms of economics, with janitors subsisting on starvation-level wages. But they both want respect and dignity and control over their jobs.

This is the challenge unions face as they appeal to a broader workforce than ever.

Second, the unions need to make friends with different kinds of workers: the very poor who can barely afford to join a union but need one desperately and the better-off, middle-class workers suddenly caught in a bind and looking for help—doctors, nurses, and other white-collar professionals. Unions need to offer themselves up as kinder, smarter places where their voices will be heard. Louder, stronger, and better connected than in a decade, organized labor has stirred new relations with college students and intellectuals and the religious community, groups that long ago left labor's side. John Sweeney was organized labor's Gorbachev: He began to dismantle the old system. But these are only starts.

Third, unions need to establish democracy, a strong antidote for apathy. Democracy creates problems for one-party unions, in which decisions are handed down from the top and the regime in power is always right. But when the top union leaders decided that they had had enough of the struggles in Decatur, when they saw that the struggles at Caterpillar and Staley were draining away money and energy, they bargained for deals that left many feeling abandoned, and betrayed. Unions in the 21st century that ask workers to fight on one day longer than the company fights, must assure their members that their unions will not desert them as the fight careens toward defeat and that they will be left with some measure of self-respect.

These steps may help to solidify the unions' ranks in the United States, but to have the needed impact on today's global corporations, American labor has to link arms with unions worldwide. If companies can plan globally, so can unions. They can coordinate their strategies on wages and working conditions so that a garment factory that flees from Louisiana to Honduras faces a workforce unwilling to let it drop to the lowest standards possible. Until now the global vision of American unions has been tainted by distrust and paternalism toward the rest of the world. That has to change.

By becoming the insurance brokers and pension advisers to their members, instead of their spokesmen on all of the other issues touching their lives, American unions severed the link to those outside their bounds and lost the chance to speak to a larger audience. They lost their history and the support they once had. They lost their roots in the liberal values that fed theirs and others' souls.

Now the American audience has to be persuaded to believe that unions have their interests at heart too.

> We seem to be waiting for someone to give us the secret to fixing all the real or perceived ills of our community. We've already got the secret. It's you and us and people who care enough about the community to make it a personal commitment to making it a better place.
> —*Decatur Herald & Review*, October 25, 1998

Epilogue

Heartbreak in the Heartland

No historical markers show where they clenched hands on Eldorado Street and waved American flags during any of the demonstrations. Or where they stood on frigid nights beside the fires of the wood-burning picket line barrels close to the Caterpillar plant. Or where the women's group collected and sorted Christmas gifts for children. No monuments were put up in places like these. But they are there.

It is a matter of looking and listening.

Annie Floyd, whom the others jokingly called the Mother Jones of the Decatur workers, earned minimum wage for a while at a small fireworks factory, then got another factory job at $8 an hour. But when her supervisor yelled at her one night because she couldn't meet her quota, despite working two or three hours overtime on top of her regular night shift, she shot back that nobody yelled at her like that—not right in her face, damn it—and walked out. She's back at the fireworks factory. Annie's husband, **Jerry**, works full-time at the granary now, making $9 an hour. With his $750-a-month pension from Bridgestone/Firestone and their combined wages, they can spend $35 on a meal out now and then and not feel crushed. That's about it.

Gary Minich felt increasingly out of place, under pressure, and unappreciated by his young editors at the *Decatur Herald & Review* and retired early. He's teaching at Richland Community College and finds that he likes teaching more than journalism.

Mary Brummet, of the Staley women's group says, "Money is not the thing. Peace of mind is," when asked how she and her husband, **Rick**, are faring on his truck driver's earnings, much lower than what he had made after 24 years at Staley.

Diana Marquis agrees with Mary, though her husband, **Gene**, is making more working as an apprentice plumber than he did at Staley. One thing they clearly agree on is that when they do not talk about what happened, they feel much better.

Sandy Gosnell says that she and **Tim**, taken on as an apprentice by the electrical workers union in town and feeling a little old to be learning a new trade, can't help thinking about the fact that the years Tim put in at Staley did not end up being the cushion for their future security as they had planned. "He had put 18 years in Staley," she says, "and it's just gone, like he was never there."

Diehard members of the **Staley women's group**, about four or five of them, get together now and then for dinner along with their husbands or on their own. The group still holds potluck dinners, and as many as 60 have shown up for the gatherings.

Ethel Ferguson says the group helped her greatly when her husband, **Jerry**, got sick and then died. She speaks as glowingly as ever of Dave Watts: how he struggled to keep the Staley workers together and always had time for everyone.

Dave and **Pat Watts** are sure that Dave's inability to find work in town is a result of employers' blackballing him. Remodeling work wasn't a solution for him, so he took a job as a union millwright, working on projects outside Decatur. Pat says taking two nursing jobs hasn't troubled her, but the way people have treated her husband has: "He was the scapegoat then, and he will be in the future."

Dan Lane ended a long journey, from Los Angeles to Mexico City to Decatur to Detroit and then back to Mexico, for various labor organizing jobs in South Bend, Indiana, working as a community organizer with a labor group—his first full-time job in five years. His marriage ended in divorce, and being in the streets with workers is lonely, yet it's where he feels he has to be. But it is like going to war, he thinks. When you go to war, you make one choice, he says, and everything else comes along with it.

Ray Rogers keeps busy serving as fireman for the small and independent unions that call him in at the last minute. Still optimistic that the major unions will "grab hold and work with us," he is less hopeful about a settlement in his suit against the paper workers' union, which claims that he was supposed to receive a share of the contributions that he helped raise for the Staley workers. He has a website that lists his major campaigns, *www.corporatecampaign.org*. Check it out. It doesn't mention what happened in Decatur.

Larry Solomon has become an even sharper thorn in the side of the UAW, intermittently publishing a several-page publication called *Kick the Cat*, which attacks the company and union leaders: "Brothers and sisters, you have been conned, flimflammed, hornswaggled into believing nothing more could be gained in our struggle with Cat."

Randy Morrell was stunned when his local voted him out of the president's seat, despite the fact that disappointment with the union's deal with the company had led Caterpillar workers in other locals to dump their officers as a form of punishment for what happened. He left the factory within months and found work as a part-time insurance adjuster. He is waiting for everything else to fall into place in retirement.

Father Mangan is supposed to be partially retired, but he is too busy to come to the phone. One of the things that keeps him occupied is his ongoing labor activities: holding seminars in nearby towns on the moral issues raised by workers and unions, helping with local union elections, speaking at union gatherings, and attending Labor Day celebrations. When he fell ill with colon cancer, those who cared for him, people like Gary Minich and Dave Watts and Dan Lane, prayed for him. After months of treatment, he seems quite recovered and as enthusiastic as ever.

Almost every day he has come across someone from the unions whom he met during the troubled times. One was parishioner Jim Moran, whose return to Staley had not been easy for him. When Father Mangan was called to the hospital to offer the last rites for Jim as he was dying after a car accident, Brenda Moran, Jim's wife, said something to her husband that seemed unusual at first but perfectly understandable upon reflection:

"Now," Brenda told her husband in an almost reassuring voice, "you don't have to go back to Staley's anymore."

Roger Gates is still the union local's president at Bridgestone/ Firestone. He thinks the returned strikers and the picket line crossers at the plant have to make peace if they ever want to achieve worker solidarity, but so far not much forgiveness has been shown to the 300-plus union members who crossed the picket lines during the strike.

Don Cottrell, not mentioned before, the only picket line crosser who has been taken back into the rubber workers local, had returned to work only a week before the union surrendered. To remain in the union, line crossers had to pay a fine of $4,500, and Don was so troubled by feeling as though he had turned his back on good people that he borrowed the $4,500 and payed the fine. "Others in the plant may think the union is a joke," he said. But he doesn't.

Richard Zerfowski has adjusted to being back at Caterpillar but no longer stops at the union hall; he tried to stay away from other Caterpillar workers, even those he had drawn close to during the long, troubled years. What preys on his mind is how to get back his good name, the one the company took away.

Don Fites's reward grew spectacularly in the years after the disputes began. He was regularly named among the nation's best corporate leaders in the business press. A leading community fund-raiser. A champion of free trade. The praise was endless.

In payment for his frugality, Fites took home $3.5 million in salary, bonus, and reward payments in 1998, his last full-time year on the job, plus $7 million worth of stock options. And because it still feared for his safety, Caterpillar also agreed to pay $185,000 a year for security guards for Fites and let him use the company's aircraft at a cost of about $75,000 a year. From the start of the company's showdown with the UAW, Fites's compensation had grown more than six and a half times. And that is not counting the stock options. He kept his silence till the end, resigning without a clarifying statement on what it had all meant to him and the company.

Tire maker **Dave Watts** is still at Bridgestone/Firestone, but he works on final inspection, earning maybe $30 a week less than he did long ago. It is a "no-brainer" job where he's just putting in his time, which is just what he wants. Several years after the strike, during the controversy over the Bridgestone/Firestone tire failures, lawyers were intrigued by inspection workers' complaints about the pressures and shortcomings of their jobs. But on the factory floor, it was a long-held belief that building a tire was far more stressful than inspecting one. One night Dave fell asleep at the wheel and wrecked his car, an accident he attributes to work exhaustion, and he carries around a little plastic card that reminds him which days he is supposed to be at work—working sometimes on weekdays and sometimes on weekends is still so confusing.

In his spare time, Dave often stops by at the Floyds' old farmhouse, and Annie and Jerry are happy that he still visits and doesn't try to forget how close Annie and Suzie had been when Suzie was alive. They worried that Dave seemed terribly lonely and hard to reach for a long time after Suzie's death. Then he began seeing a woman, and they married in September 1999.

Outside of his house in Hammond, population 500, a small place southeast of Decatur reached by a two-land road that must have been engineered by somebody who used only a ruler, Dave erected a handmade sign facing one of the few streets in town. He didn't intend to take it down. It read, "Hammond has scabs."

One night someone stole it. But that didn't bother Dave. He will put another one up soon. He won't forget. He swore on it.

Notes

GENERAL RECOMMENDED READING

Many published works were very helpful in putting the story of Decatur into a broader perspective. *Which Side Are You On?* (Farrar Straus & Giroux, 1991) by Chicago labor lawyer Thomas Geoghegan remains the best work on the dilemma facing U.S. unions. *Copper Crucible* (ILR Press, School of Industrial and Labor Relations, Cornell University, 1994), an analysis of the Arizona miners' strike in 1983 by labor lawyer Jonathan D. Rosenblum, is an insightful study of the impact of replacement workers in a strike.

A compelling account of the battle between the paper workers union and International Paper is *The Betrayal of Local 14* (ILR Press, 1998) by Julius Getman, a professor of law at the University of Texas Law School in Austin. Getman's very valuable effort chronicles the events in detail from the bottom up, from the back rows of the meeting halls where the crisis between the company and the union evolved. A companion to his overview is an oral history of the dispute: *Pain on Their Faces: Testimonies on the Paper Mill Strike, Jay, Maine, 1987–1988* by the Jay-Livermore Falls Working Class History Project (Apex Press, 1998).

Many have written about the UAW, a union with a rich legacy and complex tapestry of colorful leaders. A book that deserves more attention is William Serrin's incisive recounting of the 1970 strike by the UAW against General Motors Corporation, *The Company and the Union* (Knopf, 1973). It is a brilliant analysis of a union on the verge of change.

To understand the genetic imprint Walter Reuther left on the UAW, read *The Most Dangerous Man in Detroit* (Basic Books, 1995) by historian Nelson Lichtenstein. An essential understanding of the UAW's roots can be found in Sit-Down: *The General Motors Strike of 1936–1937* (University of Michigan Press, 1969) by Sidney Fine.

Serrin's more current work, *Homestead* (Times Books, Random House, 1992) is one of the best books in recent years about the plight faced by blue-collar towns when their pipeline of work is suddenly shut off. A longer work about the mindless destruction and collapse of the steel industry was written with great heart and excruciating attention to detail by John P. Hoerr, *And the Wolf Finally Came: The Decline of the American Steel Industry* (University of Pittsburgh Press, 1988). So, too, I would recommend *Sparrows Point: Making Steel—the Rise and Ruin of American Industrial Might* (Summit Books, 1988) by Mark Reutter. For an understanding of the issues raised by the conflict between the unions and companies in Decatur, *Locked in the Cabinet* (Knopf, 1997), by former labor secretary Robert Reich, spells out a liberal view of the dilemma. His description of the government's tangled effort to deal with the use of replacement workers by Bridgestone/Firestone serves as a critical point of reference here.

The Labor Wars: From the Molly Maguires to the Sitdowns (Doubleday, 1973) by Sidney Lens offers a priceless history of labor disputes that shaped the mindset of generations of union leaders. For a plunge into labor history as it was being made in the 1930s, few works have the dramatic presence of *Labor on the March* (ILR Press paperback reprint, 1995), written in 1937 by Edward Levinson, a labor reporter for the *New York Post*. *On Strike at Hormel: The Struggle for a Democratic Labor Movement* (Temple University Press, 1990), written by Hardy Green, is a telling memoir of Ray Rogers's efforts in Austin, Minnesota, and the strike's impact on Hormel workers.

The literature of job loss is rich with insightful tales and analyses. A recent account driven by a profoundly humane understanding of workers is *Closing: The Life and Death of an American Factory* (Norton, 1998) by William Bamberger and Cathy N. Davis. For a perceptive explanation of how jobs frame our lives and how the thinking underlining the new work rules can undermine the stability of many, read *The Corrosion of Character: The Personal Consequences of Work in the New Capitalism* (Norton, 1998) by Richard Sennett. A succinct summing of his view appears in "Work Can Screw You Up," *Financial Times*, October 17–18, 1998.

The disconnect between workers' reality and the new economy is a growing theme. It is at the core of *Illusions of Opportunity: The American Dream in Question* (Norton, 1997) by John E. Schwarz. Likewise, see *The New Dollars and Dreams: American Incomes and Economic Change* by Frank Levy (Russell Sage Foundation, 1999). A common theme in the 1990s was that the U.S. economy had changed and that the only way to survive was to move on, to embrace the new risks and let go of the past. This theme was echoed by Michael Mandel in *The High-Risk Society: Peril and Promise in the New Economy* (Times Business, Random House, 1996). A mystery of the 1990s was why workers were not reaping better wages amid desperate cries about employee shortages and a surging economy. One reason was the disconnect between how good things were and how insecure workers felt. Barry Bluestone and Stephen Rose make this point in their study, *The Unmeasured Labor Force: The Growth in Work Hours* (Jerome Levy Economics Institute of Bard College, Public Policy Briefs, No. 39, 1998).

In the 1990s the clarions of corporate America relentlessly announced new mantras and discarded old ones. They abandoned a short-lived effort at open cooperation with employees, or everyone out for himself. In an era when veteran workers could be reengineered out of a career in a flash, such upheavals seemed to make perfect sense. But they didn't. The core lost its core; companies lost the hearts and souls that drove them and quietly invited back employees let go in more thoughtless moments. Then companies openly embraced a more thoughtful form of nurturing their employees, largely because they realized that they needed workers. The bottom line doesn't seem to have changed much, however. A philosophical overview of these changes and a prescription for the route that most businesses have yet to take is described by British business philosopher Charles Handy in *The Hungry Spirit: Beyond Capitalism, A Quest for Purpose in the Modern World* (Broadway Books, 1998). Charles Heckscher writes about the dilemma of managers faced with their companies' decision to rewrite the rules of workplace bargains in *White-Collar Blues* (Basic Books paperback, 1996)

An indispensable tool for understanding the soul and history of Illinois was the *Federal Writers Project Guide* to 1930s Illinois that was updated as the *WPA Guide to Illinois* (Pantheon Books) and published in 1983. An opening to the world of blue-collar work for those who want to write about it might be George Orwell's *Road to Wigan Pier* (Harcourt Brace American edition, 1973), an unequaled description of what it is like to work in a mine. Few novels match the compelling portrayal of the loss of one's livelihood than John Steinbeck's *The Grapes of Wrath* (Knopf reprint, 1993), a work of fiction that sprang from his reporting. For a journalist's account of what happened to farmworkers in the 1930s, I strongly recommend *Factories in the Field* (1939; University of California Press reprint, 2000) by Carrie McWilliams and *Sal Si Puedes: Cesar Chavez and the New American Revolution* (University of California Press, 2000) by Peter Matthiessen. There are several anthologies on work as seen in literature. *The Oxford Book of Work* (Oxford University, 1999) is a lengthy compendium that offers an insightful historical perspective but falls short in contemporary descriptions of the work experience.

No reporter remained as loyal to or as honest and insightful in documenting what it means to work as did Murray Kempton. Read his columns in *The New York Post* and *Newsday* backward and forward; it will not be a loss. Fledgling journalists convinced there is a way to capture life's incandescent beauty and the workday world will only gain by wandering through the writings of Charles Dickens, Edmund Wilson, and James Agee. As for the small band of labor writers, nothing they write deserves to be ignored. A secret treasure that needs to be declared a public trust is the work done by the nation's labor historians. Few can match their ability to capture and analyze telling moments in the nation's story. For an example of why this is true, read "Workers' Rights Are Civil Rights" by Nelson Lichtenstein, *WorkingUSA*, March 1999.

We Americans endlessly search for ways to describe our roots and memorialize our hometowns. A shining example of this effort is *Home Town* (Random House, 1999) by Tracy Kidder.

A number of journalists have told Decatur's story. Here are some worth reading: "A Struggle for Survival," *Toronto Star*, April 30, 1995; "Town of Reagan Democrats Sour on Dole," *Tampa Tribune*, August 30, 1996; "Harley-Riding, Picket-Walking Socialism Haunts Decatur," *The Nation*, April 8, 1996; "Middle-Class Labor in U.S. Feels the Squeeze as Wages Decline. In Decatur, Ill., Locked-Out Factory Workers Square Off with Corporate Managers in a Battle over Cost-Cutting and New Labor Practices," *Christian Science Monitor*, November 29, 1995; "Labor Takes Its Lumps," *The Progressive*, March 1, 1996; "Hard Feelings in Union Fester as Staley Lockout Continues Between Workers, Decatur Firm Now Two and a Half Years Old," *St. Louis Post-Dispatch*, November 26, 1995; "Hunger Striking in the Corn Belt," *The Nation*, November 6, 1995; "Labor Wars Hit Home in Decatur," *Los Angeles Times*, September 4, 1995; "Striketown USA Making Comeback," *Austin American-Statesman*, April 29, 1998.

From the 1970s onward, it became a matter of debate among historians and union watchers as to why and when organized labor in the United States truly lost its footing and could no longer recover its position. Was it Reagan's firing of the air traffic controllers in 1981? Was it a deep trance that overcame some labor leaders? Was it the greed that infected other union leaders? Was it the selfishness of blue-collar workers, who turned their backs on the Democrats and cast their lot with the Republicans? Was it the Democrats who forgot what labor needed? Was it any one strike where, for the first time in decades, a major American company used scabs to break a strike and then handed the jobs of its veteran employees to the strikebreakers?

Where does Decatur fit? I hope others will help explain.

CHAPTER NOTES

In addition to the published sources listed below, I conducted interviews with many of the individuals discussed in the book (and others), over a number of years in New York, Washington, D.C., Pittsburgh, Miami Beach, Nashville, Detroit, Flint, Chicago, Los Angeles, Las Vegas, as well as in Peoria, Danville, Aurora, and Decatur, Illinois.

Part I. They Lead the Way

On the history of the Industrial Workers of the World, the Wobblies, see *We Shall Be All: A History of the Industrial Workers of the World, The Wobblies: The Story of IWW and Syndicalism in the United States* (1968; Ivan R. Dee, 1999) by Patrick Renshaw. On the role of corporate campaigns, see "No More Business as Usual: Labor's Corporate Campaigns," *Labor Research Review*, no. 21, 1993; *Grand Designs: The Impact of Corporate Strategies on Workers, Unions and Communities* (ILR Press, 1993), edited by Charles Craypo and Bruce Nissen; "Union Corporate Campaigns and Inside Games as a Strike Form" by Herbert Northrup, *Employee Relations Law Journal*, no. 19, Spring 1994; "Business Groups Seek Laws to Bar Smears by Union," *Wall Street Journal*, September 21, 1995; "Suit Tests Limits of Corporate Campaigns," *Legal Times*, August 7, 1995.

Mounting an incisive publicity war is a tactic that a few unions have learned well. To put pressure on the Los Angeles hotel industry, Local 11 of the Hotel Employees and Restaurant Employees Union sent out a video to potential visitors, called *City on the Edge*. It portrayed the dangers and troubles of Los Angeles. See the *Los Angeles Times*, June 23, 1992.

There have been a number of profiles of Caterpillar's former chairman, Donald V. Fites, most of them in the business press and most of them glowing. One of the most complete appeared in *Business Week*, August 10, 1992: "Caterpillar's Don Fites: Why He Didn't Blink." A highly perceptive and compelling five-part series of articles about Caterpillar's confrontation with the UAW, written by reporter Barry Bearak, appeared in the *Los Angeles Times* in May 1995. Although the workers returned and the company eventually reached a contract with the union, Fites has never talked to the news media at length about the company's view of the conflict.

For articles about Fites and his views on workers' salaries, see the *New York Times*, November 17 and 19, 1991; "Cat vs. Labor: Hardhats, Anyone?" *Business Week*, August 26, 1991; "The Cat Fight," *Fortune*, May 2, 1983; "Caterpillar Wakes Up: Corporate Excavation Uncovers a Gold Mine," *Industry Week*, May 20, 1991; "For Caterpillar, the Metamorphosis Isn't Over," *Business Week*, August 31, 1987. For the quotes from Walter Helmerich on Fites's role in Caterpillar's decision to challenge the union, see the story on Fites's retirement by Christopher Wills, Associated Press, July 28, 1997, the *Baltimore Sun*.

For an early background history on Bill Casstevens, see "UAW's Casstevens Faces Labor Day with Bleak View," *Cleveland Plain Dealer*, September 6, 1981; "Unionist Thrives on Challenge, Work for Racial Amity Praised," *Cleveland Plain Dealer*, April 27, 1972.

Part II. A Blue-Collar Legacy

Much of the history of the Midwest's industrial collapse is recounted in *Economic Restructuring of the American Midwest: Proceedings of the Midwest Economic Restructuring Conference of the Federal Reserve Bank of Cleveland* (Kluwer Academic Publishers, 1990). For the role of firms like Bridgestone in the Midwest, see "How Japanese Industry is Rebuilding the Rust Belt" by M. Kenny, R-Fla., (*Technology Review*, vol. 94, February 1, 1991). For a telling analysis of the shift of industries in search of ever lower cost labor, see *Capital Moves: RCA's 70-Year Quest for Cheap Labor* (Cornell University Press, 1999) by Jefferson Cowie. Although the results were not hard to discern, it was as if the nation were daydreaming throughout the 1980s as factories went dark forever. Some of the best research on this upheaval includes *Plant Closings and Economic Dislocation* (Upjohn, 1981) by Jean Gordus, Paul Jarley, and Louis Ferman and *Uneven Tides: Rising Inequality in America* (Russell Sage Foundation, 1993), edited by Sheldon Danziger and Peer Gottschalk.

For a description of the impact of deindustrialization on the African American community, see *When Work Disappears: The World of the New Urban Poor* (Knopf, 1996) by William Julius Wilson. For an account of how an industry's demise affected a community, see William Serrin's *Homestead* and Mark Reutter's *Sparrows Point*, both cited earlier, and *End of the Line: Autoworkers and the American Dream, An Oral History* (University of Illinois Press, 1990), edited by Richard Feldman and Michael Betzold. With colleague Marcia Stepanek, I chronicled the impact of factory closings across the United States for a series in the *Detroit Free Press* in September 1986. It was called "Blue-Collar Casualties: Life after Layoff."

On the use of the federal plant closing law, see *Labor Research Review 19*, Midwest Center for Labor Research, "WARN and EDWA: Use Them or Lose Them" by Greg LeRoy. For details on the economic slide that faced the Decatur workers as their disputes began, see "U.S. Workers Halt Productivity Slide: Gains Carry Painful Cost in Job Losses," *Chicago Tribune*, February 6, 1992; "Left Behind on the Career Track: A Growing Skills Gap Leaves Young People and Employees with a Sense of Frustration" *Washington Post*, August 24, 1992; "Low-Paying Jobs Up Sharply in Decade: U.S. Says Census Bureau Study Is Likely to Fuel Debate over Quality of New Positions Created," *Washington Post*, May 12, 1992; "The Job Drought" *Fortune*, August 24, 1992; *The State of Working America: 1992–93* (Economic Policy Institute, 1993) by Lawrence Mishel and Jared Bernstein; *Recent Job Losers Less Likely to Expect Recall* (U.S. Bureau of Labor Statistics, Summary 92-8, July 1992). On the growing gap between the rich and poor, see "Income Inequality," *Monthly Labor Review* (Bureau of Labor Statistics, August 1995). For comparisons of factory workers' compensation, see *International Comparisons of Hourly Compensation Costs for Production Workers in Manufacturing, 1995*, Report 909 (U.S. Department of Labor, September 1996).

On the use of training, see *Worker Training: Competing in the New International Economy* (Office of Technology Assessment, September 1990). For statistics on the changes in the composition of the manufacturing workforce, its impact on the Midwest and the combining impact of the global economy, see the research papers on this topic by William A. Testa (Federal Reserve Bank of Chicago, December 1998).

Ethan Kapstein, writing in *International Labour Review* (vol. 137, no. 4, 1998), makes an intriguing and compelling argument that the nation's trade adjustment assistance has continually failed to help workers, but it has persisted because politicians and others are incapable of supporting more innovative programs to help workers whose jobs have been permanently wiped out by foreign trade. For information on the impact of shift work, see "Compressed Weeks Fill an HR Niche," *HR Magazine*, June 1995; "Companies Love an Economy That Rocks Around the Clock: A Lot of Employees Can Barely Stay Awake," *Fortune*, August 21, 1995.

The sad tale of the explosion of violence that consumed the Herrin miners and the legacy it left for central Illinois was told in gripping detail by James Ballowe in "The Work of Our Fathers," *Chicago Reader*, June 30, 1995. Few companies have a written history as complete as the one about the Staley Company provided in *The Kernel and the Bean* (Simon & Schuster, 1982) by Dan Forrestal. A view of Decatur over the years is presented in *Observations from 46 Years of Newspaper Management* (Lindsay–Schaub Newspapers, 1960) by Frank M. Lindsay. He was at the time president of Lindsay–Schaub Newspapers.

Caterpillar's labor history was captured by various newspapers at the time of the dispute, but little other documentation exists. An article in the *Peoria Journal Star* on April 5, 1987, recounts the founding of the UAW at Caterpillar. The impact of 12-hour shifts and changing shifts has been looked at by medical researchers for some time. A March 25, 1998, article in the *Wall Street Journal*, "Some Employers Find Way to Ease Burden of Changing Shifts," is a handy update of the issue.

The coverage of the events taking place in Decatur by the *Decatur Herald & Review* was essential for understanding what was taking place. Covering such happenings is what local newspapers are supposed to do. Consider this excerpt from an editorial in the paper in July 1994: "As serious as Decatur's current labor–management problems is a growing sense that the community is unwilling to change. Not everyone, of course, but usually enough to torpedo projects."

On Decatur's labor history, see "Honest Men and Law-Abiding Citizens: The 1894 Railroad Strike in Decatur" by Robert D. Sampson, *Illinois Historical Journal*, vol. 85, no. 2, summer 1992. Also see Sidney Lens's *The Labor Wars*, cited earlier.

For an overview of the changes within labor unions in the context of American society, see Edward Levinson's *Labor on the March* (1938, 1995 reissue, ILR Press); *C.I.O.: Industrial Unionism in Action* (W. W. Norton, 1937) by J. Raymond Walsh; *Impatient Armies of the Poor: The Story of Collective Action of the Unemployed from 1808 to 1942* (University Press of Colorado, 1991) by Franklin Fulsome; *The Coming of the New Deal and the Politics of Upheaval* (1959; American Heritage reprint, 1988) by Arthur Schlesinger Jr.; *Labor in America* (1960; Harlan Davidson, paperback, 1993) by Foster Rhea Dulles; Carrie McWilliams's *Factories in the Fields*, cited earlier; *Labor Leaders in America* (University of Illinois Press, 1987), edited by Melvyn Dubofsky and Warren Van Tine; *Strike!* (South End Press, paperback, 1998) by Jeremy Brecher. An imaginative, detailed, and compelling history of American unionism at the end of the 19th century and the start of the 20th century is offered by J. Anthony Lukas in his monumental work, *Big Trouble* (Touchstone, 1998).

For background on the clash between the paper workers union and International Paper, see *Pain on Their Faces* (cited earlier) and Julius Getman (1998), cited earlier; *The Transformation of American Industrial Relations* (ILR Press, 1994) by Thomas A. Kochan, Harry C. Katz, and Robert B. McKersie; "IP Union in Jay Seeks Strikebreakers' Help," *Maine Sunday Telegram*, June 28, 1992; "Collective Bargaining in the Paper Industry: Developments Since 1979" by Adrienne Eaton and Jill Kriesky, an article in *Contemporary Collective Bargaining in the Private Sector* (ILR Press, 1993), edited by Paula B. Voos; "Industrial Relations in Transition: The Paper Industry Example" by Julius Getman and F. Ray Marshall, *Yale Law Journal*, vol. 102, no. 8, June 1993; "Labor Adds New Weapon to Strike Tactics: Union Targets Giant Parent of Strikebound Paper Firm in Pressure Play" by James Warren, *Chicago Tribune*, August 9, 1987.

Part III. A Call to Arms

For a brief history of the union clashes in West Virginia, see *Thunder in the Mountains: The West Virginia Mine War, 1920–21* (University of Pittsburgh Press, 1990) by Lon Savage; "The U.S. Army and the Return to Normalcy in Labor Dispute Interventions: The Cast of the West Virginia Coal Mine Wars, 1920–21" by Clayton D. Laurie, *West Virginia History*, vol. 50, 1991, pp. 1–24.

On Charles Vance and his company, see "Covering Your Assets: Charles Vance's Security Guards Area Cut above Your Typical Rent-a-Cop," *Virginia Business*, December 1989; "Picture-Perfect Strike Protection" by Charles Vance, *Security Management*, November 1991; "When Trouble Strikes," by Charles Vance, *Security Management*, January 1988. "Vance Gets Piece of Action at UPS," *Washington Business Journal*, August 18, 1997; "Teams of Guards in Wings in Case UMW Calls Strike at Pittston," *Charleston Gazette*, February 11, 1988.

On Caterpillar's actions, see "The Bitter Harvest of a Global Shift" by Frank Swoboda, *Washington Post*, April 19, 1992; "The Cat and the Mice: In the Caterpillar Strike, Don't Bet on the Union," *Newsweek*, April 20, 1992; "Caterpillar Threatens to Replace UAW Strikers," *Wall Street Journal*, April 2, 1992; "Labor Makes a Stand in Fight for Its Future at Caterpillar Inc.," *Wall Street Journal*, April 7, 1992; "Strike's Result at Caterpillar Worries Unions" by Philip Dine, *St. Louis Post-Dispatch*, April 19, 1992; "Maybe Caterpillar Can Pick Up Where It Left Off: As Its Markets Recover, Victory Couldn't Have Come at a Better Time," *Business Week*, April 27, 1992; "800 Workers Locked Out by Staley: Illinois Plant Struggle Highlights Pending Bill" by Louis Uchitelle, *New York Times*, June 29, 1993.

An exceptionally complete in-depth history of the United Rubber Workers came as a part of a yearlong project on the role of the rubber industry in Akron that appeared in 1997 in the *Akron Beacon Journal*. One of the pieces, a March 16, 1997, story, "Strike Baptizes URW," is an example of good historical reporting.

Part IV. Skirmishes and Sieges

For an article about the Reverend Martin Mangan, see "Rights are Rights, Rev. Martin Mangan Stands with the Workers," *State Journal–Register*, November 6, 1995. See "Dispatches from Decatur: Community Is the First Casualty in America's Labor Wars" by Kevin Clarke, *U.S. Catholic*, April 1996, for a description of Father Mangan's confrontation with Staley officials. Workers and the clergy have rallied to each other's side often in the last century, and this story is woven throughout labor history. Some starting points to research include the work of Dorothy Day and the Catholic Worker movement, the farmworker movement, the work of organizer Saul Alinsky with religious groups, and the connections between the Reverend Martin Luther King, Jr., and organized labor. Dr. King was assassinated in 1968 while supporting 1,300 striking garbage workers in Memphis, Tennessee. On the ties between organized labor and the Catholic Church, see "Labor and the Catholic Church: Opportunities for Coalitions" by John Russo and Brian R. Corbin, *WorkingUSA*, July–August 1999.

For the impact of permanent replacements on a strike setting, see "Permanent Replacements, Presidential Power, Politics: Judicial Overreaching" by Charles Thomas Kimmett, *Yale Law Journal*, December 1, 1996.

For a view of U.S. funding efforts for American firms overseas, see "EX-IM Bank, OPIC Spending, Charter Bills Advancing," *USIA*, July 31, 1997; "Foreign Investment Agency Is Rebuffed in House Vote," *New York Times*, September 12, 1996.

On global economics, see *The Lexus and the Olive Tree* (Farrar, Straus & Giroux, 1999) by Thomas L. Friedman. No one makes a better argument about the new reality of businesses sprawled across the globe. Friedman's flaw is that his enthusiasm on the issue blinds him to the abuses and shortcomings of global trade. Likewise, see *Has Globalization Gone Too Far?* (Institute for International Economics, 1997) by Dani Rodrik; *Globaphobia: Confronting Fears about Open Trade* (Brookings Institution, 1998) by Gary Burtless, Robert Z. Lawrence, Robert E. Litan, and Robert J. Shapiro; *Global Squeeze: The Coming Crisis for First-World Nations* (NTC/Contemporary, 1998) by Richard C. Longworth; *Global Dreams, Imperial Corporations and the New World Order* (Touchstone, 1995) by Richard J. Barnet and John Cavanaugh; *Workers in a Lean World: Unions in the International Economy* (Verson, 1997) by Kim Moody; "Can Workers Tame Unrestrained Globalization" by David Moberg, *WorkingUSA*, March 1999. See the speech by Donald Fites, *Global Competition: Is the U.S. Up to the Challenge*, Foreign Trade Association of Southern California, May 21, 1992.

When the United States blocked Japanese firms from public works projects as an effort to pressure Japan to open its doors to American firms, Caterpillar heavily lobbied to exclude Japanese construction firms, and succeeded. The reason: Caterpillar did not want to hurt its highly successful joint venture in Japan. See "U.S. Rivals' Fears Gave Birth to Japan Trade Break," *Chicago Tribune*, January 10, 1988.

On the role of the NLRB, see "Unions Increasingly Turn to Door-to-Door Organizing, Bypassing Employer Opposition," March 16, 1997, *Washington Post*; "Parting Shots by Labor Board Chief," *New York Times*, July 23, 1998; "Labor Board Chief Takes Assertive Stance," *New York Times*, June 2, 1996.

Parts V–VII. Rallying, Surrender and Retreat, Heartfelt Losses; and Epilogue

For descriptions of Dan Lane's efforts, see "Life in Lane's Fast: Hunger Strike's Effort the Rallying Point for Decatur Union," *State Journal-Register*, October 7, 1995; "Worker's Fast Sign of Union's Unusual Tactics, Staley Lockout 27 Months Old," *State Journal-Register*, September 17, 1995.

The government's uncertain battle with corporations over enforcing occupational safety and health regulations was highlighted in a May 9, 1994, article in the *Chicago Tribune* by reporter Christopher Drew. It was about the confrontation between Labor Secretary Robert Reich and Bridgestone/Firestone over industrial safety at the firm's Oklahoma City factory.

For a view of the despair within labor's left over the fate of organized labor in the early 1990s, see the winter 1992 issue of *Dissent*, "Labor's Future in the U.S.: A Time of Troubles, Chances for Renewal."

Solid, insightful reporting on the rebellion within the AFL-CIO was produced by Frank Swoboda of the *Washington Post*. For an example, see "AFL-CIO Fight Signals End of Era for Labor: Leadership Struggle Forces Debate over Future," *Washington Post*, May 15, 1995. For a view of Kirkland's early years, see "Lane Kirkland: New Style for Labor" by A. H. Raskin, *New York Times* October 28, 1979, and "Unionist in Reaganland" by A. H. Raskin, *The New Yorker*, September 7, 1981.

For reporting on Kirkland's view of his new job, see "As a New Leader Views Future of the AFL-CIO," *U.S. News & World Report*, November 19, 1979. Also see "Rocky Start for AFL-CIO's Kirkland," March 3, 1980, *U.S. News & World Report*; "Where Do America's Unions Go from Here [interview with Kirkland]," *U.S. News & World Report*, May 17, 1982.

One of the best writers in the country who cares about labor unions is Harold Meyerson of the *LA Weekly*. His March 10, 1995, article, "Bomb Throwers of Bal Harbour," was the most perceptive reporting on the conflict-ridden effort to overthrow Lane Kirkland.

An outspoken view of organized labor is found in the *Trade Union Advisor*, a New York–based publication with a small circulation. Its reporting in 1995 spoke with the authority of labor leaders who assessed the road ahead. The reporting in *Labor Notes*, a leftist publication in Detroit, regularly offers a candid view from outside the establishment. The poll results that showed deep problems for the AFL-CIO came from a confidential report, "Being Heard," prepared for the AFL-CIO by Greer, Margolis, Mitchell, Burns & Associates, with research and findings by Peter D. Hart Research, March 21, 1994.

For an overview of the role of corporate campaigns and the way the steelworkers union learned how to use this strategy, see *Ravenswood: The Steelworkers Victory and the Revival of American Labor* (ILR Press, 1999) by Tom Juravich and Kate Bronfenbrenner. On the steelworkers' effort, see "Union Leader Plans to Restore Labor's Clout," *Tire Business*, November 11, 1996; "Paying the Price for Peace Bridgestone Resolves USW Fight," *Pittsburgh Post-Gazette*, November 7, 1996.

On the NLRB and labor relations, see *The Transformation of American Industrial Relations*, cited ealier; "A Tale of Two Discourses: William Gould's Journey from the Academy to the World of Politics" by Michael Gottesman and Michael Seidi, *Stanford Law Review*, vol. 47, 1995, p. 749; *Agenda for Reform: The Future of Employment Relationships and the Law* by William B. Gould (MIT Press, 1993).To understand the thinking on labor law in the 1930s, read the Supreme Court's ruling upholding the Wagner Act, *NLRB v. Jones & Laughlin Steel Corp.*, 301 U.S.1. For a view of unions' complaints with the NLRB, see "New Bargain or No Bargain" by Richard Rothstein, *American Prospect*, summer 1993.

On the UAW's contract agreement with Caterpillar, see "Why Workers Still Hold a Weak Hand" by Aaron Bernstein, *Business Week*, March 2, 1998.

See the following sources on Bridgestone/Firestone's tire-recall crisis: "Fatalities Put Tires on Trial," *Florida Today*, July 30, 2000; "Firestone Tires Probed in 46 Roadway Deaths," *Los Angeles Times*, August 8, 2000; "6.5 Million Tires Are Target of Recall; Firestone Unable to Conclusively Explain Failures," *Washington Post*, August 10, 2000; "Ford Says Many Bad Tires Made During '94 Strike," by the Associated Press, *The Pantagraph*, August 14, 2000; "Problems at Tire Plant Alleged," *Chicago Tribune*, August 20, 2000, "How Will Firestone and Ford Steer Through This Blowout?" *Business Week*, August 28, 2000; "Tire Recalls, Tragedies Tax Ford, Firestone," *Detroit News*, September 3, 2000; "Bridgestone Boss Has Toughness, but Is That What Crisis Demands," *Wall Street Journal*, September 12, 2000;"Bridgestone/Firestone Says It Made 'Bad Tires,'" *Wall Street Journal*, September 13, 2000; "Firestone Narrows Flaw Probe," *Washington Post*, September 13, 2000; "Rollovers a Concern for Ford Explorer," *Kansas City Star*, September 30, 2000; "Firestone Idling Three Tire Plants," *Washington Post*, October 18, 2000; "Errors, Short Staffing Led to Missed Tire Warnings," *Los Angeles Times*, November 11, 2000.

For an insightful analysis of the impact of the changes taking place for workers and unions in the United States, see the *World Labor Report* (International Labor Office, 1997–98). The research on companies threatening to relocate is limited. For some of the most detailed work, see the studies by Kate Bronfenbrenner, especially *The Effect of Plant Closing or Threat of Plant Closing on the Right of Workers to Organize* (North American Commission on Labor Cooperation, 1997). There is no shortage of academic and management texts on the high road companies can take to get more out of their workers. A good starting point is *The New American Workplace* (ILR Press, 1994) by Eileen Applebaum and Rosemary Batt. A handy summary of the major issues facing workers and companies is found in *The Changing Nature of Work* (Island Press, 1998), edited by Frank Ackerman, Neva R. Goodman, Laurie Dougherty, and Kevin Gallagher.

Why do companies put the squeeze on workers? Competition? Technology? David M. Gordon raises a powerful argument that American companies put the wage squeeze on workers so they could shift the wealth to managers and shareholders. As the U.S. stock market became a game board for the rich and richest in the 1990s, it would be hard to argue that companies rewarded workers the way they rewarded themselves. Gordon's book is worth considering: *Fat and Mean: The Corporate Squeeze of Working Americans and the Myth of Managerial Downsizing* (Free Press, 1996). On the issue of union democracy, a brief but salient defense of democrats for working stiffs appears in the spring 1999 issue of *New Labor Forum*, "Is Democracy Good for Intellectuals," by Herman Benson, the head of the Association for Union Democracy, a small, struggling organization based in New York City. How well unions are cleaning themselves up is raised in an article by Mark Murray, "Labor on Patrol," *National Journal*, September 4, 1999.

On the state of American farms, see "U.S. Agriculture at the Crossroads in 1999," the *Federal Reserve Bank of Kansas City Economic Review*, vol. 84, no. 1, first quarter 1999.

Paradoxically, under John Sweeney the AFL-CIO exerted more political clout than organized labor had in decades. This is a paradox because the unions continued to bleed members. Taylor E. Dark, in his book *The Unions and the Democrats* (Cornell University Press, 1999), draws an interesting analogy to this paradox. History, he says, has often been written not by groups on the way up but by those sliding downward. He writes, "The political potency of American unionism may persist, even strengthen, as it seeks to protect its industrial sector members from the imminent ravages of a postindustrial economy."

On workers' job insecurities, see "The Decline of Job Security in the 1990s: Displacement, Anxiety and Their Effect on Wage Growth," *Economic Perspectives*, vol. 22, no. 1, 1998 (Federal Reserve Bank of Chicago). The demise of benefits for lower-income workers is detailed in a June 14, 1998, article in the *New York Times*, "Benefits Dwindle Along with Wages for the Unskilled." For steady analyses of the economic roller coaster faced by blue-collar workers, the work of the Economic Policy Institute (epinet.org) over the years is an indispensable guide.

On the growth of workplace hours, see "Working Time: Tendencies and Emerging Issues" by Gerhard Bosch, *International Labour Review*, vol. 138, no. 2, 1999; also see *Key Indicators of the Labour Market 1999* (International Labour Office, Geneva).

On the need for worldwide rules for corporations in relation to their workers, see *The Human Development Report* (Oxford University Press, 1999). The report, by the United Nations Development Program, argues that the sprawl of companies and economies from one nation to another will wither if globalization spreads vulnerability rather than growth. The report states, "Global integration is proceeding at breakneck speed and with amazing reach. But the process is uneven and unbalanced."

My own global education has taught me this: As the walls around the U.S. market vanished, U.S. firms had to take new steps to compete. The old deals with unions and workers that were reached in the cushy old days no longer fit. The workers who made television sets in Bloomington, Indiana, could no longer compete with those in Tijuana, Mexico, who earned less than one-fourth of their hourly wages. The result: They lost their jobs. Tough luck—that is the global reality. Autoworkers in Detroit and Flint, Michigan, had to set aside their old ways and match the production churned out by competitors in Japan. The result was that they mostly learned to compete on a global skill, but they also lost jobs. More tough luck.

On the generational decline in wages, and quality of new jobs, see the February 1998 issue of the *Monthly Labor Review*. Many workers' paychecks began growing in the late 1990s after years of miserly increases, or losses, when adjusted for inflation. One of the reasons they were making more money is that they put in longer hours. See "More Work, Less Pay Make Jack Look Better Off" by Louis Uchitelle, *New York Times*, October 5, 1997; see also "A Bottom-Line Blight on American Life" by R. C. Longworth, *Chicago Tribune*, October 5, 1997. For more on the growing economic inequality, see Frank Levy's *The New Dollars and Dreams, American Incomes and Economic Change*, cited earlier. For details about the Midwest turnaround, see "Reversal of Fortune: Understanding the Midwest Recovery" by William A. Testa, Thomas H. Klier, and Richard H. Mattoon, *Economic Perspectives*, the Federal Reserve Bank of Chicago, July/ August 1997, vol. 21, issue 4.

When Don Fites's retirement was announced, Gary Minich gave Decatur's view of the event in the *Decatur Herald & Review*, "Fites Leaves Huge Impact on CAT: Outgoing Chairman Has Paved the Way to Profitability, but Rankled Union Officials," November 15, 1998.

Robert Reich provided an eloquent summing up of the argument about the impact of the frayed social contract between workers and corporations and the implications of "down-waging" and "down-benefiting" in "Broken Faith: Why We Need to Renew the Social Contract," *The Nation*, February 16, 1998.

For a pessimistic view of organized labor's options, see "Union Strength in the United States: Lessons from the UPS Strike" by Richard Rothstein, *International Labour Review*, vol. 136, no. 4, winter 1997. A glum view of John Sweeney's progress in shaking up organized labor is presented in "Labor's Lost Chance" by David Whifford, *Fortune*, September 28, 1998.

Global companies say they are responsible to their shareholders, but is that really so? It is more likely that they are responsible to their executives. See "Global Trade, National Tether" by Louis Uchitelle, *New York Times*, April 30, 1998.

On the election in the UAW local in Decatur, see "Contract Unhappiness Called Key as CAT Union Selects New Leader," *Decatur Herald & Review*, May 19, 1999. On the USW strike in North Carolina, see "Steelworkers Begin Campaign against German-Owned Tire Maker," *Charlotte Observer*, January 13, 1999. See also "More Labor Strife Could Lurk Ahead," *Rubber & Plastics News*, January 25, 1999. It ends with this quote from David Meyer, management professor at the University of Akron. The view is a classic example of the pessimism about the fate of American unions in today's legal and management environment:

> Even if they lose . . . the employers are sometimes required to only make the employees whole financially, meaning the union members receive what they would have earned in a negotiated contract less what they earned in the jobs they took. . . . I don't think it's a case of winning any more, because winning isn't possible. . . . We're talking about an orderly retreat instead of a rout.

The news media's reporting of organized labor is endlessly frustrating because it is so episodic and offered with little history or perspective. For one report that goes a step further by looking at the level of corruption among unions, see "Whither Labor," *National Journal*, September 4, 1999.

In regard to union democracy, the myth is that at the bottom of all large unions there is an outspoken, local leadership flourishing. There, union leaders say, is the linchpin of union democracy and imagination. Sometimes these leaders rise up, climbing all the way to the top. But more often they are in touch with what goes on at the union's far-off headquarters. The idea is pervasive, especially among veteran blue-collar unions.

But the reality is often otherwise. In matters of life and death, in strikes, walkouts, and major organizing drives, the word often comes from higher-ups, from union headquarters or from officials located in the nearest large city. And in most cases, the word that comes from the top reflects a way of thinking nurtured over the years by a one-party leadership, somewhat like that in a Third World country. It is a leadership that has diligently maintained its control and taught everyone else what to do.

That wasn't what happened in Decatur, however. The top was stunned by how angry and bitter the bottom had become. In all three disputes the militancy that came from the bottom was boiled at the bottom and erupted, creating far many more problems than those at the top of the labor organizations wanted to deal with.

When Lane Kirkland passed away in August 16, 1999, much of the U.S. news media was kind to his memory in their obituaries and lightly dealt with the rebellion that had ousted him from the top of organized labor's ranks. For an obituary that dealt with Kirkland's life and career in depth, see "Lane Kirkland, Who Led the AFL-CIO in Difficult Times for Workers, Dies at 77" by William Serrin, *New York Times*, August 16, 1999. In the lengthy obituary, Serrin wrote: "After his resignation, Mr. Kirkland was rarely in the public eye. He never forgot or forgave Mr. Sweeney or the other insurrectionists, saying that they had engaged in 'mendacity and falsehood.' He said the labor movement had always had difficulties, given its many enemies, but was built for 'heavy weather.'

For a strong gulp of hope about organized labor's future that documents some of the changes under John Sweeney, see *Not Your Father's Union Movement: Inside the AFL-CIO* (Verso, 1998), edited by Jo-Ann Mort. So, too, for a refreshing view of what workers want from their jobs and their companies, a report based on research rather than clichés, see *What Workers Want* (ILR Press, 1999) by Richard Freeman and Joel Rogers. On the challenges facing organized labor, see S. M. Miller, "The Missing Organizational Revolution," *WorkingUSA*, November–December 1999.

On Tate & Lyle's finances, see "Sweeter Taste as Tate & Lyle Turns Corner," *Times of London*, April 12, 1999.

Index

About the Author

Stephen Franklin is a reporter for the *Chicago Tribune*, where he was a national and foreign correspondent before covering workplace issues. He previously wrote for the *Washington Daily News, Elizabeth Daily Journal, Pittsburgh Post-Gazette, Miami Herald, Philadelphia Bulletin,* and *Detroit Free Press.* He has received degrees from Pennsylvania State University and American University, and was a journalism fellow at the University of Michigan. A Pulitzer Prize finalist, he is a recipient of a George Polk award. He also served as a Peace Corps volunteer in Turkey.